indiVisible

African-Native American Lives in the Americas

General Editor
GABRIELLE TAYAC

PUBLISHED BY THE SMITHSONIAN INSTITUTION'S
NATIONAL MUSEUM OF THE AMERICAN INDIAN

IN ASSOCIATION WITH
THE NATIONAL MUSEUM OF AFRICAN AMERICAN HISTORY AND CULTURE
AND THE SMITHSONIAN INSTITUTION TRAVELING EXHIBITION SERVICE
WASHINGTON, D.C., AND NEW YORK

Smithsonian
National Museum of the American Indian

The National Museum of the American Indian, Smithsonian Institution, is dedicated to working in collaboration with the indigenous peoples of the Americas to foster and protect Native cultures throughout the Western Hemisphere. The museum's publishing program seeks to augment awareness of Native American beliefs and lifeways and to educate the public about the history and significance of Native cultures.

For more information about the Smithsonian's National Museum of the American Indian, visit the NMAI website at www.AmericanIndian.si.edu.

FIRST EDITION
10 9 8 7 6 5 4 3 2

The name of the "Smithsonian," "Smithsonian Institution," and the sunburst logo are registered trademarks of the Smithsonian Institution.

National Museum of the American Indian

Associate Director for Museum Programs: Tim Johnson (Mohawk)

General Editor: Gabrielle Tayac (Piscataway)

Co-editors: Tanya Thrasher (Cherokee Nation) and Arwen Nuttall (Four Winds Band of Cherokee)

Senior Designer: Steve Bell

Editorial assistance: Amy Pickworth, Chris Gordon, Anna Wilkinson, and Jane McAllister

Design assistance: Sara Lynch-Thomason

Library of Congress Cataloging-in-Publication Data

IndiVisible : African-Native American lives in the Americas / [general editor, Gabrielle Tayac]. – 1st ed.
 p. cm.
 Includes bibliographical references and index.
 ISBN 978-1-58834-271-3 (alk. paper)
 1. African Americans—Relations with Indians. 2. Indians of North America—History. 3. African Americans—History. 4. United States—Ethnic relations. 5. America–Ethnic relations. 6. Indians of North America—Ethnic identity. 7. African Americans—Ethnic identity. 8. Indians of North America—Mixed descent—History. 9. Indians of North America—Social conditions. 10. African Americans—Social conditions. I. Tayac, Gabrielle. II. Title: Indi Visible.
 E184.A1I463 2009
 305.800973–dc22

                              2009034290

As the *IndiVisible* project delves into history, certain terms are quoted within essays that are considered racist and archaic by contemporary standards. Such usage is in no way meant to validate racist language or to offend readers, but merely to document historic realities in context.

COVER IMAGE TOP: Comanche family, early 1900s. Back row, from left: Ta-Tat-ty, also known as Qu-vuh-tu; Wife-per, or Frances E. Wright; Ta-Ten-e-quer. Front row: Henry (left) and Lorenzano, also called Moots. COVER IMAGE BOTTOM: Foxx family (Mashpee Wampanoag), 2008. From left: Anne, Monét, Majai (baby), Aisha, and Maurice Foxx.

TITLE PAGE IMAGES: Studio portrait of Mrs. Zerviah Gould Mitchell (Wampanoag), ca. 1872. N15198. Emancipation certificate of Ben Vann, 1889.

CONTENTS

COMMUNITY

CREATIVE RESISTANCE

LIFEWAYS

POEM

Alfred Young Man (Cree), *I'd Love My Mom if She was Black, Brown, or White*, 1968. Oil, acrylic on canvas, 71 x 44 in. Museum of Contemporary Native Arts Collection: CE-15.

FOREWORD

Since the early days of U.S. history, Native Americans and African Americans have been linked by fate, by choice, and by blood. Terrible and remarkable things have passed over and between our communities, as well as the communities we have created together. This book—and the exhibition it complements—tells some of those stories.

Many museums see it as their primary role to serve as a repository for beautiful objects. This is important work. We are also proud stewards of very important collections. But that is only a part of the work of the Smithsonian's National Museum of the American Indian and the National Museum of African American History and Culture. We represent hundreds of dynamic contemporary communities, and as such we serve as forums for conversations of all kinds. The topic of African-Native Americans is one that touches an enormous number of us through our family histories, tribal histories, and personal identities, and a conversation with and about them is long overdue. With this in mind, we have assembled *IndiVisible: African-Native American Lives in the Americas*—a multivoice project that acknowledges and honors the histories and contemporary lives of our African-Native American brothers and sisters.

Radmilla Cody, Miss Navajo Nation, and her grandmother, 2006. Radmilla Cody became Miss Navajo in 1997. Although she proved her cultural knowledge, her selection was controversial in the Navajo community because she has mixed-race heritage. © 2009 John Running.

This volume explores how Native and African American lives have been inextricably linked by the binds of systematic oppression, the freedom offered in the expression of creativity, and the displays of bravery by countless individuals who chose to define family, love, or simply *themselves* differently than those around them dared. It affirms how blacks and Indians see one another in our shared histories of genocide and our alienation from our ancestral homelands, and it acknowledges the strength and resilience we recognize in one another today.

We believe this book is both timely and vastly important, not only in terms of illuminating our past and present, but also in terms of what our communities intend to become. We also have no doubt that the project as a whole will be questioned and debated in multiple circles, and we welcome that. *IndiVisible* is not so linear in its approach, nor does it offer tidy solutions. Material drawn from so near the heart seldom is tidy. But it begins to plumb great depths, examining the complicated and very human concept of identity: who we are and where—and to whom—we belong. We are very pleased that the National Museum of the American Indian, in partnership with the National Museum of African American History and Culture, has engaged in a conversation that will help lead to a greater appreciation of African-Native American peoples. And we emphasize that this is the beginning of that conversation. Additional research and programming, together with the multi-city tour organized by our project partner, the Smithsonian Institution Traveling Exhibition Service (SITES), will lead to an increased understanding of these members of our community and the most excellent vitality that they bring to our national cultural fabric.

As Mwalim (Morgan James Peters [Barbados/Mashpee Wampanoag]) points out, "The big myth of the United States is that the races are kept separate." Looking at the face of Native America today, we know that this is, indeed, a "myth." There is a multitude of perspectives to be shared in any conversation about being Indian, about being black, and about being both, and we realize that *IndiVisible* can only hope to scratch this surface. But from a place of respect and gratitude, we say: This is a beginning.

Kevin Gover (Pawnee), Director
National Museum of the American Indian

Lonnie G. Bunch, III, Director
National Museum of African American History and Culture

The Crow Nation's Black Eagle family adopted Barack Obama in May 2008 while he campaigned for the presidency. A Crow leader wondered, "We have called the president The Great White Father, so we are not sure what to call you." Photo by James Woodcock.

Jimi Hendrix, The Royal Albert Hall, London, February 18, 1969. Hendrix, who spoke proudly of his Cherokee grandmother, was one of many famous African Americans in the 1960s who cited family traditions linking them to Native ancestry. Photo by Graham F. Page.

GABRIELLE TAYAC

INTRODUCTION

"When the power of love overcomes the love of power, the world will know peace."

—Jimi Hendrix

Jimi Hendrix, virtuoso guitar artist: Cherokee grandmother. Crispus Attucks, sailor and martyr of the American Revolution: Natick mother. Paul Cuffee, a founder of the American Colonization Society, which settled African Americans in Africa: Wampanoag mother. Edmonia Lewis, renowned sculptress: Ojibwe mother. The full stories of their identities cannot be separated from the story of the Americas.

And that story is vast—its full telling just starting to be heard. At the foundation of societies that came to be the Western Hemisphere's modern nations, three major ethnic strands came together in the early colonial period across the Atlantic—Europeans, Natives, and Africans. European colonization of the Americas occurred through the devastating cataclysm of chattel slavery and largely violent dispossession of Native peoples from land, life, and culture. For centuries, history was written by the victors, and the perspectives of African Americans and Native Americans told in their own voices were nearly non-existent. While contemporary attention has been focused more closely on the separate experiences of African Americans and Native Americans, and educational efforts have taught about Indian-white relations and black-white relations, there has been a missing side. An invisible experience with an indivisible reality found in the illumination of centuries-long relationships between African Americans and Native Americans.

In many indigenous conceptions, creation emerges from the ground—the underworld—through the log tunnel from blindness to sight, from being unseen to being visible. Such was the case with this project, as it blossomed after many heroes banded together to bring truth to light. Our work here is not the first step on the path; there has been critical work done by scholars, artists, and family culture bearers to bring us great distances. Quite notably, Jack Forbes, Tiya Miles, Sharon Holland, and Loren Katz are among the groundbreaking scholars who fully embraced the inquiry into, as Dr. Forbes describes, "the language of race and the evolution of red-black peoples." The term African-Native American, after extensive thought and debate among our curatorial team, was determined to be the most accurate term to represent the lived realities of individuals and communities in the intersections of African American and Native American worlds. The signifier "Black Indian" certainly resonated with some of mixed heritage, but many felt that it obscured the complexities of tribal affiliation and African American identity as well as the historic ties to aboriginal landbases.

IndiVisible: African-Native American Lives in the Americas emerged from the deepest grassroots of our museum's host city, Washington, D.C. Soon after the National Museum of the American Indian (NMAI) opened in 2004, a visitor closely scrutinized a wall of faces in the exhibit *Our Lives: Contemporary Native Identity*. These faces of contemporary Native people show the incredible diversity of current indigenous peoples and demonstrate, after centuries of intermarriage and cultural dynamism, that there are many ways to look like a "real Indian." This visitor, Louise Thundercloud, noted that there were several individuals on the wall who appeared African American. She most closely zeroed in on the photo of my longtime friend Penny Gamble-Williams, a striking woman with long dreadlocks clearly showing her African American heritage while her wampum shell earrings represent her membership in the Chappaquiddick Wampanoag tribe. Louise quite rightfully wondered: the museum shows that mixed African American and Native American heritage exists, but where is the story behind the picture?

Armed with the question and determined to move NMAI to action, Louise located Penny, an artist, and her husband, Thunder, an Afro-Carib lawyer now retired from the Justice Department. The couple had been a powerhouse of activism on behalf of Native causes in the D.C. area for decades. Starting in the office of the American Indian Movement's Longest Walk in 1978, Penny and Thunder eventually focused their work on the revelation of the Black Indian

Buck Colbert Franklin (right) **and his older brother Matthew**, ca. 1899. Buck Colbert Franklin, the father of renowned African American historian John Hope Franklin, was named after his grandfather, who had been a slave of a Chickasaw family in Oklahoma. Buck Franklin became a lawyer, notably defending survivors of the Tulsa Riots in 1921 which had resulted in the murder of 300 African Americans. Courtesy John W. Franklin

Choctaw Freedmen roll, ca. 1907–08. Buck Colbert Franklin's father was a Chickasaw Freedman and his mother was one-quarter Choctaw. His family is listed on the roll shown here.

experience and they frequently probe the topic on their radio show, *The Talking Feather.* Of particular concern was the healing from historic trauma as well as the building of awareness, spiritual strength, and pride. In the D.C. area, there had been various organizations over a number of years formed specifically to bring African-Native American people together. So when Penny and Thunder put together the proposal for NMAI to formally engage a project to address the history and contemporary cultures of mixed heritage people, with the input of Louise and others galvanized by common cause, there was simply no other response but for the museum to say yes. NMAI was not alone in answering the call—the newly chartered National Museum of African American History and Culture (NMAAHC) and the Smithsonian Institution Traveling Exhibition Service (SITES) joined the project as well.

This was not work to be done by an "expert" alone. Traversing the hundreds of years of racism, fear, and denial which has left communities, families, and individuals deeply scarred at many levels requires collective courage to bring a hidden history to light. Thus, it was fortunate that the intrepid Fred Nahwooksy, who has extensive experience in community museum work as well as in curating exhibitions, fully launched the project at NMAI. Using a collaborative approach learned from his work in the Smithsonian's Center for Folklife and Cultural Heritage, Fred cast a wide net which quickly caught me in it. When he first asked me to serve as the coordinating curator for the exhibit, I was hesitant. The topic can be excruciatingly controversial in both Native and African American communities. Coming from a small Chesapeake regional tribe with mixed European and African American heritage, I was intrigued by the fact that only the latter had been submerged for centuries; I was not so sure I was ready to face what could become a racialized storm. Previous meetings on the topic at other institutions had degenerated into divisive and emotional shouting matches about who was a "real Indian," who "did not want to be black," and who won the vote for most oppressed. Later academic sessions, such as those at Haskell Indian Nations University in 2006 and at the first meeting of the Native American and Indigenous Studies Association in 2007, had pushed beyond the initial explosive engagements, demonstrating perhaps how those dealing with these issues were processing historic grief. So, on a more lucid second thought, I knew that this was the moment for an advancement of truth and reconciliation. Much solid scholarship and clear thinking had been done in the past years, and by providing opportunities for constructive dialogue through an internationally positioned venue, the Smithsonian had made it clear that *IndiVisible* was ready for primetime.

Five great thinkers who center their life's work on understanding identity at the crossroads of race and tribal sovereignty honorably took up the challenge. Penny Gamble-Williams and Thunder Williams have keen insight into the emotional, spiritual, and political ways that African-Native American lives are lived. Judy Kertész, a doctoral student at Harvard University, had demonstrated profound understandings of the intersections of power, racism, and representation. Angela Gonzales, a Hopi sociologist on the faculty at Cornell University, has deeply analyzed the impact of identity policy on American Indians at the macro-level. Robert Keith Collins, a Choctaw/African American anthropologist at San Francisco State, has worked on more fully describing how personal identities can be categorized among race, tribal status, culture, and sovereignty. Rob came up with the insightful title *IndiVisible*.

We realized that neither a small traveling exhibit nor another book on African-Native American experiences could ever completely fill out the history and contemporary situations of African-Native people. By not limiting ourselves to case studies, we were able to provide a series of cornerstone themes so that those who want to pursue further understanding could process new information and findings in an organized way. Readers will find four main lenses through which to consider African-Native American lives: racial policy, community, creative resistance (both peaceful and militant), and lifeways. These four themes framed the publication and provided the outline for identifying contributors.

This book brings together twenty-seven scholars who formed for us a brain trust from which to develop the content of the exhibit. They crafted a solid academic foundation for both the exhibition and the publication. We also valued community culture bearers as much as academically trained writers in the formation of the project. The book and exhibit complement, rather than replicate, one another.

Ultimately, *IndiVisible* goes beyond its subject matter. All human beings express the basic desire for being and belonging. Revealing a particular aspect of this fact through the examination of African-Native American lives can help everyone to more deeply look into their own identities, origins, and the forces that make us who we are. May we all overcome with the power of love, not the love of power.

THEDA PERDUE

NATIVE AMERICANS, AFRICAN AMERICANS, AND JIM CROW

Generalizations about relationships between American Indians and African Americans are difficult to make. Time, place, and circumstance shaped specific interactions, but European imperialism and colonization set the overall parameters. The nature of relations was neither inevitable nor uniform, and interactions ran the gamut from amity to enmity. European power in the South rested initially on African labor and Indian land, so from the very beginning colonizers had a vested interest in regulating the races. By the time the United States emancipated its slaves, a pattern of interaction had developed that pitted the two peoples against each other. Southern whites then tried to classify them as "colored," a category in which African Americans overwhelmingly outnumbered the surviving remnants of southern Indians. In the late nineteenth and early twentieth centuries, legislatures passed Jim Crow laws that mandated separate transport, public accommodations, schools, hospital wards, prison cells, and so on for white and colored. These laws usually did not distinguish between African Americans and Native Americans, and in the face of biracial segregation, southern Indians struggled to maintain their identities and establish institutions that expressed that identity.

New Bethel Indian School, New Bethel Township, Sampson County, North Carolina, early twentieth century.

Alexander de Batz (1685–1737), *Desseins de Sauvages de Plusieurs Nations*, 1735. PM 41-72-10/2. The caption reads, "Indians of several nations bound for New Orleans." The artist labeled each *esclave* (slave) by tribe; an African boy is also noted.

Except in Louisiana, race relations in the South grew out of the English colonial experience.[1] Commerce formed the basis of early English relations with Indians, and the production of tobacco, rice, and other agricultural commodities soon eclipsed the deerskin trade in profitability. Native people unwillingly contributed both land and labor to this enterprise. Until the 1720s, Indians comprised a significant proportion of the enslaved labor force on southern plantations. Captured by enemy warriors or colonial militias, many Indian slaves were deported to the Caribbean, but others worked alongside African slaves on mainland plantations. Even as their proportion relative to African slaves declined, their identifiable presence remained until the end of the eighteenth century.[2] The imbalance in the sex ratio—a higher proportion of African men and Indian women—encouraged marriage, and both the people and the culture that slaves produced on colonial plantations, especially in the South Carolina Low Country, owed much to Native America.[3]

Outside slavery, relations between Indians and Africans were more complicated and more varied. Southern Indians had no inherent antipathy for Africans and initially regarded Africans, like Europeans, merely as outsiders. The nature of encounters depended on specific circumstances, and Indians fought Africans, traded with them, married them, captured them, adopted them, and enslaved them. Colonists, however, feared collusion, and they worked to divide Indians and Africans—especially in South Carolina, where the two groups dramatically outnumbered the colonists—by employing Indians as slave catchers and terrifying African slaves with tales of Indian savagery.[4]

Indians were astute observers and quick learners. By the late eighteenth century, southern Indians increasingly adopted the views of the colonists: Africans were the last human link in the great chain of being, decidedly inferior to both Europeans and Indians. By the nineteenth century, intermarriage with African Americans had declined in most southern Indian communities, and some Indians were acquiring African American slaves as part of a more general cultural reorientation. Cherokees, Chickasaws, Choctaws, and Creeks had the most formal, legalistic, and clearly articulated racial codes, and they not only legalized slavery but also restricted the rights of free African Americans and Indians of African descent. Cultural values changed slowly, however, and Indians continued to forge bonds with African Americans beyond the master-slave relationship.[5] Unlike the other large southern Indian nations, the Seminoles developed a tributary system in which African Americans lived in their own villages but paid rent to the tribe and joined them in armed struggle against removal.[6]

Removal of the Cherokee, Chickasaw, Choctaw, Creek, and Seminole nations in the 1830s to what is today eastern Oklahoma eliminated most Indian slaveholders from the Southeast. Those who remained, such as Greenwood Leflore (Choctaw), tended to identify with white southern planters, and their descendants often became ethnically white. Like their relatives in Oklahoma, most of them supported the Confederacy in the Civil War (Leflore, however, flew the United States flag over his Mississippi mansion throughout the war). Perhaps more surprising, southern Indians who were not planters and owned few slaves also joined the Confederacy. Today, a monument in the central plaza of the Alabama-Coushatta reservation in east Texas commemorates their service to the Confederacy, as does a memorial in Fort Mill, South Carolina, which celebrates the twenty Catawbas who wore the gray. Landless and impoverished Mississippi Choctaws and Cherokees from the mountains of western North Carolina also served in the Confederate army.[7] Other Indians declined. Regarded as "free people of color" by North Carolina, Lumbees in the eastern part of the state resisted forced labor on coastal fortifications. Instead, they fought a guerilla war against the Confederacy, and joined by African Americans and poor whites, the conservative Democratic regime that arose during Reconstruction.[8]

At the end of the Civil War, only the Alabama-Coushattas in Texas, the Chitimachas and Tunica-Biloxies in Louisiana, the Catawbas in South Carolina, the Cherokees in North Carolina, and the Pamunkeys and Mattaponis in Virginia had tribal land, and no Indian tribe in the old Confederacy enjoyed any sort of federal protection. Congress recognized the Eastern Band of Cherokees in 1868 in order to file suit on their behalf to clear land titles, but no other southern tribe gained federal recognition until after World War I. In the absence of a federal status, all southern Indians—with the possible exception of the Cherokees, whose status was contested until 1930—were subject to state laws.

The brief period of Reconstruction offered some hope for a racially equitable society, but the opportunity ended with the "redemption" of state governments by Democrats. In the absence of slavery, they imposed their racial order through Jim Crow laws. Because these politicians sought to protect whiteness, they rarely distinguished between Indians and African Americans, lumping all non-whites together as "colored." Only Florida included Indians specifically in a Reconstruction constitution by providing them with one representative in each house of the legislature, but the constitutional convention of 1885 omitted this provision.[9] Florida also recognized the Seminoles' presence by prohibiting the sale of alcohol to Indians—a demeaning concession to stereotype.[10]

Most laws concerned miscegenation.[11] In 1873, North Carolina prohibited unions between whites and African Americans or Indians, and in 1879, South Carolina declared, "Marriage between a white person and an Indian, Negro, mulatto, mestizo, or half-breed shall be null and void."[12] Subsequent laws, including one that prohibited marriage between African Americans and the Lumbees of North Carolina, augmented these early antimiscegenation statutes.[13] Virginia prohibited intermarriage between Indians and whites, but to enforce the law, the state had to delineate race very carefully. The legislature defined as white a person who had no African American ancestry and was one-sixteenth or less Indian, thereby affirming the whiteness of prominent citizens who claimed descent from the state's most famous Indian—Pocahontas. In the 1920s the state decided that it had no Indians at all except the few who lived on two tiny reservations established by the colonial government in the seventeenth century. Everyone else was black or white.[14] In addition to these three states, Louisiana outlawed "concubinage" between Indians and African Americans in 1920, but in 1942 dropped this provision from its code because it "had little social utility."[15] Few states established separate schools or other institutions legislatively. Mississippi and North Carolina passed laws in the 1880s to provide separate schools for Indians, but only North Carolina consistently offered segregated state facilities for Indians.[16] Otherwise, Jim Crow law codes were silent on the subject of Indians.

Southern states enforced Jim Crow laws with violence and intimidation rather than judicial action. African Americans bore the brunt of such treatment, but Indians suffered as well. The most brutal assault on Indians took place in 1901 in Charenton, Louisiana, where a white mob attacked a Chitimacha family living on tribal land and murdered a woman and two men. The assailants apparently intended to kill all the Indians in the small community, but local priests stopped them.[17] The NAACP log of lynchings in the New South included no Indian victims, but the danger was both omnipresent and real.[18] Thwarted attempts to lynch a Cherokee man accused of rape and murder in North Carolina and three Lumbee men under indictment for robbery and murder in Georgia suggest that Indians were, like African Americans, victims of vigilantism.[19]

Most Indians, however, did not make common cause with African Americans in their struggle against Jim Crow. Clearly defined Indian communities began to police their own racial boundaries, discouraging unions with African Americans but generally not whites. Native people also usually refused to patronize institutions established by and for African Americans. As southern states established public school systems, enacted compulsory school-attendance laws, and created public services such as mental hospitals and schools for the deaf and blind, they declined to provide separate institutions for Indians. Although the United States furnished schools and medical care for the Cherokees before World War I and the Seminoles, Chitimachas, Coushattas, Alabama-Coushattas, and Mississippi Choctaws between the world wars, most southern Indians had neither the treaties nor trust land that required such services. When the Office of Indian Affairs tried to pressure states to assume responsibility for Indians, the states replied that "colored" institutions were open to them.[20]

Indians, however, refused to attend schools with African Americans or avail themselves of other "colored" services. In many cases, they set up their own subscription schools by collecting funds to hire a teacher who held classes in their churches. In the early twentieth century, for example, Coharie people in the Shiloh community of North Carolina paid two or three dollars each a month to hire a teacher for their school.[21] Missionary societies also set up segregated schools strictly for Indians. Episcopalians, for example, established missions among the Seminoles, Monacans, and Poarch Creeks; Baptists supported schools among the Houmas and MOWA Choctaws; Catholics operated a church, school, and farming program among the Mississippi Choctaws; and Mormons provided most teachers for the Catawba school.

Despite official commitment to a biracial system, some southern states provided schools for Indians. In the 1890s, Mississippi established an Indian school system for Mississippi Choctaws, who had sustained literacy in their own language through instruction in Choctaw Baptist churches. Texas supported a separate school for the Alabama-Coushattas, and South Carolina contributed to the support of the Catawba school. Alabama offered some funding to Indian schools, but as was the case in most southern states, mission societies and parents bore much of the burden of educating Indian children in Indian schools.[22] Virginia provided a school for the Pamunkeys and Mattaponis who lived on small reservations and also contributed to some other Indian schools, although the 1924 Racial Integrity Law denied the existence of nonreservation Indians.[23] Further belying this law, Virginia paid North Carolina to permit members of the tribe now known as Sappony, who lived across the state line, to attend the High Plains Indian School in Person County. The only state to consistently provide Indian schools was North Carolina, which established a school system for the Lumbees in Robeson County in 1885 and a normal school to provide teachers in 1887. Subsequently, other Indian communities in the state managed to open segregated schools with state or county support.[24]

In their own schools, Indians carefully monitored the color line and resisted any link to African Americans. The Pamunkeys, ethnologist John Pollard observed in the late nineteenth century, "probably acknowledge the whites as their equals, [but] they consider the blacks far beneath their social level. Their feeling toward the negro is well illustrated by their recent indignant refusal to accept a colored teacher, who was sent them by the superintendent of public instruction to conduct the free school which the State furnishes them."[25] In the 1920s the Waccamaw community in Horry County, South Carolina, objected to the school board's attempt to classify their school as "colored" but accepted a "white" classification, the only alternative in the state's biracial system.[26]

The absence of institutions for the higher education of Indians severely limited their educational opportunities. Admission to Croatan Normal School, established for the people now known as Lumbees, was open only to them. For tribes whom the United States had recognized, some opportunities existed in federally supported schools. The superintendent of the Cherokee reservation for example wrote in 1916 that Moses Owl, who wanted to learn a trade, needed admission to Carlisle because he was "by reason of his blood barred from attending such a school in North Carolina outside of a Negro institution."[27] Hampton Institute, founded for African American Freedmen, had an Indian department, but it was separate from the program for African American students and therefore carried none of the shame associated with attending a strictly "colored" institution.[28] A few students risked opprobrium by attending African American schools. A young MOWA Choctaw man concealed his whereabouts from his people when he enrolled in an African American school because he recognized that "there is much race prejudice even among themselves. . . . [H]e knows how they will feel toward him should they know he is going to a Negro school."[29]

Indians and whites carefully scrutinized the ancestry of those who attended Indian schools. Indeed, public funding of separate schools rested on the Indians' willingness to discriminate against people with African ancestry. The North Carolina legislature established a school for the Coharies in Sampson County in 1911 but repealed the legislation two years later when the Coharies admitted the children of an Indian man who had married a woman of known African ancestry. Subsequently, Coharie parents had to convert their public school to a subscription school.[30] In 1921, the North Carolina legislature created a "blood" committee, composed of tribal members, to determine whom to admit to their Indian schools.[31] In the 1920s, the Cherokees demanded that the children of an African-Cherokee family be excluded from the federal boarding school on their reservation. "Some of the more self-respecting Indians among the full bloods have told me," their superintendent wrote, "that the minute the Colemans were enrolled in the Cherokee Boarding School they would withdraw their children from the school." Furthermore, he anticipated the reaction of local whites: "If we take into our school a bunch of to all appearances Negroes we will have lost the respect of the whites and our school will be classed little better than a Negro school."[32] Among the Mississippi Choctaws, the federal government withheld a school from the Choctaw community in Union County out of fear

A Seminole Indian elder and historian (Billy Bowlegs III, 1862–1965), said to be a descendant of an African American intermarriage with a Seminole, adopted the name of the legendary resistance fighter Billy Bowlegs II (1810–1864). The "patchwork" pattern covering his turban expresses the influence of African *ovpispisi* (bits and pieces)—sewing typical of the Suriname Maroons and Ashanti who married into the tribe.

that it might become associated with a local minister who was "believed to be a Negro by great many of the people of that community."[33] As late as 1954 the Poarch Creeks in Alabama insisted that an Indian woman whose children had an African American father withdraw the youngsters from their state-funded Indian school.[34]

The negative reaction of southern Indians to African Americans has several sources. First of all, Indians took pride in being the original inhabitants of the continent. Philip Martin, a long-time Mississippi Choctaw chief, explained: "The Choctaws were here in Mississippi before anybody. When the white people came they brought with them the Negroes as their slaves."[35] Indians also had always been free, many believed, another factor that distinguished them from people of African descent. In their appeal for reinstatement of their public school, the Coharies emphasized their status: "These people were never slaves and from the memory of the oldest white inhabitants have always been free men. There is no record that they ever purchased their freedom from former white men. They were never born nor sold into slavery; they were found living in this country as free and separate people as long ago as we have any record of them."[36] The acceptance of the same status as the descendants of slaves would have challenged the foundation of Indian identity.

The European intellectual legacy distinguished between Indians and Africans. The institution of slavery, for example, gradually eschewed the enslavement of Indians (except under fictions that defined them as African), and the acquisition of African slaves by many southern Indians simply reiterated the message that Africans were suitable for slavery and Indians were not. The attempt of the New South to simplify its racial hierarchy ran counter to that longstanding conception of the races. Indians had learned from Europeans to despise Africans, and Indians dashed white expectations that they would accept assignment to the category of "colored" along with African Americans. Indeed, the lesson grew more compelling in the postbellum world, where race rather than status—slave or free—shaped the contours of individual lives. The Seminoles in Florida, for example, had been more likely to accept African Americans into their society before the Civil War than afterward, when they outlawed intermarriage with people of African descent—even those of Seminole ancestry who had always lived among them.[37]

Recognition of a distinct Indian identity also rested on the survival of cultural traditions. In the late nineteenth century, a host of Native languages were still spoken in the Southeast. These included nearly extinct languages such as Ofo, Biloxi, and Atakapa; threatened languages such as Chitimacha and Catawba; and perfectly healthy languages such as Alabama, Coushatta, Miccosukee, Muskogee (Seminole), Choctaw, and Cherokee, which are still spoken today. Southern Indians continued Native craft traditions that ranged from the basketry of the Cherokees and Chitimachas to the pottery of the Pamunkeys and Catwabas to the house construction of the Seminoles and St. Tammany Parish Choctaws. Southern Indians hunted with traditional tools such as rabbit sticks, blowguns, and clay lanterns, and they ate traditional foods such as *coontie*, *sofkee*, bean bread, and *sochani*. Native religious beliefs and practices remained strong in some Indian communities, especially among the Seminoles, who completely rejected Christianity until the 1930s and even today are sharply divided between Christians and non-Christians. Some Choctaws and Seminoles even wore distinctive clothing into the last half of the twentieth century, perhaps so that whites could readily distinguish them from African Americans.[38]

Native people also realized that they constituted an extremely small minority among the "colored" population of the New South.[39] Their identities and whatever cultural traditions expressed those identities were at risk if southern Natives were redefined as African American. Therefore, southern Indians scrupulously guarded their racial boundaries. One of the patrons of the Chitimacha basketmakers recognized the danger of racial reclassification when she wrote in 1916 that they "refuse to send their children to the schools for negro children, holding themselves as a superior race, and realizing that intermarriage with negroes would mean their extermination."[40] This was not a baseless fear. In 1969, a lawyer in Marksville, Louisiana, home of a community of Tunica-Biloxi Indians, told a representative of the National Congress of American Indians that "all the Indians have gone. They've either married white or black, and that's what they are now—either white or black."[41]

The African American response to Indian insistence on separateness is not clear. A survey of the *Richmond Planet* (1883–1938) reveals few articles on Indians, no doubt because other issues loomed far larger for the African American community. At least two prominent late-nineteenth-century African American writers seem to have regarded the Lumbees not as Indians but as mulattoes. African American journalist Jack Thorne labeled the Lumbee hero Henry Berry Lowry (who resisted the Confederacy, Republicans, and Redeemers) an "octoroon" and named his people descendants of "free negroes." Thorne conceded that Lumbee ancestry was "Saxon, Indian and negro" and that they had an "aversion for social mingling or intermarriage with blacks," but he clearly considered their racial category to be "Negro."[42] The African American characters in novelist Charles Chesnutt's *Mandy Oxendine*, a novel about passing for white in eastern North Carolina, have surnames characteristic of the Lumbee community.[43] Chesnutt, who recognized that Lumbees had Native ancestry, which he described as

Husband and wife Richard (1933–1975) and Mildred Loving (1939–2008) embracing at a press conference the day after the Supreme Court ruled in their favor in *Loving v. Virginia*, June 13, 1967. The court, in a unanimous verdict, overturned Virginia's antimiscegenation statute, which had resulted in the Lovings' arrest shortly after they married in 1958. Widely recognized as African American, Loving also asserted her Rappahannock Indian ancestry.

Tuscarora "blood," nevertheless regarded them as descendants of "free colored people."[44] Whoever their ancestors might have been, the members of this community are generally considered African American in his writings.

The belief that eastern North Carolina Indians were really mulattoes survived into the twentieth century and endures even today. A particularly bizarre expression of this conviction came from Clyde Pulley, an African American man who tried legally to force his estranged Haliwa-Saponi wife to renounce her Indian identity in favor of an African American one. In the 1970s, he peppered North Carolina officials and the Bureau of Indian Affairs with demands that they respond to the fraud he believed tribal leaders had committed in 1965 when they obtained a court order to change the birth certificates of tribal members from "colored" to "Indian." During the era of segregation, the county registrar had refused to register Indians as such, and when attitudes changed, leaders of the Indian community succeeded in having the error corrected. When Pulley married his wife, Ella Richardson, she was legally "colored," but unknown to her husband, she had changed her official race, just as the rest of her family had. Pulley was outraged: "I am very proud of my own race, yet found out after we were married that my wife's race had been changed from Colored to Indian." He was quite certain that her family's objective was "to pass from the black world into the white world and for other reasons to suit their personal desires."[45]

Other African Americans reacted differently to their Indian neighbors. Sociologist Brewton Berry examined the attitudes of African Americans toward Indians in South Carolina in the mid-twentieth century. He found that African Americans were quite willing for Indians to attend their schools, but they were wary of social interaction with them. People he interviewed regarded Indians as clannish, lazy, and mean. Berry's informants also resented the "attitude" of local Indians: "They think they are too good." Several informants thought that the Indians were trying to be white and that they avoided interaction with African Americans to curry favor with whites: "If there are any white people around they tend to snub Negroes, because they like to pretend they are white." Some felt sorry about the fact that the South's biracial system had no place for Indians, but one person expressed disgust that Indians would not enlist in the common struggle against racial discrimination: "They think they can solve their problem with feathers. . . . They ought to forget all that foolishness and join with us. We could do more for them than anybody else."[46]

With a few exceptions, antagonism between Indians and African Americans largely obviated cooperation in the civil rights movement. In Robeson County, North Carolina, Lumbees and African Americans cooperated on voting rights, and Tunica-Biloxis secured the right to vote in Louisiana's Avoyelles Parish as a result of the broader civil rights movement.[47] But generally, Indians thought that their interests did not coincide with those of the movement. Choctaw chief Philip Martin expressed the views of many: "In a nutshell, the white and Negro problem is one of their own making. In my opinion, the basis of the Indian problem is entirely different. History can prove that the Indians once were the owners of these lands. The white people came here as intruders."[48] As Vine Deloria, Jr., pointed out in *Custer Died for Your Sins*, the civil rights movement sought to incorporate African Americans into the American mainstream, while Indians wanted recognition of the sovereign rights of Native nations.[49] For that reason, many Indian people actually advocated segregation. The Lumbees protested the integration of their schools, and the Poarch Creeks supported the campaigns of George Wallace because, as their chief phrased it, "We believe in voluntary segregation. We believe people should be allowed to associate with others on a voluntary basis that is mutual."[50]

The failure of Indians and African Americans to join together to battle Jim Crow was a legacy of European imperialism. Europeans had fostered and exploited divisions between Africans and Indians in the colonial period. With the removal of most southern Indians in the 1830s, southerners no longer needed to promote hostility. After the Civil War, when slavery had ceased to regulate race relations, elite white southerners turned instead to the segregation of white and "colored." Classifying Indians and African Americans together as members of a "colored" underclass provoked Indian resistance, which they expressed not so much by assailing Jim Crow as by demanding their own separate institutions. In doing so, Indians transformed the racism they had learned under European tutelage into a nationalist struggle for sovereignty.

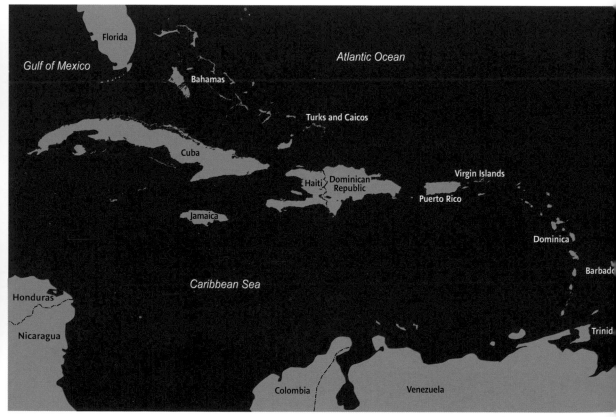

Map of the Greater Antilles (Cuba, Jamaica, Hispaniola [Haiti and the Dominican Republic], and Puerto Rico).

JOSÉ BARREIRO

TAINO-AFRICAN INTERSECTIONS
Elite Constructs and Resurgent Identities

In the Caribbean, a thirty-year resurgence of indigenous identity has challenged the thesis of extinction. Undeniable and growing interest in indigenous roots has coalesced disparate families and individuals and is reflected in numerous self-determined groups with designations such as Taino, Taino Nation, Taino people, Siboney, and Caribe. The movement's depth is amply documented by scholar Maximillian Forte and others.[1] But one opposing viewpoint deserves attention: a current of elite academic thinking that puts forth a claim of anti-African motivation as part of the Taino resurgence.

The assertion of cultural or generational legacy as the basis of a contemporary indigenous identity challenges the historical narrative accepted by most of the Caribbean's intellectual elite—however, it has persisted in "rooted" community bases. Dominated by metropolitan erudites, the identity-from-above discourse is built upon the interpretation of historical text; very little fieldwork on indigenous survival either in remote or urban areas has taken place.

With wider-spread recognition of indigeneity as a viable quotient in the Spanish-speaking countries of the Greater Antilles—Cuba, the Dominican Republic, and Puerto Rico—and their diasporas in the United States and elsewhere, the Taino communities are increasingly empowered. This growing universe of contemporary institutions is dedicated to the preservation and restoration of mutually recognized insular indigenous heritage. It is important to note that in remote places, particularly mountain ranges in Cuba, Dominica, Trinidad, and perhaps the Dominican Republic, actual *sui generis* communities are identifiable. Marginalized from international outreach and reflective of *mestizaje* (interracial or interethnic marriage), these mostly rural communities sustain numerous spiritual and material traditions of indigenous origin.[2]

Being Taino today means relating to a reality that has been acutely denied over time and constantly addressing assumptions of Taino extinction. Despite the political and physical decapitation of the large *cacicasgos* (chiefdoms) following European conquest in the early 1500s, the theory of Taino extinction has been proven incorrect. Throughout the Greater Antilles, historians point out the substantial strength of Taino cultural traits, knowledge of the natural world, and customs of daily living in the formational cultures of the islands. Of course, the blow "that paralyzed the Indian" (to paraphrase the Cuban poet José Marti) led the descendant populations to blend in rather than draw the fire of supremacist social regimens. Clearly, cultural and biological legacies from ancestors can lie seemingly dormant while buried in layered marginality, sometimes for decades at a time, then be triggered into movement by particular historical conditions.

The Caribbean population's genetic trail, increasingly of interest in the past decade, has turned up substantial evidence of continuous genealogical lines—most widely the result of early intermarriage between Taino women and Spanish and, later, African men. Of particular note is Juan Martínez Cruzado's significant finding of Taino mitochondrial DNA in 61 percent of the Puerto Rican population.[3] New scholarship in ethnohistory, ethnography, and archaeology increasingly deepens our understanding of the intangible, everyday culture introduced to the *guajiro, indio, criollo, jibaro,* and Afro-Caribbean subcultures of the Greater Antilles by the Taino grandmothers. A quest to understand the role of this foundational culture in the ethnic formation of the contemporary populations of these countries is active today. In Cuba, the small enclaves of Indian descendant populations, in quiet consistency, are studying and articulating their history and recording their lifeways.

Most prominent in the Taino network of Puerto Rico are the Taino Nation of the Antilles and the United Confederation of Taino People (UCTP), interconnecting dozens of other groups. The Taino Nation of the Antilles, which publishes the *Taino Nation Bulletin*, maintains a registry of people revitalizing Taino legacies; manages cultural recovery projects in music, language, dance, and decorative and other visual arts; and operates Wanakan, a Taino cultural center in Manhattan. The extended reach of the Taino Nation, which is Puerto

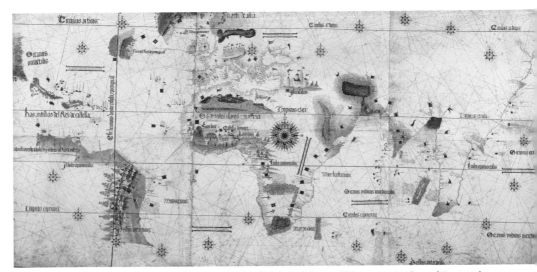

Cantino Planisphere, 1502. This map illustrates the division of the world between Spain and Portugal.

Rican, or Boricua, at its core, ranges from large cities and rural areas in the U.S. to Puerto Rico (known traditionally as Boriken) and various tribal communities throughout the Caribbean. Significantly, the United Confederation of Taino Peoples also incorporates many organizations throughout the Caribbean and the diaspora and follows the activist international (United Nations) work of its founding president, Roberto (Mucaro) Borrero, also of Boricua Taino origins. At odds over some issues, the Taino Nation and the UCTP nonetheless collaborate on global policy at international events. Many distinct smaller groups, mostly based on family and mutually supportive friendships, continue to surface.

Salient arguments leveled against the notion of a resurgence of indigenous or indio identity in the Caribbean always deserve attention. In particular, one faction accuses the Puerto Rican reflection of the Taino movement of inherent hostility against the island nation's African heritage. A volume reacting to the movement edited by professor Gabriel Haslip-Viera, for example, asserts that the Taino resurgence in Puerto Rico—and by implication the Greater Antilles—is the offspring of a core group of national intellectual elitists who propagandized Taino symbology and study over the past half-century. Prominently targeted is Ricardo Alegria, foremost among Puerto Rico's intellectuals in generating cultural interest in and governmental recognition for indigenous origins. Haslip-Viera states that Alegria's efforts led to the contemporary Taino movement, which he considers "a significant by-product of the cultural nationalism promoted by various Commonwealth agencies." He continues, "The neo-Taino have created new and self-serving histories for themselves."[4]

Of greatest interest here is the authors' position that the Taino movement is a detriment to the well-being of African Caribbean people and legacies. In an article regrettably titled "Making Indians Out of Blacks," contributor Jorge Duany writes, "The re-creation of Indigenous past has entailed the denigration of 'the third root,' as African culture is commonly called in Puerto Rico."[5] In another volume, Duany asserts that "the revitalization of the Taino Indians has helped to erase symbolically the racial and cultural presence of blacks in Puerto Rico."[6]

Idalis Ramirez with her son Yasmani Zoler, Caridas de los Indios, Cuba, 2003. The Taino of the Caribbean were the first Native people to bear the brunt of European colonization. Despite the popular belief that Caribbean Native peoples died in the wake of conquest, the Taino people and culture remained alive by blending with Africans and Europeans.

The proposition in this academic current is that the claim of Taino identity and any reorganization of Puerto Rican families as Taino *yucayeques* (communities) is inexorably linked to elitist, romantic, and even reactionary ideas emanating from anti-black motivations in the island nation. The presentation of this thesis surprises not only for its virulence but also for how it imposes a definition intent on corralling the resurgent movement. Undeniably, the discourse described that has counterposed the "indio" to deny the African is a fact of Caribbean history, but to ascribe it so vehemently and aggressively to the Taino movement seems prejudicial. It is also important to note that this type of negative response to the rise of Native consciousness in previously marginalized groups is not limited to the Caribbean.

Within the indigenous experience, in any case, "essential" feelings of identity link inexorably to familial lineage, place of birth, ceremony, adult family culture, and community, as well as shared childhood culture and experience. The greater Caribbean islands have sustained until recently a rich tradition of small agriculture, including widespread cultivation and medical use of herbal medicines and root crops. Great spiritual tradition, much of it indigenous, attaches to this folk agriculture, crossing race and ethnicity. All of these legacies are part of today's Taino resurgence, with the added contemporaneousness of indigenous participation in regional and international arenas.

A turn to reporting...

Mocking the Taino movement as being in "ideological competitiveness" with "Scientology," "Norse revivalists," "Promise Keepers," and other "movements of that type," Haslip-Viera warns that the indigenous identity movement poses a danger of division to the *criollo* identity of Puerto Rico. He accuses Taino revivalists of being anti-Christian, in favor of religious "polytheism" or of "spiritual philosophy based on pre-Columbian Caribbean." He ridicules them for their "preoccupation with Taino pedigree ... [their] focus on the land, the forests and the indigenous animal life of Puerto Rico, along with environmental concerns." Haslip-Viera considers these ostensible faults to be plentiful evidence that the "neo-Tainos" have a "desire for self-enrichment" and again, most objectionably, that Tainos make their claims "at the expense of any African, European, or Asian . . . ancestry." Finally, he complains that "fixation on the revival [of] Taino language, culture and lifestyle clearly demonstrates accommodationist and politically conservative orientation."[7]

The Haslip-Viera essays irritated the journalist in me. Their easy accusations of "essentialism" as a direct assumption of racialist intents within the Taino resurgence movement lacked adequate field research with the population presently asserting itself.

My involvement with the Taino resurgence movement, though naturally grounded in the Cuban experience, has provided direct connection to much of the Taino leadership and community, in both the islands and the diaspora. Given my personal experience as well as my perspective as a journalist and scholar, I am disturbed by the accusations of essentialism and their direct assumptions of racialist motivations within the Taino resurgence. Although the claims thoroughly examined narrative texts by national elites and properly described how African origins are marginalized therein, they ignored the realities of families and individual leaders involved in the resurgence. From the prism of community, the accusations of being elite driven and racialist are incongruent with the realities of Taino self-expression.

Panchito Ramirez, the elder *cacique*, or chief, of the Taino Caridad de los Indios community located in the Guantanamo Mountains of Cuba, leads a repatriation ceremony, 2003.

I have talked at length with many people at the center of this discussion, both casually and in formal interview sessions. I recently interviewed five men and three women, all identifiable opinion leaders of Taino communities and organizations, representing four main groups and currents of community movement in the Greater Antilles. It is safe to say that each of these currents involves hundreds of people, while some *sui generis* descendant communities have been estimated in the thousands. I initially interviewed four of the leaders at the National Museum of the American Indian's George Gustav Heye Center in New York City, where they gathered for a consultation on the proper use of Taino objects housed in the museum's collections. Another leader, Cacique Francisco Ramirez, has granted me extensive interviews over the past decade. In Cuba, I interviewed two women elders among Taino descendants, Reina Mongo and Reina Rojas. More recently, I interviewed Vanessa Pastrana (Inarunikia/ Boriken), director of Presencia Taina, an arts and performance group in New York City. Our discussions covered a range of topics, including the above asser- tions of divisionism by the Taino movement, attitudes and positions relative to Afro-Caribbean currents, and the impetus for reclaiming Taino identity, searching for foundational or culturally essential motivations.

Many more opinion leaders are available to engage in this significant and worthy discussion. In my immediate survey of Taino leadership, from which the following brief but telling remarks are selected, none expressed antipathy for another people or movement. The social approaches identifiable among the Taino opinion leaders so far focused on mutual inclusion and development of supportive relations with other ethnicities. If scholars are intent on defining the Taino (or any other indigenous revival movement) and by implication, its leadership, it seems only sensible to talk with them, or better yet, to let them speak for themselves.

Five Taino Leaders

I am Indian, natural from Boriken. The African culture, the African blood, also runs in my veins. In fact, being Taino does not diminish my pride of the African in me. I wonder if that is Zulu, is it Masai, I don't know. But they too were strong, heroic warrior peoples. In fact, quite similar to the indigenous cultures of the Caribbean. So I am proud to have African blood. I am Taino. Yet, in saying so, I do not deny, how could I, the fact of my African blood.

—Rene Marcano (Cibanakan), b. 1941. An office worker at the Department of Health in New York and the father of seven, Marcano is a principal *cacique* of the Taino Nation of the Antilles.

I find it interesting that Puerto Ricans can take part in the affirmation of African character—even the most white, even from elite families. Cultural transfer is all right there. And a black or Afro or Negro, a moreno can play and sing a bolero or even a flamenco, anything, say, from Majorca or Seville, and that is all right, it's part of our national culture. But when we see Taino people affirming themselves, whether of lighter or darker skin, suddenly there is an uproar about affirmation of heritage. Why is the bringing up of indigenous heritage attacked as a negative side of cultural legacy? Why must we look through a lens of racial purity to be a people?

—Roberto Borrero (Mucaro), president of the United Confederation of Taino peoples and a cultural outreach specialist at the American Museum of Natural History, New York City

I recently ran a biracial support group. The focus was precisely on reaching acceptance of all parts of one's self. You are not half this and half that. You are all of this and all of that. That's my philosophy about our identity as mixed peoples.

—Daniel Rivera (Wakonax), age 68, Taino Nation ceremonial leader

There is mestizaje, with African, with Español. Racially, if you accept the term, we are a blended people. But Taino is not about race. It is about culture. Taino and African were slaves together and together fought against the colony. In our movement, there is not racism; there is not a wish to deny the black nor the white in us or outside us. We come from our own memory in our families, not from books. We cannot accept such an argument. I identify with my culture, not with a race.

—Vanessa Pastrana (Inarunikia), director, Presencia Taina, elder of the Bohio Atabey

My sons have married Indians and also white and black. It changes our original race, but that is natural. One, my son, he married an African Cuban woman. They have children. They are my grandchildren. They belong to us, to our community. We know who our people are.

—Panchito Ramirez, age 72, Guama Cacique, Caridad de los Indios, Cuba

BETHANY MONTAGANO

BLACKING OUT HISTORY

Definition of indivisible: not separable into parts; incapable of being divided. Definition of invisible: not accessible to view; hidden.

In many cases, the histories and shared experiences of African and Native Americans are so intertwined, they are *indivisible*. At the same time, however, the shared history and the people that make up its chapters have become *invisible*. One might be compelled to ask how an entire shared history can be rendered invisible. A stunning example that brings the idea of invisibility to the forefront in a tangible and dynamic way is the side-by-side comparison of two images. The original albumen print *Kickapoo to the Emperor's Court*, commemorates a Kickapoo delegation's visit in 1865 to the court of Maximilian, emperor of Mexico. August Schoefft's painting *Six Kickapoo Indians, Chief and Family* is an artistic interpretation of the same event. Two men of African descent stand in the center of the albumen print wearing large-brimmed hats. By contrast, these individuals have vanished from the scene in Schoefft's work. An examination of the historical context surrounding the albumen print will shed new light on the possible identity of these prominent figures, rendering them visible again. Furthermore, an investigation into Schoefft's experience as an artist, and social commentaries on those in a position to influence Schoefft's work, will provide plausible explanations for his omission. Finally, an analysis of three similar artworks will help facilitate a better understanding of why this important event and all its implications are unknown to so many today.

Kickapoo to the Emperor's Court (detail), ca. 1865. Albumen print, carte-de-visite.

Kickapoo to the Emperor's Court, ca. 1865. Albumen print, carte-de-visite.

August Schoefft, *Six Kickapoo Indians, Chief and Family*, ca. 1865. Oil on canvas.

Historical Context: The Kickapoo

Examining the image of the Kickapoo delegation for the first time, two questions come to mind: How did the Kickapoo, originally from the Great Lakes region, find themselves in the court of the Austrian-born emperor of Mexico and moreover, in an interracial alliance, at the height of the American Civil War? And who *are* the Kickapoo individuals depicted in the image?

In the fall of 1862, nearly six hundred Kickapoo, under the astute leadership of Chief Machemanet and exhausted by the ravages of the Civil War, fled southern Kansas and set out for northern Mexico.[1] Chief Machemanet said, "We do not understand what these white people are wanting to fight about; none of them have injured us, so why should we stain our hands with their blood?"[2] This was not the first time Mexico had become a refuge for the Kickapoo; Kickapoo bands had arrived in Mexico as early as 1838 and again in 1850, when they forged an alliance with Seminole leader Wildcat (Coacoochee) and Black Seminole leader John Horse of Florida.[3]

As conditions brought on by the war worsened, the remaining southern Kansas Kickapoo also decided to follow Machemanet and head for Mexico. Led by chiefs Pecan, Papicua, and Nokohat, this second wave of Kickapoo left southern Kansas in the fall of 1864.[4] Their journey to Mexico was fraught with hardship. On January 8, 1865, they were attacked without provocation by members of a Confederate regiment and Texas militia. This deadly altercation would become known as the Battle of Dove Creek. Its timing is crucial to pinpointing the identity of the chief shown in the albumen print.[5]

On January 6, 1865, only two days before the Battle of Dove Creek, Emperor Maximilian wrote a letter to his brother detailing the visit from the Kickapoo delegation, which had transpired only a week earlier.[6] His testimony places the delegation at Maximilian's court close to New Year's Day of 1865. It further establishes that Pecan, Papicua, and Nokohat are not the Kickapoo featured in the albumen print, given the fact that they were still on the migration route during the delegation's visit. Machemanet is thus left as the only plausible candidate.

An artist who documented the delegation's visit noted about the Kickapoo chief: "Suspended from his neck, as a sign of superiority, [is] a medal bearing the effigy of Louis XV."[7] This medal dates to 1756 and celebrates the Kickapoo's alliance with the French.[8] It is well known that Machemanet was the architect of the tribe's relocation to Mexico. More than any other Kickapoo leader, he had the political experience to comprehend that the medal would communicate good faith to Maximilian, a French-appointed leader.[9] Using historical context, established timelines, and process of elimination, therefore, one can make a strong case that Machemanet is the chief featured in the albumen print. If this is the case, the Kickapoo men dressed in regalia are likely Machemanet's closest advisors.

Historical Context: The Black Seminoles

Questions remain as to the identity of the men of African descent in the albumen print. Who are these men and how did they become associated with the Kickapoo? Newspaper accounts of the delegation indicate that the deputation consisted of twenty persons, including "two negroes from Texas, who understood the Kickapoo idiom pretty well but could not speak Spanish."[10] Most likely, the men described here and depicted in the albumen print were Black Seminoles. Before one can confirm the presence of Black Seminoles among the Kickapoo delegation, however, one must first determine how Africans became associated with the Seminoles and what circumstances brought them to Mexico.

Early encounters between Africans and Seminoles can be traced to seventeenth-century Florida, with the Spanish serving as a proxy connecting the two cultures. Enslaved Africans in the British colony of South Carolina found refuge and greater freedom under Spanish rule in Florida. The Seminoles, who had broken from the Creek Confederacy and settled in Florida, also found more friendly allies in the Spanish. Africans soon began to live in Seminole communities and establish alliances with Seminole towns. Some Seminoles took Africans as slaves, although their practice differed dramatically from that of invading colonizers.[11]

When the Seminoles were removed from Florida in the 1840s and '50s and made their way west, Black Seminoles in their communities became targets for slave hunters. Tribal leaders decided that the risk of losing black members to kidnappers was too great in Indian Territory, so they sought refuge in Mexico.[12] Their migration there soon led to encounters with Machemanet and his band of Kickapoo in the municipality of Muzquiz. Although the exact timing is unclear, Black Seminole leader John Kibbetts and his followers moved to this same location from another area in Mexico shortly thereafter.[13] Thus, one can deduce that geographical proximity, shared interests in land, and prior alliances most likely brought the Kickapoo and the Black Seminoles together in the mid-nineteenth century.

One way to go about establishing the identity of the Black Seminole men in the albumen print is to peel back the layers of relationships noticeable in the original image. Given the mix of men, women, and children, the relationship that immediately surfaces is that of a family. The delegation comprised approximately twenty people: a chief, his advisors, and their respective families.[14] It is reasonable to believe that because the Kickapoo chief and his advisors brought their families, the Black Seminoles were likely extended the same invitation.

Cross-referencing the idea of family with census reports, and entertaining an exciting theory from a leading authority on Black Seminoles, Kevin Mulroy, one can arrive at probable identities. It is highly possible that the two men standing center in the albumen print are Black Seminole leader John Kibbetts and his son, Robert Kibbetts, while the youth in front is John's younger son, George Kibbetts.[15] It is important to note that John Kibbetts was the only Black Seminole leader living in Nacimiento, near Machemanet's band.[16] Because of their keen interests in land rights in the region, it would have been advantageous for the Black Seminoles to send their leader with the deputation. In summary, it seems likely that John Kibbets accompanied the delegation and is prominently featured in the albumen print.

Deconstructing Schoefft's Omission

The circumstances that brought the Kickapoo and the Black Seminoles together are remarkable, and it seems strange today that August Schoefft would deliberately minimize the value and rarity of their partnership. Schoefft's refusal to capture the momentousness of the event begs the question: what compelled him to do such a thing?

August Theodor Schoefft, a Hungarian painter, was born in 1809. He studied at the Academy of Fine Arts in Vienna and was well traveled as an artist, having spent time in India painting the Sikhs. In Mexico between 1864 and 1866, Schoefft painted other works for Maximilian, including a portrait of the emperor and a landscape featuring the emperor and empress.[17] In effect, Schoefft served as an artist to the court. As a result, Maximilian was in a position to influence the artist's choice.

During Maximilian's reign, nearly three quarters of Mexico's population was indigenous, and it is well documented that the emperor and his wife sympathized with their plight. Maximilian even wrote an Indian manifesto entitled *Cuestion India*, lambasting the conquistadors for their destruction of the

August Schoefft, Six Kickapoo Indians, *Chief and Family* (second version), ca. 1865.
Courtesy Gilcrease Museum, Tulsa, Oklahoma.

ancient civilizations of Mexico and offering a relief plan for Indian families. It is reasonable to assume, then, that the emperor communicated his enchantment with the Indians to Schoefft and that the artist was influenced by Maximilian's stereotypical view of Indians. In a letter to his brother Maximilian wrote, "Last week we received a deputation of genuine, wild heathen Indians from the Northern border, all of them Kooperian [sic] figures in the true sense of the word."[18] Another passage from Maximilian's letter reads, "Soon deputations will also come from the Southern border from the Yucatan's primeval forest. How they will be dressed is still unknown at the palace."[19] Mirroring these romantic sentiments in a second version of *Six Kickapoo Indians, Chief and Family*, Schoefft adds a nude Indian girl to the scene. Although it is not known whether he did so to appease Maximilian, the addition does point to the possibility of a sympathetic collusion between Schoefft and the emperor.

Maximilian was captivated by the exotic peoples who visited his court and was eager to boast about them. Both versions of *Six Kickapoo Indians, Chief and Family* allude strongly to Maximilian's fascination with everything about the Kickapoo, from their world view to their ethnic dress. Schoefft may well have deleted the Black Seminoles for the simple reason that Maximilian was solely interested in perpetuating the romantic image of Indians exemplified so distinctly by the Kickapoo members of the delegation.

It is also likely that Schoefft's stylistic treatment of the subject matter was colored by his earlier experiences painting the Sikhs in India.[20] Schoefft's affinity for adornment is clearly demonstrated in his painting of the Maharaja Sher Singh. His highly ornamented renderings from India reveal the lasting impact his time in India had on his artistic values. With this in mind, it is conceivable that Schoefft found the elaborately dressed Kickapoo more interesting subjects than the more plainly dressed Black Seminoles. Whether Schoefft was influenced by Maximilian or chose to omit the Black Seminoles in his painting because of his own artistic predilections, the omission diminishes the Black Seminoles' value, status, and role in the deputation.

Analyzing a Selection of Similar Artworks

After looking at Schoefft's work, one can't help but wonder how often these kinds of omissions occurred. Was it common practice to overlook black agency in Native life, culture, and history? By evaluating depictions of the Kickapoo delegation executed by other artists, one can gain a better understanding of how the Black Seminoles were perceived and why this history is unknown to so many today.

In the print *Indios Kikapoos Presentados a Maximiliano* by an unidentified artist, notice how the artist embellished the skin color of the Black Seminole. This particular artist was not shy about accentuating the racial and cultural differences among the group. It is quite possible that he or she used those racial signifiers to reach his or her own conclusions about the rank of the Black Seminole man in the gathering. Notice also that the Black Seminole man has been shifted away from the center, signifying his perceived inferiority to the chief. This composition differs from the original image, which shows Chief Machemanet and John Kibbetts directly in the center. The artist may have misunderstood John Kibbetts' role as a Black Seminole leader who was as revered by his followers as Chief Machemanet was by his Kickapoo tribesmen.

There appears to be one identifiable Black Seminole present in a wood engraving from the *London Illustrated News*, dated 1865; he is recognized solely by his large brimmed hat. Otherwise the artist made little effort to highlight any racial distinction between the Black Seminole and the Kickapoo. Notice that the Black Seminole man is seated, implying a perceived inferiority to the standing chief and advisors. His communicative expression and raised hand suggest that the artist believed him to be an interpreter rather than a leader representing the interests of his people.

Conclusion

Taking a final look at the original albumen print, it is interesting to contemplate the positioning of the delegation, the interaction that might have taken place between the members, and how the photogapher arrived at his composition. In this moment they were given a rare opportunity to define themselves, which renders this image a true cultural reflection of their shared experience. It is telling that none of the artists who subsequently depicted the event chose to portray the historic moment with accuracy or saw value in the way members of the delegation had elected to identify themselves. Instead, the artists re-created the scene, thus redefining the individuals and their roles in the delegation. In each instance, the paintings illustrate an obvious distance between the artists' perception and the lived experience of the subjects.

Whatever the motivations of the artists who portrayed the Kickapoo delegation, it is clear that widely held stereotypes of the mid-nineteenth century distorted the reality of that moment in history. The members of the delegation were depicted through a lens of racial prejudice common to that era, and not as they saw themselves.[21] In the great divide between how the world viewed the intersecting lives of African and Native Americans and how they identified themselves exists a history to be rendered visible again.

Unknown artist, *Indios Kikapoos Presentados a Maximiliano*, ca. 1865. Hand-colored engraving. Courtesy James H. Nottage.

Unknown artist, *Embassy of Kickapoo Indians to the Emperor of Mexico*. Wood engraving. *London Illustrated News*, March 1865.

Unidentified buffalo soldier, between 1860 and 1870.

HERMAN J. VIOLA

THE BUFFALO SOLDIERS

Plains Indians coined the nickname "buffalo soldiers" to identify the black troopers who manned several of the military garrisons in the American West after the Civil War. It is believed the term originated with the Cheyenne Indians—others say it was the Comanche—who saw a similarity between the curly, black hair and dark skin of the soldiers and the shoulder hair and coloration of the bison, the cultural heart of the Plains people. Since tribes admired the stamina, strength, and courage of the bison, identifying the black troopers as "buffalo soldiers" was in no way meant to be derogatory.

A bison is the dominant feature of the regimental crest of the 10th Cavalry, one of the six all-black regiments formed in the regular U.S. Army after the Civil War. The others were the 9th Cavalry and the 38th, 39th, 40th, and 41st regiments—each containing about 1,000 soldiers, most of them Civil War veterans. In 1869, the Army reorganized the four black infantry regiments into two: the 24th and 25th infantries. The term "buffalo soldiers" eventually came to identify all African American soldiers, who continued to serve in segregated units until the Korean War.

The original black regiments—usually commanded by white officers—served at a variety of posts across the American West and earned an exemplary record for bravery and devotion to duty. Whereas desertion was endemic in the peacetime army, it was almost unknown in the black units, despite their serving in some of the most inhospitable parts of the country and enduring discrimination and racism both within the military and in nearby white communities.

Often divided into small detachments stationed at isolated posts, including Fort Sill (Oklahoma), Fort Leavenworth (Kansas), and Fort Clark (Texas), the lives of the buffalo soldiers were far from romantic. They performed routine garrison chores, patrolled empty wastelands, built roads, mapped vast areas of the Southwest, strung hundreds of miles of telegraph lines, escorted mail coaches, and handled a variety of other often mundane and thankless civil and military tasks. One such little-known task was to serve as the nation's first "park rangers." At the turn of the twentieth century buffalo soldiers stationed in California patrolled and protected the newly established Yosemite and Sequoia national parks. But they also participated in most of the major frontier military campaigns of the period and distinguished themselves in battle against the Apache, Arapaho, Cheyenne, Comanche, Kiowa, and Lakota Indians. Thirteen enlisted men and six officers from these four regiments earned the Congressional Medal of Honor for their actions during these bitter engagements.

The irony, of course, is that one abused minority helped crush another, and both were victims of racism in America. Romantic legend prefers that the black soldiers sympathized with their dark-skinned adversaries and exercised restraint in combat, but little evidence supports that reality. The buffalo soldiers wore their uniforms with pride. As veterans of the Civil War, they were soldiers first and showed little mercy to their enemies on the battlefield. On the other hand, many of the black soldiers remained in the West after completing their tours of duty. Given that both groups were racially excluded from socializing with their predominately white neighbors, intermarriage between the buffalo soldiers and their former Indian adversaries became commonplace. Many of the black soldiers—some of whom were descendants of slaves owned by members of the Five Civilized Tribes—already shared Indian blood and so were often welcomed into nearby tribal communities. Today, in fact, many Native Americans boast of having a "buffalo soldier" in their ancestry.

Amelia "Kitty" Cloud and John Taylor, 1907. As a child, Kitty was adopted by Utes when her starving Hispanic parents insisted on trading her for food. Her Ute parents called her "Little Woman," but because the Bureau of Indian Affairs (BIA) insisted on English names, she became Kitty of the Cloud family. She married buffalo soldier John Taylor when she was eighteen.

ANGELA A. GONZALES

RACIAL LEGIBILITY
The Federal Census and the (Trans)Formation of "Black" and "Indian" Identity, 1790–1920

Throughout the Americas, statistics, averages, and probabilities permeate the ways we talk and describe modern nation-states and their citizenry. Whether in the United States, Canada, or Latin America, the nation-state arose from colonial settings and the resolve of ruling elites to categorize populations by setting boundaries across preexisting identities. James Scott, professor of political science and anthropology at Yale University, explains the process as the state's attempt to make society legible by imposing categories and simplifications, and he argues that these categories, "begun as the artificial inventions of cadastral surveyors, census takers [etc.] . . . end by becoming categories that organize people's daily experiences precisely because they are embedded in state-created institutions that structure that experience."

In the United States, the significance of official state certification of individual and collective identities can be charted historically through the U.S. Bureau of Census' decennial enumeration of the population. As articulated by its framers in 1787, the purpose of the census was to determine apportionment of political power based on population, and tax responsibility based on wealth. The

Constantino Brumidi, *Portrait of Bartolomé de las Casas*, 1876. Dominican priest Bartolomé de las Casas (1484–1566) denounced the subjugation of Native Americans. Although he initially kept enslaved Africans at his missions, Las Casas changed his views after 1543, when he witnessed the Portuguese slave trade, and began writing in vigorous opposition to the practice.

former, however, proved problematic in terms of who was to be included as part of the "population" that deserved the right to political participation and had the responsibility of paying taxes. Although an expansive definition was used to include women, children, and the poor, questions quickly arose about whether to include slaves and Indians. At the time, Southerners considered slaves property for purposes of tax assessments, while Indians, as members of foreign states, were generally considered outside the purview of U.S. polity. Despite these precedents, slaves and "Indians not taxed" (meaning Indians who were not citizens subject to state law) were soon counted in the U.S. Census. Beginning in 1910, census forms included the categories of "black," "colored," and "Indian," and the census emerged as the most visible and arguably the most politically important means by which states and the federal government statistically depict collective identities.

The centrality and importance of the decennial U.S. Census in the classification, quantification, and enumeration of the population raise a number of questions concerning the historical construction of American Indian and African American individual and collective identities and the politics of their representation. If these identities are to be understood as the product of social imagination and construction, then we are compelled to ask how these ways of sorting and counting people reflected the strategic needs of U.S. polity and society. Moreover, what roles have these techniques of enumeration played in the formation and transformation of American Indian and African American identity and self-understanding? This essay addresses these questions through an examination of the techniques of enumeration used in federal census-taking between 1790 and 1920, and reveals that the U.S. Census, rather than serving as a passive instrument of data gathering, has long encoded and enforced an understanding of identity and difference through a pseudo-science of race. Charted historically, this form of racialized reasoning not only (trans)formed American Indian and African American self-understanding and identity, but also continues to reinforce notions of race and racial difference despite disclaimers that the racial categories now used by the U.S. Census Bureau are sociopolitical constructs that reflect self-identification.

Techniques of Enumeration

In the United States, the practice of counting people and property has a long history closely linked to apportionments and taxes. Article 1, Section 2, of

1721 Louisiana census, listing "Negro/Indian" slaves. Written in French, the census demonstrates that African Americans and Native Americans were sometimes enslaved together during the colonial era. Note the French word for savage (*sauvage*), referring to Native Americans.

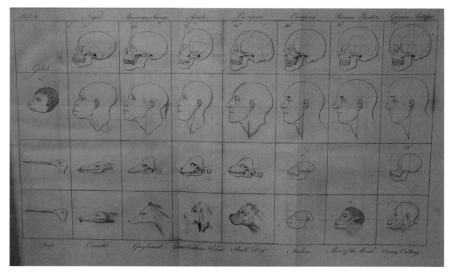

Charles White, *The Gradation in Man*, 1799. Dr. Charles White, a noted physician, was influential in promoting the idea of racial hierarchy despite his personal opposition to slavery. In his opinion, Africans were violent and primitive while Native Americans were childlike—White considered both incapable of the higher intellect of Europeans.

the U.S. Constitution requires that a census be taken every ten years so that seats in the House of Representatives can be apportioned among the states. Paragraph 3 of Section 2 specifies that the representatives and direct taxes are to be "apportioned among the several States which may be included within this Union, according to their respective numbers." The dilemma concerning whether to consider slaves and Indians as part of the population was solved with the following two provisos: "Respective Numbers [of the population] . . . shall be determined by adding to the whole Number of free Persons, including those bound to Service for a term of Years, and excluding Indians not taxed, three-fifths of all other Persons." At the same time that the three-fifths compromise required the enumeration of slaves separately as three-fifths of a free person, it excluded from the census altogether, based on the recognized status of Indian tribes as sovereign, Indians who did not pay taxes. These constitutional provisions both defined the populations to be included and excluded, and determined who would be counted either as a whole person or a fraction, according to that person's civil status. Only those Native people considered assimilated enough to be called "civilized Indians" were to be included in the decennial census count and, hence, in the apportionment totals.

From the years 1790 to 1840, the census enumerated the population using several simple but discrete categories: free white males and free white females (subdivided into age groups), free colored persons and/or all other free persons except Indians not taxed, and slaves. If representation depended, however, on civil status—whether one was free or slave, and whether or not one was taxed—why did the census categorize according to race? At the time, race was understood to be a natural and self-evident component of human identity and factored into a number of popular theories based on ideas of inheritable characteristics and racial hierarchy. In 1735, Charles Linnaeus had established a classificatory system of human life, separating homo sapiens into four categories based on origin, physical appearance, and supposed behavior. *Homo sapiens americanus* was supposedly red skinned with black hair and a sparse beard, stubborn and prone to anger, "free," and governed by traditions (and thus inferior and uncivilized). *Africanus,* identifiable by black skin and curly hair, was cunning, passive, inattentive, and ruled by impulse. By contrast, *Europeaus* was characterized as clever, inventive, and governed by laws and therefore, the most civilized and superior subspecies.

1850–1920

The 1850 census marked a watershed in census-taking in several ways. Much significance rests on the inclusion of the "mulatto" category and the reasons motivating its introduction and use. Theories emerging from the European Enlightenment—such as polygenesis (both scientific and religious), which posited that each race was actually a separate species springing from a different origin—had already established a widespread acceptance of the concept of innately and permanently superior and inferior races. By 1850, the deepening entrenchment of slavery in U.S. economic and political life coupled with "scientific" validation enabled slave owners to lobby Congress successfully for the inclusion of the mulatto category for persons of mixed heritage. On the 1850 census, instructions to enumerators of the slave population read: "Under heading 5 entitled 'Color,' insert in all cases, when the slave is black, the letter B; when he or she is a mulatto, insert M. The color of all slaves should be noted."[1] For the free population, enumerators were instructed: "In all cases where the person is black, insert the letter B; if mulatto, insert M. It is very desirable that these particulars be carefully regarded."[2] In 1870 and 1880, census enumerators

Studio portrait of Mrs. Zerviah Gould Mitchell (Wampanoag), ca. 1872. N15198

Cherokee family, ca. 1907. From left to right: Mrs. Stacy Welch, her baby, and an unidentified woman. Photo by Colonel Frank C. Churchill. N26830

were further instructed also to count "quadroons, octoroons, and all persons having any perceptible trace of African blood," and in 1890 enumerators were ordered to record the exact proportion of the "African blood." By 1900, the census bureau specified that "pure Negroes" were to be counted separate from mulattoes, a population then defined as "all persons with some trace of black blood." In 1920, the mulatto category was dropped, and black was defined to mean any person with any black ancestry.

The enumeration of mulattoes, quadroons, octoroons, and all persons having any perceptible trace of African blood parallels the rise of scientific racism, which held that the "races" were distinct genetic populations. In the United States, the acceptance of "races" as distinct genetic populations objectively determined and quantified by blood was aided by Francis Galton's theory of fractional inheritance, which stated that every person received one-half of their hereditary endowment from each parent, one-fourth from each grandparent, and so on.[3] In the South, legislated race codes, some predating the work of Galton, quantified racial identity based upon a percentage of blood.[4] The related concept of hypodescent, which formed the basis of the "one-drop rule," defined as black anyone with any known African ancestry. Reflected across the long history of slavery, this paradigm was central to Jim Crow segregation.[5] The one-drop rule for determining the identity and categorization of persons of mixed black ancestry was applied in policies that classified and assigned identity based on the race of the more socially subordinate parent. But where *hypo*descent assigned racial identity based upon any known black ancestry, Indian identity followed the logic of *hyper*descent, which required a minimum amount of Indian blood, usually one-quarter or more.[6]

Blood quantum as a method for classifying American Indians proved even more influential than the earlier designations of taxed and not taxed. The intellectual roots of this metaphorical description of ancestry and identity through the use of fractional measures of different types of "blood" are well known and traceable back to Spanish colonial America, where the concept of *sangre pura* (pure blood) was central to a highly variegated, complex classificatory schema that took into account not only the parentage of the offspring, but the degrees of color admixture. Acknowledging the three "pure" original racial types recognized under the Spanish empire at the time—European, Indian, and African—racial classifications, based on maternal lineage and ranked by the amount of European blood, included, for example, the gendered distinctions of *mestizo* (Indian Spanish), *mulato* (African Spanish), and *zambo* (African Indian). The degree of racial admixture was further denoted in terms such as *cuarterón* (three-quarters Spanish, one-quarter African), *cuarteado* (one-half Spanish, one-quarter Indian, and one-quarter African), *cambujo* (three-quarters Indian, one-quarter African), and *cambur* (one-half African, one-quarter Spanish, and one-quarter Indian).[7]

By 1850, notions of fractional inheritance and concerns over taxation and the civil status of American Indians resulted in the first official enumeration of Indians who were considered assimilated enough to be called "civilized Indians." Later, this determination was generally applied to Indians on reservations who received land allotments under the General Allotment Act of 1887 (or Dawes Act). However, enumerating Indian people was further complicated by Indian people of mixed blood. It was eventually decided that persons of mixed white and Indian blood, living in white communities, who were assimilated would be counted as white. However, if the mixed bloods lived among Indians, they would be counted as Indian. These definitions of Indians were applied in the federal censuses of 1850, 1860, and 1870, in determining the country's population.

Juan Rodríguez Juárez, *De negro y de india, produce lobo* (Black and Indian Produce a Wolf), ca. 1715. Oil on canvas, 80.7 x 105.4 cm. Spanish authorities created more than fifteen categories to classify racial background. Casta (or caste) paintings popularized notions that those not of "pure" Spanish blood had lower status—how low depended on how much non-white ancestry. The term *lobo* (wolf) suggests that black and Indian coalitions could be dangerous.

It was not until 1890 that the census attempted to enumerate all American Indians, this time counting as "Indians taxed" those American Indians who were living in or near white settlements, away from their tribal community, and working as farmers, laborers, or in some sort of trade. In other words, prior to 1890, "Indians taxed" meant, in terms of the U.S. Census, those Indians who were not tribal members but state citizens, and therefore subject to state laws and taxes. In 1890, "Indians taxed" came to be understood as individuals who had more or less assimilated into white culture. Data on race in the 1890 census estimated that about 59,000 out of the 248,000 American Indians enumerated were adequately civilized to justify their taxation.[8] Twenty years later, largely as a result of allotment, the number of "Indians taxed" had risen to 194,000, about three-fourths of the total Indian population.[9]

Seminole men, ca. 1920. Photo by L. Winternitz. P08256

Thus, prior to 1890, only those Indians deemed "civilized" enough to own property or "assimilated" into white society were enumerated in the U.S. Census. From 1890 onward, all American Indians were included in the census, although problems remained in terms of who was to be included in the category. In 1910 and 1930, all mixed-blood Indians were enumerated as "Indian." The impetus for this inclusiveness can be traced to two events. The first was the passage of the Indian Citizenship Act of 1924 that conferred U.S. citizenship on all Indians born within the territorial limits of the United States. The second was the 1935 Supreme Court decision (*Superintendent v. Commissioner*) which held that all Indians are subject to federal taxation regardless of land ownership.

This systematic categorization of race, with its blood-based rules establishing identity, not only maintained white supremacy but also reflected the difference in how blacks and Indians were viewed during the early period of colonization. It also provided justification for the dispossession of land from Native peoples. Enslaved persons of both African and Indian ancestry were viewed as property alienable through purchase and possessing a status releasable through emancipation. American Indians, on the other hand, were considered the collective owners of property coveted by white settlers.

Conclusion

As a product of the ideology of colonial and modern states, the project of dividing, classifying, and counting the population by racial categories shares a common logic, a kind of imperative, that suggests people *must* be assigned to a category or race. This history of racial thinking seized certain physical character-istics and inscribed them with meaning based on a biological understanding of identity and difference. In devising racial categories, federal census makers and takers employed a subjective understanding of racial difference and hierarchy that unilaterally distinguished Indians and blacks based on pseudoscientific notions of race once thought to be natural but now regarded as unscientific and morally reprehensible. In the United States—in its continuous history, until recently, of placing its entire population into mutually exclusive "races"—people were pigeonholed into official governmental divisions, which gave legitimacy to these divisions and to the racialized modes of thinking inherent in them. Insofar as the U.S. Census is presented as an instrument of objective scientific inquiry, the persistent racial categorization in the census provides an aura of scientific legitimacy for the continued racialization of the population.

The historical examination of the U.S. Census richly reveals the relationship between racial ideas and public policy and teaches us that the racial categories listed on the census do not merely capture demographic realities but rather reflect and help create political realities and ways of thinking and seeing. By dividing people into official governmental categories, the census gives legitimacy to the categories themselves and to this mode of thinking. Not merely a means of mak-ing society "legible," the census also provides the "authoritative tune to which most of the population must dance."[10] The realization that governmental statistics gathering and census taking have been influential in creating and manipulating identities requires an understanding of the evolution of the census enumeration process and the role it has played in constructing American Indian and African American individual and collective self-understanding and identity.

KIMBERLY TALLBEAR

DNA AND NATIVE AMERICAN IDENTITY

Since the early 1960s, genetic techniques have been applied to traditional anthropological questions, including those concerning ancient human migrations and the biological and cultural relationships between human populations. By drawing blood from people around the world, geneticists and anthropologists investigate the "origins" of and genetic relationships between geographically disparate populations. Native American (Amerindian) peoples are heavily studied, and in their genomes researchers search for molecular sequences—or genetic signatures—of the first peoples of the Americas.

In the last decade, these types of molecular sequences, also called ancestry DNA, have become salient beyond the lab and now feed a commercial phenomenon. Since 2000, nearly half a million people have purchased genetic ancestry tests, and public interest continues to grow.[1] So-called Native American DNA markers are now detectable through self-administered cheek-swab tests marketed by more than a dozen companies. In the U.S., those interested in Native American genetic ancestry include genealogists, applicants to Ivy League and other competitive schools, and former citizens of Native American tribes (such as Seminole Freedmen descendants) whose ejection is usually related at least in part to the financial stakes of membership. While no tribes or First Nations currently use DNA fingerprint tests to confer citizenship, these tests are reconfiguring concepts of Native American race and identity in the twenty-first century.

Blake-Scott family (Assonet Wampanoag), Mashpee, Massachusetts, 2008. From left: Lascelles Scott, Eva Blake, and Qunônuw Scott (child).

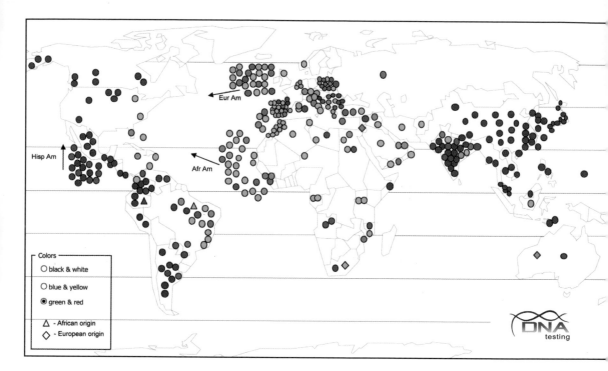

A map from a DNA Fingerprint Ancestry Report showing populations around the world. Red dots indicate absence of a match, green dots presence of a match, and brown dots weak or ambiguous matches. This pattern means the individual has a combination of European, African, and Native American ancestry. Genetic assessments can be disappointing, however, as they sometimes disprove family oral traditions of Native ancestry. Positive genetic presence of Native American ancestry does not necessarily confer tribal membership.

In narrow circumstances, some genetic ancestry tests are highly reliable, but they examine only about 1 percent of the user's DNA. These tests fall into two categories: mitochondrial DNA (mtDNA), passed from the mother, and the mother's mother, and so on, and Y-chromosome tests (which reveal only the DNA passed from the father, and the father's father, and so on). The results of these tests—while helpful to genealogists seeking verifiable biological links between specific individuals or information about the deep geographical history of a genetic line—are limited to strict matrilineal or patrilineal progressions and do not adequately account for gene flow between populations or the high-genetic variation present within human populations.

A third type of test attempts to account for overall ancestry by surveying for 175 autosomal markers (inherited from both parents) from across all 23 chromosome pairs. Each marker occurs in higher and lower frequencies in different groups across different parts of the world. Surveying for markers inherited from all of one's ancestors is an important selling point in a highly racialized society such as the U.S. After analyzing markers in the test taker's genome, a complicated algorithm compares the results to the frequencies of those markers in populations including Indo-European, East Asian, Native American, and sub-Saharan African, and reveals what percentages of those ancestries they possess.

This highlights a big problem, or set of problems, with genetic ancestry tests: despite disclaimers, they suggest a linear, deterministic link between genetics and race that simply does not exist. Genetic ancestry tests involve assumptions of uncomplicated social continuity between present-day ethnic/national/racial groups and groups in the past, even if those groups are genetically related. Genetic sequences, named according to today's salient racial or ethnic categories, correspond to ideas of continental origins. Companies purport to tell consumers where in the world their genetic ancestors "originated" and which races or cultural and social groups (e.g., "tribes") they belonged to, with the implication that the test takers themselves originated in those places and can claim affiliation with those groups or tribes. Genetic markers come to stand for the individual and the race, group, or tribe. Patterns of residence today, however, are rarely synonymous with patterns of the past. Human beings move around. Social groups organize themselves and are organized, and name themselves and are named, in different ways from era to era. Genetic databases built from living human beings' biological samples offer interesting but incomplete genetic views of the deep past and certainly should not be seen as anything approximating a cultural or social snapshot.

DNA tests, aside from their use in very specific cases, compel us to conflate genetic ancestry with racial, ethnic, national, tribal, and kinship identity categories, but these categories are embedded in one another, and all have been shaped by colonialism. The twenty-first-century use of genetic markers to weigh in heavily on these categories is a practice not disentangled from colonialism's, which dates from the sixteenth century. The genetic knowledge that enables us to do this—and our intellectual and emotional receptiveness to doing it—are predicated on the power relations of colonial history.

At least two companies have marketed the DNA fingerprint, or parentage, test directly to U.S. tribes and Canadian First Nations for purposes of enrollment. Commonly sold as a paternity test, it is both more and less informative than genetic ancestry tests because it gauges relatedness at a different biological level (e.g., mother, father, siblings) with a very high degree of probability. DNA fingerprints are often used in conjunction with blood requirements and are currently employed by many tribes on a case-by-case basis. The parentage test can help fill gaps in the documentary record—for example, when proof of biological paternity is needed to ascertain blood quantum and process a child's enrollment application. This situation poses fewer risks to tribal sovereignty, both political and cultural. Another option that accounts for some tribes' traditional kinship values is found in the Sisseton-Wahpeton Oyate (SWO), for example. It uses affidavits from enrolled relatives who testify about their respective relationships with an enrollment applicant whose biological parentage was in question. SWO reviews both DNA fingerprints and affidavits, thus preventing genetic evidence to trump familial testimony about kinship.

Much more risky to the historical and political foundations of contemporary tribal governance is the shift by some U.S. tribes and Canadian First Nations, especially those that distribute financial benefits from gaming and other economic windfalls to members in the form of per-capita payments, to across-the-membership DNA fingerprint testing. The research and documentation of biological relationships are time-consuming for applicants and cumbersome for tribal enrollment offices, but it is not only the missing or hard-to-track records that pose problems in tribal enrollment. Critics of blood rules (including would-be tribal members) talk about inaccuracies and discrimination in the tribal base rolls constructed many years ago. If ancestor(s) were left off the rolls because they were absent from the reservation during their construction or wrongly judged to be racially other than Native American, the DNA fingerprint test cannot rectify that documentary problem.

Speaking in support of using DNA fingerprint tests for purposes of enrollment, a representative from one company says DNA fingerprints ensure that there is "no possibility of incorporating a subjective decision into whether someone becomes a member or not." But whether or not someone is verifiably a biological kin of the type indicated by a parentage test is not an "objective" enrollment criterion. Allowing a parentage test to trump other means of reckoning kin (e.g., blood quantum as a way of counting relatives, or signed affidavits of family relatedness) for purposes of enrollment gives priority to techno-scientific knowledge of certain kinship relations over other types of knowledge and relationships. Across-the-board testing does not solve every problem related to

Comanche enrollment card. In 1935, the U.S. government established "blood quantum" laws to measure Native ancestry and define who was considered Native. Today, Native tribes use versions of blood quantum to regulate who can be accepted as a member.

establishing membership. Moreover, it often creates new problems for existing families, considering the not-uncommon situation in which false biological parentage is exposed, even when it was not questioned in the first place.

It's been said that we are a nation governed by science.[2] Genetic studies carry tremendous cultural weight and seem far more precise and scientifically valid than the old-fashioned ideas of blood quantum still common in tribal enrollment. DNA testing and gene metaphors are now expanding into territory long claimed by blood and blood metaphors. Yet important material differences between blood and genes differentiate the symbolic work that they do in relation to Native American identity. Those differences, in addition to the scientific authority of genetics, make it difficult to see why the science is actually more problematic than blood at this historic juncture.

Native American tribes have shown that they are deeply attached to kinship, much of it biological, in determining citizenship.[3] Exceptions to biologically based tribal citizenship include the Seminole and Cherokee Freedmen—descendants of freed slaves and not necessarily "blood" relations of the tribe—who have long been eligible for tribal enrollment owing to post–Civil War treaty provisions. Nonetheless, Freedmen descendants continue to struggle against blood rules, and their tribal citizenship has recently been put at risk or revoked.

Critics of blood quantum recognize the difficulties in completely overcoming biological bases for Native American identity. Even among those who advocate concepts of tribal citizenship that ultimately extend beyond biology (e.g., residency, cultural requirements, adoption, and other allowances for naturalization), many also argue for more inclusive blood rules, especially for lineal descent. By standard tribal lineal-descent regulations, an applicant need only document his or her biological descent from one individual named on the tribe's base rolls. (In a very few tribes, that ancestor must be strictly maternal or paternal, but descent can usually occur in either line.) Often portrayed as less essentialist because it is more inclusive than blood quantum, lineal descent can also be seen as more essentialist than blood quantum because it traces identity through a single line, basically following the same kinship concept underlying genetic ancestry testing.

Genetic ancestry tests gauge linear biological descent along strictly maternal and paternal lines—or bloodlines, in the language of blood—a method of reckoning that is valid in some contexts but culturally narrow. This type of multigenerational lineal blood relationship tends to dominate thinking about family in the U.S., but it can be at odds with the concept of the tribe.[4] By privileging such narrow, often distant links to unnamable ancestors whose cultural and political ties are impossible to establish, genetic ancestry tests, ironically, undermine the sovereignty and self-governance of today's tribes and First Nations.

Blood quantum stands for the probabilistic social link between an individual and a land-based group, meaning the higher the blood quantum, the greater the likelihood a person has relatives that are Native American or from a specific tribe, and the greater the probability of actual group affiliation. In short, blood quantum attempts to capture a networked set of social and cultural relations based on biological relatedness. (Again, the DNA fingerprint—unlike genetic ancestry tracing—is intelligible in the context of tribal blood rules and confirms genetic connections between closely related and named individuals.) Clearly there are problems with blood quantum. But ideas other than biological essentialism—that go to the heart of what is unique about the tribe—also ground its use.

Blood is unlikely to be redeemed, however, even as a placeholder, until a time when it is not the only way to citizenship but rather one among multiple ways—when tribes and First Nations enjoy the economic, political, and cultural power to truly remake enrollment as citizenship. In the meantime, genetic-testing companies assertively seek out not only private individuals looking for Native American ancestry but also tribal and First Nation governments hoping to "precisely" and "objectively" construct their tribal membership. To be Native American is to be simultaneously categorized according to racial, ethnic, and sometimes citizenship terms. DNA is reconfiguring those categories, and as we consider involvement with genetic testing, we must think carefully about the implications of our understandings of what it is to be Native American. Do we want it to be a genetic category after all? What, then, are the implications for tribes and First Nations as complex governing and kinship entities? What are the risks to the historical and political foundations upon which contemporary tribal governance and land rights are based? We have much at stake.

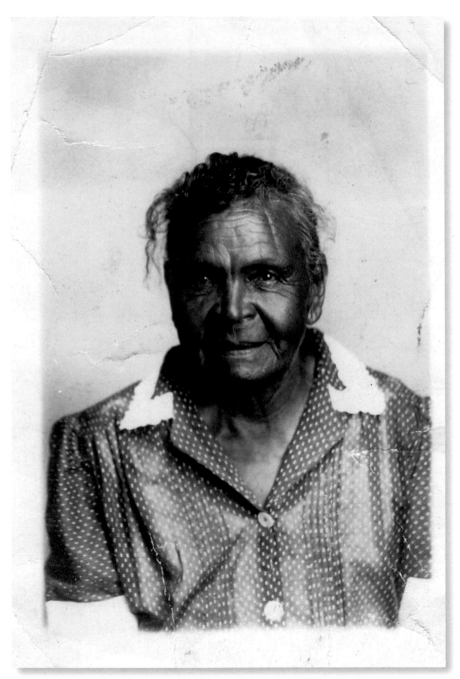

Sallie Walton, great-grandmother of educator and author Angela Walton-Raji, ca. 1950.

ANGELA WALTON-RAJI

BLENDED FAMILIES, BLENDED HISTORIES
Documenting Black Indian Families

Genealogy is a journey into the past, documenting the historical trails taken by a family and the persons sharing that past and preserving it for future generations. To research mixed-race or "blended" families that are both black and American Indian—for which there are distinct methods and documents—the investigation requires a variety of techniques related to both communities. Despite its inherent complexities, learning about one's blended heritage can result in personal reflection and the desire to share the rich and compelling stories.

For family histories in which two cultures are known to be present, it is important to begin by asking questions that will elicit specific data while employing sound genealogical methods. When researching families of dual black and American Indian heritage, for example, the process should include conducting an oral history; collecting family memorabilia, documents, and records; and carefully documenting and analyzing the resulting data.

Oral History
Collecting a family's story is the first critical step to genealogical research. Speak and listen to the elders and record the stories they tell. The oral-history interviews can be taped, but it is more important that they be transcribed. A good transcription, clearly indicating the date and the full name of the person interviewed, is a critical part of the family history and will serve as an important artifact for future generations.

Conducting an oral-history interview requires asking the right questions of elders, ones that can lead the genealogist to critical documents. Possible questions include: Who is the oldest person in the family that you remember? Who is the specific ancestor that is said to have been of American Indian ancestry? Why was he or she said to have been of Native ancestry? Did he or she have connections to a particular nation or tribe? Was there a tribal community in the area? Did he or she visit that community? Did this ancestor speak a language other than English? What kind of religion did he or she practice? Did he or she ever speak about the family's elders?

Family Memorabilia

Photographs and documents such as licenses, tribal-allotment certificates, military records, and funeral programs hold fascinating details. Marriage, birth, and death records are the basic documents that connect generations, and family records such as deeds and allotment records are particularly useful as they tie families to the land, sometimes indicating tribal and community affiliations. Land records may also present insights into land use and allocation, and homestead records reflect citizenship, literacy, and in some cases even economic status.

Documentation of Blended Families

When researching families that share more than one culture, it is important to address the history, geography, and culture of the region that the family calls home. Learn about the local history of the places the ancestors lived and identify which ancestor(s) lived near specific American Indian settlements. Identify the appropriate American Indian nation affiliated with the family and research all public documents available from that nation. Learn also the methods particular to researching African American families. A critical step when researching former slave families, for example, is identifying the last known slaveholder. The historian must then research that family using the same methods they would to research any other. This strategy will provide insight into both the movements of slave owners and the history of those held in bondage. Critical documents include wills, deeds, and estate records, which often identified slaves by name and family. Work backward in time from the most recent to the oldest documents.

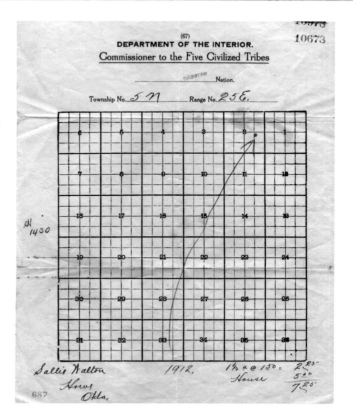

Above: Land allotment certificate issued to Choctaw and Chickasaw Freedmen, 1907.

Right: Plat map of a Choctaw Freedmen land allotment, 1912. The diagram indicates the location of the allotment given to Sallie Walton in present-day LeFlore County, Oklahoma; she kept the map tucked into the family Bible.

Page from federal census, Giles County, Tennessee, 1870. The enumerator noted at the bottom of the document, "One male Indian counted as colored."

The United States Census is the engine that drives the genealogical process. Every ten years since 1790, the federal government has conducted a census, or count, of the general population. Before 1900, there was no pattern to the method of recording American Indians. Indian people were sometimes listed as "mulatto," sometimes accurately identified as Indian but "counted" as part of the colored population, and sometimes counted as white. In mixed communities, white, black, and Indian were listed on the same standard census schedules. In cases of blended families, individuals from the same household were identified as having different racial backgrounds.

During the census years 1870 to 1900, people were identified simply as white, black, or mulatto, with few exceptions. One, in the 1870 census, for example, was the identification of American Indian people as "Ind" or simply "I," with no tribal affiliations attached. Until 1900, no regular census was conducted of the Indian populations; after that time, Indians were identified on a Special Indian Census schedule that occasionally noted mixed heritage. In 1900, for example, many Indian families with African ancestry were identified simply as black; ten years later, the same individuals were enumerated on the Indian census schedules.

The Indian census schedule captured many families whose members were of Indian and black ancestry. The Special 1910 Indian Census schedules listed the possible family mixtures as Indian, white, and Negro. On that form, the census enumerator made a mathematical "calculation" of Indian blood—a wholly inaccurate accounting of mixed heritage but an important inclusion nonetheless. Mixed families from various states, including Massachusetts, New York, Pennsylvania, North Carolina, Mississippi, and Oklahoma, are included on the 1910 census.

In addition to tracking census records, identifying family connections to specific Indian communities through tribal records can yield excellent results. For Black Indian genealogy research in particular, a number of records are available for the Cherokee, Choctaw, Chickasaw, Creek, Seminole, Mississippi Choctaws, and Eastern Cherokee communities. These records, such as the Dawes Rolls from Oklahoma, can be highly detailed and include interviews taken under oath. Earlier rolls, established periodically between 1867 and 1900, also hold the names of family groups.

Accumulated by the federally appointed Dawes Commission between 1898 and 1914, the Dawes Rolls are the largest Indian record set and contain hundreds of entries for individuals with mixed black and Indian heritage. Documents known as Rolls by Blood and Freedmen Rolls, as well as a subcategory of documents known as the Minors and the New Born Rolls, are useful in genealogical research. Freedmen, the slaves held by the southeastern Indian communities known as the Five Civilized Tribes, sometimes had blood and cultural ties to individuals listed on the blood rolls. In some cases, siblings appear on both the Rolls by Blood and the Freedmen Rolls. These families were blended.

In addition to the Dawes Rolls, many other rolls record mixed-heritage families and individuals, including:

- Tompkin Roll, Cherokee Nation (1867)
- Dunn Roll, Creek Nation (1869)
- Cherokee Census of 1872
- Wallace Roll, Cherokee Nation (1880)
- 1880 Authenticated Cherokee Roll, Cherokee Nation
- Hester Roll, Cherokee Nation (1883)
- Choctaw-Chickasaw Freedmen Census (1885)
- Cherokee Census (1890)
- Kern Clifton Roll, Cherokee Nation (1896)
- Authenticated Roll, Cherokee Freedmen (1896)

Other records that can be of use to the genealogist and that document many blended families are the rejected files of the Mississippi Choctaws and the Eastern Band of Cherokees. The rejected files represent data provided by applicants who had ties to Indian tribes based on family histories but were not approved by government authorities. As a result, the descendants of many of the mixed-heritage families who submitted applications were later identified as being only black or white.

Military records from the eighteenth and nineteenth centuries—pension files and service records being the most valuable—are also informative resources. For more recent genealogical data from the twentieth century, researchers should attempt to locate both standard census records and personal family records.

While blended black and American Indian heritage can be documented in some cases, it is important to understand the limitations and challenges of the research process. Not everyone will successfully identify or document their "Indian heritage"—for some, the stories heard from childhood are simply not true and the claims of Indian ancestry unfounded. Not all Indian communities created tribal rolls, and not every community has easily accessible records. Census records are limited, especially in relation to the enumeration of Indian people. In Louisiana in the 1870s, for example, some Indian communities were recorded only by naming the head of the household; the rest of the family was labeled simply "wife," "son," or "daughter." In some cases, self-identification for individuals and communities changed over time; in North Carolina, persons enumerated as Croatan in 1900 are later referred to as Lumbee, and Indian communities in Virginia were simply terminated on paper and referred to as white, black, or mulatto, with no reference to their cultural identity.

The effort to document family history is a rewarding venture but not without its challenges. Much is still to be explored in Black Indian genealogical research. But by adhering to sound methodology and keeping the integrity of the research in focus, the journey can be a successful one.

Ho-tul-ko-mi-ko (Silas Jefferson or Chief of the Whirlwind, 1835–1913), ca. 1877. Of mixed African and Creek heritage, he served as an interpreter for the loyal Creeks during the Green Peach War (1882–83) and became the official interpreter for the Creek Nation. Photo by Colonel Frank C. Churchill. P01199

BRIAN KLOPOTEK

OF SHADOWS AND DOUBTS
Race, Indigeneity, and White Supremacy

Indivisible? It is not the word that comes to mind when I think of black-Indian relations. Indeed, whether we are divisible seems a less pertinent question than how we might overcome the chasms that have divided us. Given the history of Indian-black relations, particularly in the South, whence my own Choctaw ancestors hail, we have an arduous task before us. Black and Indian communities have undermined each other's best interests many times over. Why? Typically because we have failed to recognize the unique but common impact white supremacy has had on each of our communities. Thinking about why Indians in the South have consistently sought to separate themselves politically from African Americans obliges us to grapple with issues that touch on our most sensitive nerves, our most basic sense of who we are.

Of central concern in this essay is a pattern of anti-black racism evident in many Indian communities in the southeastern United States. Arica Coleman discusses the identity of Mildred Loving, one of the plaintiffs in the famous court case that struck down Virginia's antimiscegenation laws. While widely understood solely as an African American, Loving herself denied having any African ancestry in a 2004 interview.[1] Helen Rountree discusses how Virginia's racial-purity laws became a veritable cornerstone of Indian self-identity in that state because of the way they distinguished the legal rights of Indians with no African ancestry from those with African ancestry.[2] In another example, a southeastern tribe whose council includes individuals with black, white, and Latino heritage—seemingly indicating a significant degree of racial harmony—some light-skinned tribal members subtly express contempt for their darker-skinned relatives.

If we are to make sense of this broad and deeply set pattern of anti-black racism among southern Indians, we need to understand that the pattern reaches beyond the southeastern U.S. and beyond indigenous communities. At some point in its history, every community in the U.S. has subscribed to some version of anti-black and anti-Indian racism; we are inundated with these ideas from birth. Histories of black-Indian relations in this case simply allow us a way to see the problems we face more clearly. That we are all in this narrative together provides, I hope, some consolation for the fact that I am discussing here what many would rather bury. This is our common heritage, and this is my humble attempt to contribute to our decolonization.

The origin of anti-black racism among southern Indians clearly rests in Anglo-American racism and colonialism, two phenomena that are based on an ideology of white supremacy—one in which white people are understood to be morally, intellectually, politically, and spiritually superior to non-whites and therefore entitled to various forms of privilege, power, and property.[3] A number of scholars have documented southern Indian adoption of Anglo systems of racial thinking as one component of a multifaceted response to U.S. aggression; in mirroring the peculiar notions of civility held by southern Anglos around race and gender, southern tribes hoped to protect themselves against conquest based on constructions of Indian savagery.[4]

Regulating Racial Categories

After slavery was legally abolished, segregation policies were the arena in which the boundaries of race and white privilege were officially policed. Educational segregation became a key way for Indians in the South to distance themselves as much as possible from blacks. When they wanted access to education, southern Indians fought to have their children enrolled in white schools and refused to send them to black schools. Rather than challenge the existence of the color line, most tried to position themselves on the most beneficial side of it. Clearly, tribes hoped there would be economic and political value to distinguishing themselves from blacks in the U.S., but the significance of the distinction goes further than that. Losing their status as Indians altogether would threaten their legal claim to sovereignty and political equality. Overall, tribes saw distancing themselves from blacks as a useful political strategy. Consequently, anti-black racism seeped deeper still into the construction of Indian identity.

More recently, policies surrounding federal recognition of Indian tribes have highlighted the boundaries of Indian identity and by extension black and white identities as well. Numerous indigenous communities in the U.S. for one reason

Class of 1895, Hampton Institute, Virginia. From 1877 to 1923, Native children from Plains tribes were sent to Hampton Institute—a "colored school"—as part of a national policy to eradicate indigenous cultures. Hampton's white founder believed that blacks would be the ideal instruments of "civilization" for Indians, whose memories of wars with whites were still fresh.

or another have not been acknowledged by the federal government. The Bureau of Indian Affairs (BIA) established in 1978 a process by which nonfederal tribes could petition to have their status as Indian tribes affirmed if they could prove through genealogical, historical, and anthropological research that they had always had social and political cohesion as an Indian community.

At first glance, federal recognition policy seems fair enough, but problems have emerged in practice that have resulted in constant criticism of the process by those familiar with it.[5] Notably, African ancestry and its absence come into the federal recognition discussion in several ways. A primary concern is the previous recognition from governments, surrounding communities, and social scientists, each of which helped establish tribal persistence under federal regulations.[6] Because of Anglo-American conceptions of race and the one-drop rule, anyone with visible or known African ancestry (one drop of African blood) was considered black for most purposes. An Indian community with even a small degree of black ancestry is much less likely to have been acknowledged as Indian than a community with even greater degrees of white ancestry, making it far more difficult for them to establish claims.[7]

A look at the census provides a good example of this bias in historical records. The census enumerators in 1910, for instance, were instructed to use so-called Indian Schedules "principally for the enumeration of Indians living on reservations or in tribal relations."[8] They were given further instructions on how to group mixed communities. "Every family composed mainly of Indians should be reported entirely on this special schedule, and every family composed mainly of persons not Indians should be reported entirely on the general population schedule."[9]

This presented a problem for some Indian communities, particularly those with any African ancestry. People of mixed black, white, and Indian ancestry were classified as mulattoes by the 1910 census, undifferentiated from people of solely white and black ancestry. Surrounding populations in Louisiana acknowledged Indian ancestry in multiracial tribal communities by addressing them as Redbones, a derogatory term that denotes Indian, black, and white ancestry. The official census record, however, did not have a category to reflect that distinction, leading one to conclude that the record stated they were solely black and white instead of Indian.[10] Often, the extent to which a community designated as Redbone had mixed at all was questionable, as in the case of one Louisiana tribe, who were dismissed from consideration for federal services in 1938 by anthropologist and BIA official Ruth Underhill not so much because they had mixed with blacks but because local whites *said* they had.[11] This characterization of them as a group with an ambiguous identity leaves the impression that they are not, in fact, a legitimate Indian tribe and therefore not worthy of federal assistance. It was a means of disempowering Indians. Tribes knew this and sought to avoid it.

Similarly, in terms of previous federal acknowledgment of Indian communities, the BIA of the 1930s was, because of the one-drop rule, extremely disinclined to treat communities with black ancestry as Indian tribes. Considering that previous acknowledgment from the federal government is the gold standard and is supposed to establish tribal existence at every point prior, African ancestry becomes a considerable barrier to recognition. BIA officials expressed concern in 1934, for example, that they might be called on to serve Louisiana Indians who were "mixed with negroes."[12] Bureau records indicate that black ancestry among *some* Louisiana Indian groups made officials less inclined to serve *any* of the Louisiana tribes. Thus, tribes with black ancestry petitioning for federal recognition are clearly at a disadvantage.

Perhaps the most difficult rejection to deal with comes from other Indians. While many tribal leaders throughout the U.S. have in recent years expressed support for tribes with African ancestry, there are still those who have a hard time accepting people with black ancestry as "real" Indians. Tribes with minimal black ancestry will have a more difficult time gaining acceptance from other tribes than will tribes with similar degrees of white ancestry because of the ways in which Indians have been encouraged, through the twin processes of colonization and racial oppression, to adopt anti-black racism.

Special Indian census schedule showing Chickahominy family records from Virginia, 1910.

Indians who appear to have black ancestry bear a unique burden in being discriminated against even within their own tribes and families. Doubts about tribal authenticity that are linked to accusations of blackness are placed on their shoulders, or more accurately, on their faces. Such is the power of race that it leads us to disown our own kin, undermining the most basic human bond and principles of tribal people.

We are dynamic people with the power to change and adapt our strategies as new information comes to light. Once we understand that the ideology of white supremacy performs many tasks, diverting multiple resources away from blacks and Indians alike, we can see more clearly that anti-black racism, when manifested by Indians, undermines tribal well-being. How else could we describe a system that perpetuates a racial formation with whites at the top of a racial hierarchy?[13] When we finally see ourselves in this way, as truly responsible for each other's freedom and implicated in each other's oppression, it will become easier to forge alliances and free ourselves from the behaviors that have held us back in the past. And then we may find that we are truly indivisible after all.

Jack Arzu and Georgette Lambey, Garifuna immigrants to the U.S., dance during the Garifuna Hudutu gathering, California, 2008.

JOSEPH O. PALACIO, SR.

HISTORY AND CONTINUITY
Being Garifuna and Black Indian in the United States

Millions of immigrants from Brazil, the Caribbean, Central America, Columbia, and Venezuela are of Black Indian heritage. The Garifuna people have been migrating to cities such as New York, Boston, Chicago, Los Angeles, and New Orleans since the early 1900s. Among the approximately 300,000 Garifuna in Central America, most have at least one close relative from Belize, Guatemala, Honduras, or Nicaragua living in the United States.

Several studies have centered on the differences in Garifuna cultures in St. Vincent Island, Central America, and the United States, but with little focus on their shared Black Indian roots.[1] This essay begins with a fictional sketch of the life of a young Garifuna woman in Brooklyn, New York, who is unaware that she and thousands of her fellow Americans share Black Indian blood. Following that is a discussion about the rise of Garifuna nationhood and some observations about the continuity and culture of Garifuna and Black Indians in the United States.

Being Garifuna in Brooklyn

Bernardina Alvarez is a fifteen-year-old first-generation American whose parents came from Dangriga, Belize, in 1980. She is caught between two strong cultural currents—her home life and her African American peer group. Her father reinforces her cultural heritage as the anchor that keeps her from straying into what he refers to as *gudémei lídan samínü* (which translates idiomatically as "short-sightedness") among her friends. Her closest reminder of being "different" comes from the Garifuna language, which her parents speak to each other and several relatives who visit often. Bernardina knows only a few words in the language, although her parents send her for classes on weekends with an elderly relative. Another reminder is the food that her mother prepares on the weekends: plantain, *eréba* (cassava bread), coconut, fish, green banana, and yams. Although Bernardina does not care much for the dishes, she eats a little bit to show her appreciation. She is more at home at parties with her Garifuna friends where they play the latest *punta* rock songs they receive from Dangriga.

What Bernardina questions most about her culture, however, is the reverence her parents maintain for the ancestors. She attended a *dügü* (ceremony of placation) in Dangriga one summer, and it took her months to recover from the culture shock of the rites taking place in the *dabuyaba* (temple)—the endless chanting and dancing, the trances that took place when ancestral spirits periodically overpowered some of the dancers, the roosters flapping around and cackling, and so on. She would have dismissed this "never-again exotic adventure into her ancestors' spirit world" if it were not for a miracle that unraveled before her eyes. After the *dügü*, her uncle, who also lived in Brooklyn, was cured of an illness that had afflicted him for months, despite the efforts of specialists. Bernardina's namesake appeared through an aunt of hers and vowed to cure her sick son as a show of gratitude for the *dügü* feast he had sponsored. Bernardina's uncle took all the remedies recommended, including ritual baths, herbal brews, and dietary abstinence, and gradually got better.

Understanding Garifuna Nationhood

Bernardina's experiences in Dangriga found some grounding in a history class she took the following fall. A young teacher introduced her to the study of indigenous peoples in the Americas and assigned a group project to discuss how indigenous peoples interact with one another. One of Bernardina's group members was Robert Williamson. To their mutual surprise, they discovered that they both shared Black Indian blood, although Robert's family is from Oklahoma. As part of their assignment, they interviewed me about the origins of the Garifuna, which served as a prelude to a similar session related to Willamson's nation.

The conjoining of runaway African slaves and Carib-Arawak Indians in the eastern Caribbean was not meant to result in the formation of and ultimate consolidation of both groups into one socioculture. Within the cauldron of African

Augustine and Simeona Palacio, Barranco village, Belize, 1979. Courtesy Dr. Joseph O. Palacio, Sr.

and Indian slavery, the frequent escapes of both groups from the relentless search by Europeans for more chattel labor resulted in unions between the Africans and Carib-Arawaks. The children created through these unions joined the increasing ranks of mulattoes, who formed their own Hispanic creole culture practiced today by their descendants all over the Caribbean and South America.

The blending of African and Garifuna blood and culture occurred on Yuru-mei (the name given St. Vincent by the Garifuna ancestors) as groups struggled against a common enemy—Europeans—and sought to maintain possession of a common resource—land—which the British subdivided into plantations in the late 1770s. With an inexhaustible supply of fleeing slaves and a dwindling number of the original Carib-Arawaks, the population became increasingly black in skin color.

Patterns of culture, which no doubt recurred in the formation of similar groups in the New World, developed through the mixing of Indians and blacks on St. Vincent. The blending of Arawaks and Caribs is one of the many inter-mixtures in the history of the Garifuna people, and highlights the fact that the mixing of peoples had been happening long before Africans and the Garifuna ever came into contact with each other. Originating from two Amazonian forest peoples in present-day Venezuela, the Arawaks and Caribs remained distinct in language, belief systems, and material culture as they moved into the Caribbean. The Arawaks are Taino people who still live today on the Greater Antilles islands of Cuba, Jamaica, Hispaniola, and Puerto Rico. They passed their language to

Pen Cayetano
(Garifuna, b. 1954),
Triumph of Unity, 1994.
Oil on canvas, 150 x
100 cm. Cayetano is
a self-taught painter
and musician who
infuses much of
his artwork with
Garifuna history,
folklore, and culture.
People of African
descent—including
the St. Vincent
island Garinagu, or
Garifuna, formerly
known as Black Caribs
(mixed African and
Carib Indian)—form
part of the population
of Belize today. The
British imported
African slaves during
the eighteenth
century to fell lumber,
cut sugarcane, and,
later, to erect colonial
buildings. Since
emancipation from
slavery, the Garifuna
have contributed
widely to the history
and culture of Belize,
including combining
traditional music
with modern rock
to create the music
phenomenon *punta*
rock.

their descendants, some of whom became the Garifuna. Most present-day Caribs, or Kalinago, live in the Carib Territory on the island of Dominica. More research is needed to better understand how the Arawaks and Caribs joined to form the people called Yellow Caribs, who inhabited the eastern Caribbean and became the immediate ancestors of the Garifuna.

Much discourse about African civilizations in the pre-Columbian Americas has developed, with special mention of St. Vincent in Ivan Van Sertima's book *They Came Before Columbus: The African Presence in Ancient America*. The debate ranges beyond the origins of the Garifuna people to that of all Africans in the New World. Certainly, as the spotlight on Black Indians increases, the search will intensify for specific regions in Africa where particular cultural traits originate. Little has been done in this regard for the Garifuna, apart from the generic reference to West African origins. The Garifuna recognized both the humanity and suffering of African runaway slaves and their own similar role to the Carib-Arawaks as culture bearers.

Another pattern found in the formation of Black Indian culture is the deliberate construction of heritage, often taking cues from the larger society. Black Caribs emphasized their Indian heritage to distinguish themselves from the African slaves the British used as scouts during the Carib Wars. They wrapped boards around the heads of their infants to make them look like Yellow Caribs and adopted the primary language of St. Vincent.

Indians and blacks mixed mainly owing to circumstances beyond their control. The Europeans held political power over both the Indians and the blacks, and manipulated the two peoples to their benefit. The British turned their full wrath toward Black Caribs in their determination to take full possession of all lands on the island. They argued that because interloping blacks had forced the Indians from their lands, they were justified in taking over those same lands. Focused on their own desires, Europeans resorted to wars and forced removal to achieve their ends. To create more plantations, the British eventually placed the Garifuna on ten ships destined for Central America, exiling them forever from their homeland. Nancie Gonzalez's *Sojourners of the Caribbean: Ethnogenesis and Ethnohistory of the Garifuna* describes in great detail the Garifuna's defeat, capture, transport, and arrival on the island of Roatan.

The Garifuna brought to Central America the marronage characteristic of remaining in isolated communities along the coast, where they secured their food from the land and sea and relied on their neighbors for trade goods and wage labor. It was in these communities, numbering more than fifty from Nicaragua to Belize, that Bernardina's parents' self-identified culture developed. The Black Indian culture that orginated in the eastern Caribbean reached its apogee in coastal Central America.

One of the Garifuna's greatest adaptations is retaining their identity while being exposed to and assimilating traits from others—explorers, adventurers, state workers, multinational companies, and missionaries—all bringing along the trappings of Western civilization. Adopting the designation "indigenous people" is an example of such adaptation. While the Garifuna have always been self-conscious as one people formed in the subregion, others have had problems accepting them as a socioculture indigenous to the circum-Caribbean. When the indigenous peoples movement extended itself from North America to the rest of the Americas in the 1980s, not only did the Garifuna join it, they also went a step further and spearheaded the indigenous peoples movement in the English-speaking Caribbean.

Leadership in the Caribbean Organization of Indigenous Peoples (COIP) marked the Garifuna's first effort to mobilize their people beyond Central America. The contemporary sociopolitical context within the English-speaking Caribbean could not have been less promising. The struggle among the islanders had been dominated by the evolution from black slavery through British colonialism and eventual independence into the 1980s postindependence era of the indigenous peoples movement. The first response from academia and the rest of the society was to ask, "Didn't the Arawaks and Caribs all disappear into extinction hundreds of years ago?" The second wave of responses wondered why, "If they and their black descendants did still exist, they would seek recognition during a historic period when the islands were building seamless creole societies in which everyone could enjoy the equal rights promised by political independence?" The composition of the microstates, many measuring less than 1,000 square kilometers in territory and with populations of less than 200,000 each, is the answer to this last question. These characteristics were far different from those in Canada, where cultural and political pluralism were accepted and scores of aboriginal nations are still living. Leaders from the microstates were at the forefront of the movement within the Caribbean, and the Garifuna Nation assisted with the initial implementation during the movement's difficult founding years, from 1989 to 1993.

History and Continuity

Bernardina and Robert listened intently and had questions to ask, each from their own perspective. Bernardina wanted confirmation of the continuity of her culture for herself and her future children. Robert, on the other hand, kept looking back, comparing what he had just heard with what he had gathered from his grandfather, his main source of information about his heritage. For Robert, the account of the initial mix between Carib-Arawaks about to lose their land and the African runaways was not enough. Why did the two groups not continue fighting each other and retain their separate colors? He had heard about the vicious quarrels among his grandfather's siblings, some of whom were of lighter complexion, with one holding fast to being Indian while loudly disclaiming any ties to the others. As a result, this particular ancestor was able to live on the reservation and retain Indian status from the federal government.

The larger context of blending was so significant that it is difficult to attempt any quick comparison from one case to another. The overpowering influence of white racism, which was encoded into laws within the United States against both blacks and Indians, greatly affected the social status of their shared progeny. The result was that the chromatic shade of individuals made it almost impossible for them to form a sense of nationhood.

Furthermore, while the Garifuna have a strong sense of culture and history, their leaders have deliberately submerged the significance of color as a building block for nationhood. Thomas Vincent Ramos—the pioneer of Garifunaduo (loosely translated as Garifunaness) in modern Belize—was greatly influenced by Garveyism, the black nationalist movement that took root in the United States and extended into black communities in Central America. Also, the leaders active in the indigenous peoples movement influenced by North America and those who pioneered the Central American Black Organization, which represents black people throughout Central America, did not see themselves in opposition to each other—together they spoke for one people, the Garifuna. Host countries, however, have not extended to the Garifuna the same statutory recognition given to blacks in countries like Brazil, Colombia, and Venezuela or to Native peoples such as those in Guatemala and Honduras. They have been pushed between the cracks for being both black and Garifuna. This lack of governmental support has lead to poor education, extreme poverty, malnutrition, landlessness, and a high incidence of disease, such as HIV/AIDS, diabetes, and hypertension.

On the other hand, the capacity to integrate seemingly contradictory elements has made the Garifuna unique to the rest of the world. That inimitability has been validated with the highest level of global recognition. In 2003, UNESCO formally proclaimed Garifuna music, language, and dance a world heritage. Andy Palacio, born and raised in a small coastal village in southern Belize, projected his music onto the world stage in his own language and won the World Music Expo (WOMEX) award in 2007. That same year, he won the coveted UNESCO Artist for Peace Award. Such validation signified that the synergy that seemed impossible between blacks and Indians could result in the highest form of aesthetic expression.

RICHARD W. HILL, SR.

ROTIHNAHON:TSI AND ROTINONHSÓN:NI
Historic Relationships between African Americans and the Confederacy of the Six Nations

In August 1749, Onondaga speaker Canassatego met with Governor Hamilton of New York and asked him to allow the Nanticoke to leave their Maryland homelands and join the Six Nations: "We further tell you that the People of Maryland do not treat the Indians as you & your other do, for they make Slaves of them & sell their Children for Money, and this makes us more importunate with you to get the rest of our Couzins from among them, and to urge this we give you a Belt of 7 rows."[1] The concept of slavery was part of founding dialogues between Native nations and the colonizing governments. The first slaves we were aware of were our own people, forced to serve advancing whites.

While we have numerous references to Indians held as slaves, considerably less-reliable information about Rotihnahon:tsi and Rotinonhsón:ni relationships is available. Rotihnahon:tsi, the Mohawk name for African Americans, means "people who have dark skin." In addition to the more common use of Haudenosaunee, or Six Nations, Mohawks call themselves Rotinonhsón:ni, or "people of the longhouse." I prefer to use these Mohawk terms, as they seem to be less layered with meaning than the common English words. You will have to read carefully and remember who I'm speaking of as I briefly trace several historical accounts related to the relationships between our peoples.

John Trumbull (1756–1843), *Captain Joseph Lewis (or Louis) of the Oneida Indians*, (detail) ca. 1785–86. Colonel Louis Cook, the son of an Abenaki and an African, was adopted out of slavery by Mohawk chiefs as a boy. He became a leader of the Mohawk people, an officer in the Revolutionary War, and is an ancestor of the Cook family at Akwesasne (Mohawk territory).

The First Rotihnahon:tsi

We were introduced to the Rotihnahon:tsi by the Dutch. By 1626, the Dutch West India Company had imported black slaves from Africa for use in the fur trade and building their new colony, New Amsterdam (New York); occasional trips to trading posts there most likely brought the Mohawks into contact with blacks for the first time. In 1644, a number of black slaves in New Amsterdam who had worked for the West India Company for a number of years were granted conditional emancipation. They were free on a bond, payable in labor, while their children remained slaves. It is not clear how the Rotinonhsón:ni viewed such measures, nor is it clear if the Dutch term *negerslaven* shaped Rotinonhsón:ni views of blacks. The fact that blacks came as slaves might have influenced our collective image of the Rotihnahon:tsi.

The French also made reference to slaves held by both Indians and themselves. These captives were forced to work for their captors and often treated poorly. Records indicate that our ancestors agreed with the idea that slaves were the property of their owners, and their loss required compensation.[2] The Rotinonhsón:ni are known to have placed some captives into slavery during the seventeenth century, treating them quite cruelly, at least initially. Jesuit Father Louis Hennipen said, "Those whose Lives they spare, live amongst them, and serve them as Servants and Slaves, but in the process of time they recover their Liberty, and are held in the same Esteem as if they were of their own Nation."[3] In 1699, Rene-Robert Cavelier de La Salle hoped to obtain slaves from the Senecas to serve him as guides as he looked for new trading routes. The Senecas asked him to wait, as most of their slaves were returning from a trip to the Dutch, which suggests slaves were critical to the operation of the fur trade. La Salle also discovered that there were cultural protocols to the transition of captives into slaves and that the Seneca women decided the final fate of any captives.[4]

Rotihnahon:tsi and Rotinonhsón:ni Becoming One

At the same time in other colonies, different power dynamics were at play. An act of the Virginia Commonwealth in 1705 reduced all slaves—whether black, Indian, or mixed race—to the same fate, stating "that from and after the passing of this act, all negro, mulatto, and Indian slaves, in all courts of judicature, and other places, within this dominion, shall be held, taken, and adjudged, to be real estate (and not chattels;) and shall descend unto the heirs and widows of persons departing this life, according to the manner and custom of land of inheritance, held in fee simple." Through slavery, the Rotihnahon:tsi and Rotinonhsón:ni became brothers.

When my daughter Brenda was performing research for the Mashantucket Pequot Museum in Connecticut, she went to the Bahamas and visited with the descendants of Pequots, who in the 1600s had been shipped there as slaves, along with Mohawks and other Native people. She found that many of these "Black Indians" thought of themselves as Mohawks. Although they knew little of what it actually meant to be Mohawk, it had become a socialized identity, a self-made way of coping. While some may think of their assumption as inauthentic, consider for a moment the concept of identity. Mohawk is not our own word but rather an imposed identity. Another of the "real" names for the Mohawks is Kaniekeha, or "people of the land of the flint," and while the Bahamas are a long way from those lands, some of our blood still flows there. If culture and identity are tied to blood, we cannot stop the course of that blood, which will reveal itself through the spirit of the people. Such traces of black blood have, however, been erased from our collective memory. In a similar narrative, some black families became "cousins" with Rotinonhsón:ni families at Grand River and lived there with them for many generations, until federal law forced the black families to leave the reserve in the mid-twentieth century. Some Mohawk families are in denial about any mixed blood, and our histories have been tainted by modern-day racism.

Joseph Hodge: Ascent from Slavery

We do know that over several centuries a number of Rotihnahon:tsi men rose to prominence in tribal politics, among them Tachanuntie (also known as Tocanontie, or the Black Prince), who became an Onondaga chief, and Captain Sunfish (O-gah'qaah) and Duck (So-wak), "free black" brothers who lived among the Senecas. Another of these was Joseph Hodge, who was also known as Black Joe. When Presbyterian minister Reverend Samuel Kirkland met with the Rotinonhsón:ni at Buffalo Creek in 1788, he was accompanied by a black servant who some historians believe was Hodge, who had been taken prisoner by the Seneca during the Revolutionary War.

During various treaty negotiations with the new United States, the Senecas were required to deliver up any captives. Mary Jemison, the so-called "White Woman of the Genesee," was among them. So too was Hodge, who was taken to Fort Stanwix (near present-day Rome, New York) and given over to Ameri-

Lewis Foy (1757–1825), *The Great Indian Council*, ca. 1793. Watercolor, gouache, graphite, brown pen, 33 x 50.7 cm. Gift of Messrs. G. Ronald Jackson and Michael Jackson. Courtesy The Montreal Museum of Fine Arts.

can officials. Returning from the treaty council, he chose to live among the Senecas and soon became a fur trader and had children with a Seneca woman. Having a Seneca wife certainly would have helped in his business. When Colonel Thomas Proctor visited the Buffalo area in 1791, he reported that a white trader, Cornelius Winne, and his business partner, Hodge, were the only two non-Indian settlers living in the area. Soon after, Hodge was operating a tavern near Buffalo Creek, near the site of a large Six Nations reservation. He was well known and apparently well liked. Stories of his having more than one Seneca wife have been told.

In 1793, a drawing was made of a council at Buffalo Creek, and one of the speakers appears to be African American. Most likely it was Joseph Hodge. By all accounts, within five years Hodge had gone from slave to translator. That he served as an interpreter is important, as it showed a level of trust and respect. Hodge, however, served at a time when the U.S. was looking westward, and his role in interpreting fairly for the Rotinonhsón:ni has subsequently come into question. Unfortunately, his role has been overlooked by historians.

Gilbert Stuart
(1755–1828), *Joseph Brant*, 1786. Oil on canvas, 30 x 25 in. N0199.1961.

The Brants: Mohawk Slave Owners

Oneida warriors fighting for the Americans in the Revolutionary War often offered captives to their allies for use as slaves. One of these warriors, Joseph Brant, received a handsome allowance and a captain's pension after the war and lived quite comfortably; several Rotihnahon:tsi slaves served him at his home in Brant's Ford and later in Burlington, Ontario. It is said that he captured these slaves from American colonists.[5] Joseph Hodge was likely one of his captives.

Joseph Brant and his sister, Molly, mimicking the British model, used black "servants" to tend to their needs. Molly had been the common-law wife of British Indian Agent Sir William Johnson, and Joseph remained loyal to the British crown all his life. A list of Loyalists who moved to Canada in 1783 included three black members of Molly Brant's household: Abraham Johnston, Juba, and Jane Fundy. They were likely the same slaves who escaped with her when she fled colonist aggressions and left her home in the Mohawk Valley in 1777. Molly's "husband" had willed her Jane Fundy and one-quarter of his other slaves.

In the Mohawk language, Molly's slaves would have been referred to as *yontatehnahskwa*, meaning "she has them as pets." The term applied not only to Rotihnahon:tsi but to anyone in servitude. Slaves were seen as not unlike domestic animals that were expected to work for their masters. It also reflects Haudenosaunee complaints to officials that they were themselves treated "like dogs" by the colonists. This was not a good state to be in. Interestingly, Molly's household also included a white captive named William Lamb. The Roti-nonhsón:ni made a distinction between captives and slaves. The Dutch, French, and English had held some Haudenosaunee captive, refusing to let them go but not necessarily mistreating them. Some were turned into slaves forced to labor for the colonists, some executed, and others held for ransom.

Were Brant's "servants" slaves or employees? It appears that Brant was quick to assure his peers that his workers were not slaves in the traditional sense. About a visit in 1797 with Brant, Jeromus Johnson recalls Brant stating that "they were entirely willing to live with him, pleased with the Indian habits and customs, and never expressed a wish to return into civil society, where they were sure to be slaves to the white people, as they had been before the war."[6] Other accounts written by visitors to the household make it appear that these Rotihnahon: tsi were happy to serve their Mohawk captors. But we do not know the real thinking of the "servants," nor Joseph Brant's attitude, other than that he felt he should be served by them.

Captain Louis Cook

In 1802, the New York state legislature passed a law that allowed the Mohawk chiefs at Akwesasne to appoint three trustees with the power of entering an agreement with the state to lease a ferry, purchase a bell, and build a school. The first trustees were Louis Cook, who was half Abenaki and half African American; William Gray, a white man adopted by the tribe; and Loran Tarbell, a descendant of the Tarbell brothers who had been kidnapped in Massachu-setts. That none of these men was Mohawk by matrilineal descent was not a coincidence: the state was less interested in tribal members loyal to Mohawk concerns than in trustees who might support the state's own agenda for taking Rotinonhsón:ni land.

As a young man, Cook—also known as Louis Atiatoharongwen or Atayatagh-ronghta—fought for the French in the Seven Years' War, and by 1760 was leading an Indian force with outstanding skill and bravery. He returned to Kahnawake

John Trumbull
(1756–1843), *Captain Joseph Lewis (or Louis) of the Oneida Indians*, ca. 1785–86.

and later moved to the Mohawk community at Akwesasne. He became allied with the Americans, and after visiting with General George Washington in 1775, served them as a scout and messenger. Washington noted a second visit in January 1776, during which Cook tried to wrestle an officer's commission, promising that he would try to persuade Kahnawake and Seven Nations of Canada warriors to support the Americans. Cook convinced Washington to form the Company of Indian Rangers, which was attached to the 1st New York Regiment, and he led a party of Oneidas and Tuscaroras in the victory over Major-General John Burgoyne. In August 1777, Cook led the Indian Rangers as they battled their Rotinonhsón:ni relatives—Joseph Brant's Mohawk, Seneca, and Cayuga warriors—who had sided with the English; that bloody day at Fort Schuyler caused generations of animosity between the two factions. After the war, Cook lived with the Oneidas and Onondagas, married, and raised several children.

In 1787, at the site of present-day Geneva, New York, forty-seven Rotinonhsón:ni chiefs and warriors were persuaded to sign two leases for 999 years which relinquished twelve million acres to a group of associates including white politicians and prominent citizens who were collectively known as the New York Genesee Company of Adventurers. One principal behind the negotiation was Cook. Cook returned to the land he held at Akwesasne and became a chief of the Mohawk. In 1792, the Americans called on him to help pacify Indians in the Ohio Valley, and in 1796 he was asked to help negotiate a treaty with the Mohawks. The result of the treaty was the cession of all Mohawk lands, save for a few square miles, and the establishment of the St. Regis Mohawk Reservation. This situation brought the ire of the Mohawk people upon Cook, who in turn sought to blame Joseph Brant for the bad deal. Missionary Roderic MacDonell wrote in 1801 that Cook "makes away with the greatest part of the money and disposes of lands on the American lines without consulting the Indians." He became known as *thiathoharonkwen*, meaning "one who pulls down the people," and died fighting for the Americans in the War of 1812. The Cook name survives today at Akwesasne.

The Rotinonhsón:ni Underground Railroad

The Rotinonhsón:ni were involved in a version of the Underground Railroad long before the abolitionist networks of the early nineteenth century. By the time they began assisting fugitive slaves in the late 1600s, the Rotinonhsón:ni had already witnessed slavery up close and personal for nearly a century, and they equated the master-slave dynamic to *yontatehnahskwa*, or the master-dog relationship. There was generally a disdain for slavery, and many Rotinonhsón:ni communities offered a safe haven for runaways.

The Rotinonhsón:ni Underground Railroad was, however, not without complication, and the system was not always a perfectly benevolent one. The colonies had repeatedly petitioned the Rotinonhsón:ni for the return of escaped slaves, and they sometimes were returned, used as bargaining chips, or traded for Rotinonhsón:ni captives, while others were provided safe passage from southern colonies to northern borders and, later, across to Canada. The escape routes followed ancient Indian paths connecting the Tuscarora Territory of North Carolina to the lands of the Seneca, Cayuga, Onondaga, Oneida, and Mohawk nations in New York State. The Warrior's Path and the Forbidden Path served as woodland expressways for hundreds of warriors, countless bundles of trade goods, and an unknown number of fugitive Rotihnahon:tsi.

The Tuscarora were engaged in contentions with colonists and other local North Carolina tribes. Competing trade interests contributed to conflicts with other Native nations, but colonial records show that so many slaves sought sanctuary among the Tuscarora that this also became a point of political tension. The Tuscarora were themselves put into slavery or shot on sight, and after the wars of the early eighteenth century and a denied petition for sanctuary in Pennsylvania, most Tuscarora headed north to New York. This development ended the main north-south route of the network, but it did not put an end to an east-west portion.

One east-west route into Canada led from Lockport, New York, and along the Niagara Escarpment, crossing the Niagara River into Ontario at Lewiston. This journey led Rotihnahon:tsi right through newly established Tuscarora Territory. The Tuscarora were legendary canoemen, capable of safely crossing the rapids of the lower Niagara. One oral history mentions Rotihnahon:tsi hiding on the Tuscarora reservation near Lewiston before continuing on to St. Catherines and Hamilton, Ontario. Some even made their way to the Six Nations Reserve along the Grand River, near Hamilton. Harriet Tubman lived in St. Catherines for eight years after 1850, and surely must have been aware of the Tuscarora–Six Nations connection to the Underground Railroad.

I have seen an old photograph, taken about 1880, of the Ohsweken Baptist Church choir. In it, standing with my great uncle, Josiah Hill, are two black women. Seneca historian Tom Hill told me that these women were former slaves who made their way north and ended up on the Six Nations Reserve. In the past, both individuals and communities could be adopted by the Rotinonhsón:ni. By living amongst the Haudenosaunee, they could earn their place in tribal society. They would be given new identities and assigned to specific clans and female relatives. In these ways, Rotihnahon:tsi blood was subsumed by Rotinonhsón:ni identity and oral history. The individual stories have been lost.

Conclusion

Since the 1600s, at their own peril, the Rotinonhsón:ni have offered escaped Rotihnahon:tsi refuge, returned them to their white owners, and kept them as their own slaves. Each group has betrayed and been betrayed by the other. We have also regarded each other as family. Intermarriage and children were the inevitable result, but in the past, Rotihnahon:tsi blood merged silently into Rotinonhsón:ni identity.

Today, few blacks live on the reserves in Canada or the reservations in New York, and many contemporary Rotinonhsón:ni have racist attitudes toward their Rotihnahon:tsi relatives. A growing number of Rotinonhsón:ni women are having children with Rotihnahon:tsi men, however. Time will tell how these new children will shape—and be shaped—by Rotinonhsón:ni culture.

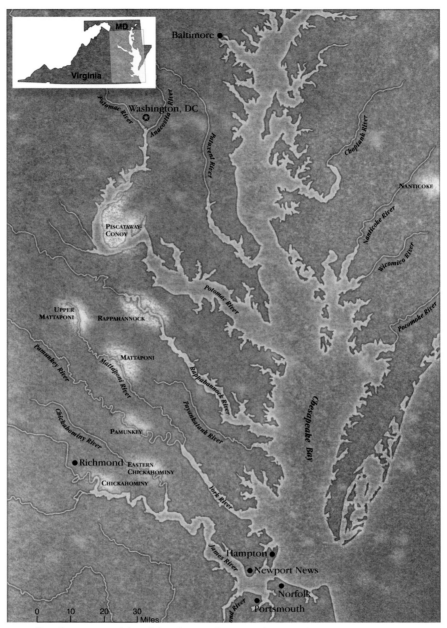

Map of Native communities of the Chesapeake Bay region, ca. 1610.

GABRIELLE TAYAC

CLAIMING THE NAME
White Supremacy, Tribal Identity, and Racial Policy in the Early Twentieth-Century Chesapeake

Mooney's Mongrels

"Those who remained in Maryland are represented today by a few negro mongrels who claim the name." These are the words of noted ethnographer James Mooney in the 1911 *Catholic Encyclopedia* as he describes the fatal finale of the Piscataway people. This essay will place Mooney's archaic and racist assessment of indigenous Piscataway identity in a historic context, which explains how Native peoples throughout the Chesapeake region were officially detribalized through white supremacist racial policy and attitudes. It will then address the interior experience of maintaining tribal identity in this often-terrifying environment, as well as the degradation of this identity within the larger societal context. Finally, it will argue that antiquated racial concepts still persist as key obstacles towards tribal recognition. This essay will focus primarily on the Piscataway histories but will also draw comparisons with the related peoples of the Chesapeake region.

Who and Where?

The most persistent Native peoples still in the Chesapeake region include the descendants of three powerful Algonquian-speaking chiefdoms: Piscataway on Maryland's Western Shore (of the Chesapeake), Nanticoke on Maryland's Eastern Shore (in present-day Delaware and southern New Jersey), and Powhatan in the coastal plain of Virginia. All of these peoples occupied riverine, agricultural communities—characterized by a centralized high chief and a sacred seasonal cycle—in one of the richest biospheres in the world. The Piscataway—also known by the Haudenosaunee name, Conoy—trace descent from the Nanticoke, who in turn trace descent from the Lenape.

Attempting Social Murder

According to sociologist Orlando Patterson, slavery is social death. Although the communities under consideration were not collectively enslaved, they were radically transformed through the institution of slavery, which led to the eventual tightening of race laws marginalizing non-white people. A law outlined in *Bacon's Laws of Maryland*, enacted in 1717, for example, illustrates the erosion of the Piscataway's already meager rights:

> II. Be it therefore Enacted, by the Right Honourable the Lord Proprietary, by and with the Advice and Consent of his Lordship's Governor, and the Upper and Lower Houses of Assembly, and by the Authority of the same, That from and after the End of this present Session of Assembly, no Negro, or Mulatto Slave, Free Negro, or Mulatto born of a White Woman, during his Time of Servitude by Law, or any Indian Slave, or Free Indian Natives of this or the neighbouring Provinces, be admitted and received as good and valid Evidence in Law, in any Matter or Thing whatsoever, depending before any Court of Record, or before any Magistrate within this Province, wherein any Christian White Person is concerned.

The recasting of Indians throughout the Chesapeake region as mulattoes and free people of color, at the same time that reservations were being eradicated in the 1700s and 1800s, resulted in the dissolution of treaty rights (often known as Articles of Peace and Amity). This racialization of Indian people set into motion the death of their recognized sovereignty.

Letter sent to other states by the eugenicist Walter Plecker, Virginia's Registrar of Vital Statistics, 1943. Virginia's Racial Integrity Act of 1924 prohibited people from identifying their race as Indian because it was believed that Indians who were "tainted" by African American ancestry were attempting to "sneak into the white race" in order to "pollute" it. All Native people were reclassified as "Negro" until 1967, when the act was repealed.

has special file

Dr. Plecker

COMMONWEALTH OF VIRGINIA
Department of Health
Bureau of Vital Statistics
Richmond

January 1943 .

Local Registrars, Physicians, Health
Officers, Nurses, School Superintendents,
and Clerks of the Courts

Dear Co-workers:

Our December 1942 letter to local registrars, also mailed to the clerks, set forth the determined effort to escape from the negro race of groups of "free issues," or descendants of the "free mulattoes" of early days, so listed prior to 1865 in the United States census and various types of State records, as distinguished from slave negroes.

Now that these people are playing up the advantages gained by being permitted to give "Indian" as the race of the child's parents on birth certificates, we see the great mistake made in not stopping earlier the organized propagation of this racial falsehood. They have been using the advantage thus gained as an aid to intermarriage into the white race and to attend white schools, and now for some time they have been refusing to register with war draft boards as negroes, as required by the boards which are faithfully performing their duties. Three of these negroes from Caroline County were sentenced to prison on January 12 in the United States Court at Richmond for refusing to obey the draft law unless permitted to classify themselves as "Indians."

Some of these mongrels, finding that they have been able to sneak in their birth certificates unchallenged as Indians are now making a rush to register as white. Upon investigation we find that a few local registrars have been permitting such certificates to pass through their hands unquestioned and without warning our office of the fraud. Those attempting this fraud should be warned that they are liable to a penalty of one year in the penitentiary (Section 5099a of the Code). Several clerks have likewise been actually granting them licenses to marry whites, or at least to marry amongst themselves as Indian or white. The danger of this error always confronts the clerk who does not inquire carefully as to the residence of the woman when he does not have positive information. The law is explicit that the license be issued by the clerk of the county or city in which the woman resides.

To aid all of you in determining just which are the mixed families, we have made a list of their surnames by counties and cities, as complete as possible at this time. This list should be preserved by all, even by those in counties and cities not included, as these people are moving around over the State and changing race at the new place. A family has just been investigated which was always recorded as negro around Glade Springs, Washington County, but which changed to white and married as such in Roanoke County. This is going on constantly and can be prevented only by care on the part of local registrars, clerks, doctors, health workers, and school authorities.

Please report all known or suspicious cases to the Bureau of Vital Statistics, giving names, ages, parents, and as much other information as possible. All certificates of these people showing "Indian" or "white" are now being rejected and returned to the physician or midwife, but local registrars hereafter must not permit them to pass their hands uncorrected or unchallenged and without a note of warning to us. One hundred and fifty thousand other mulattoes in Virginia are watching eagerly the attempt of their pseudo-Indian brethren, ready to follow in a rush when the first have made a break in the dike.

Very truly yours,

W. A. Plecker, M. D.
State Registrar of Vital Statistics

Indeed, in census records for the Nanticokes on the Eastern Shore of Maryland, clear cases of racial reassignments took place up to the early nineteenth century, at the moment of reservation dissolution. For example, as anthropologists Rountree and Davidson report, "The loss of a legally recognized Indian identity can be seen clearly in the case of one Choptank Indian named Abraham Bishop." In 1790, Bishop was clearly identified as a Choptank Indian. That same year, he moved off of the Locust Neck Reservation, which was formally abolished by 1800. By 1797, Bishop was classified as a "free Negro" and also counted among "other free colored." All of his descendants were classified as free Negroes or free colored persons in Dorchester County.

On the Western Shore of Maryland, in Piscataway Territory, a picture emerges of an indigenous community continuing to live on the last reserved land for Piscataway peoples at a site called Choptico, also known as Calverton Manor. An English Jesuit Indian mission, Calverton Manor was seized in the Protestant Rebellion of 1689. With the Catholics expelled, Protestant overseers eventually deeded Indian lands to their own descendants while at the same time acted as legal representatives for the Chopticos before Maryland authorities. As nominal Catholics and a dispossessed minority in their own homeland, the Piscataway likely found eligible marriage partners among the free people of color who were the children of white indentured servants and enslaved Africans. This is the situation with the children of Elizabeth Proctor, a white English indentured servant who married an enslaved African. They both lived on the estate of the Indian agent, William Boarman. In the Piscataway case, a bit different perhaps in its originating state from the Choptank, marriages between Indians and mixed-race free people were highly likely. At the same time as the dissolution of the Choptico reservation, there emerged a free colored people who carried the surnames of English settlers who lived on the reservations and identified themselves quite distinctly as descendants of the old chiefdom. And as with the Choptank, any association of African identity to Native people undermined their sovereignty.

Thomas Jefferson's notes on the Powhatan in Virginia reflect a similar sense of diminished tribal integrity relative to the level of black appearance. He states: "There remain of the Mattaponies three or four men only, and they have more Negro than Indian blood in them. They have lost their language, have reduced themselves, by voluntary sales, to about fifty acres of land, which lie on the river of their own name, and have, from time to time, been joining the Pamunkies, from whom they are distant but 10 miles." In other notes, Jefferson lauds the Pamunkeys for their "purer" blood.

Eunice and Levin Sockum (Nanticoke), ca. 1860. In 1856, storeowner Sockum was found guilty of violating a law that prohibited "mulattoes" and "Negroes" from owning firearms. The Nanticoke identified as Indians but also had a history of intermarriage with whites and blacks. Exasperated by white racism, Sockum closed his store and moved to New Jersey.

By Any Other Name

Mulatto. Wesort. Moor. Triracial Isolate. All these terms appear with increasing frequency in the late nineteenth and early twentieth centuries in reference to Chesapeake Native communities. Sometimes, during that period, as in the case of the Powhatan and Nanticoke in Millsboro, the communities defended their tribal names through legal actions. Moreover, in church writings from the old mission at Choptico, the Native community still referred to itself as Indian.

When in the 1890s, James Mooney sent circulars from the Bureau of American Ethnology to research Indian remnants, reports came back from families who identified as members of the Piscataway chiefdom tribes. These same peoples were identified by their neighbors as being "part Negro." By 1910, however, the designations of "free colored" or "mulatto" gave way to the bifurcated classification of either "black" or "white" on the census reports. Despite this narrow categorization, the church continued to identify the community as Indian. Numerous stories still exist among contemporary Piscataways about how the census man was hated, and how the "census man changed our names."

Chickahominy family, 1918. Photo by Frank G. Speck. N12600.

Among Mooney's papers at the National Anthropological Archives, Suitland, Maryland, is an article from a 1912 edition of the *Washington Star*. It describes a group of people in Prince George's County with the surname "Proctor" who have brown complexions and straight black hair and trace their ancestry back to the old Piscataway empire. There also exists a series of studies on triracial isolates by William Gilbert. Articles describing this community as "mysterious" or as an "outcasted clan" are seen throughout the first half of the twentieth century. The Indianness of the community is speculated upon, but continuous references to ranges of blackness in phenotype serve to publicly undercut any acknowledgment of the community's tribal heritage.

Staying Together, Falling Apart

The Piscataway community maintained strong ties to the original site of the Jesuit mission at Choptico and actively participated in St. Ignatius Church, where they were able to maintain their unique spiritual traditions. Seasonal ceremonies were adapted to fit the Catholic calendar. The Green Corn Ceremony, for example, became associated with the Feast of the Assumption, and the Feast of the Dead took place near All Saint's Day. Unlike their Protestant counterparts in the Nanticoke and Powhatan communities, however, the Piscataway could not maintain a separate church. At St. Ignatius, the seating arrangement reflected and enforced the racial order. Whites sat in the front, Indians and light-skinned blacks downstairs at the back, and blacks on the balcony. This arrangement remained in place until 1964.

The Piscataway also practiced high rates of endogamy (marrying within their own community) to an extent that they were often selected by medical researchers for studies of genetically transmitted diseases. From the late eighteenth to the mid-twentieth century, community members married within only very specific surnames. This boundary maintenance served to minimize intermarriage with blacks and frequently led to disownership of family members who married outside the community. Endogamy is declining today. While racism persists in the selection of marriage partners, it is also in decline.

Thus, a community that was characterized by its lack of discrimination in the seventeenth century was molded by white supremacist race laws and social orders into a closed society that soundly policed its color lines. While those practices once served to protect a sense of Indianness in a violent world, I contend that to continue to deny the realities of our history and disavow our African American ancestors does not serve us well. The deliberate manipulation of history paralyzes our communities by suggesting that African ancestry cancels Indian claims to a collective right to inherent sovereignty. We may be "hybrid" in composition, but we are enduringly rooted in indigeneity. By claiming our names, we can bite back.

Emancipation certificate of Ben Vann, 1889. After the Civil War, Cherokee Freedmen and their descendants were given citizenship in the Cherokee Nation.

Chad Smith speaking after the film *The Trail of Tears: Cherokee Legacy* at the National Museum of the American Indian, Washington, D.C., 2007. Principal Chief of the Cherokee Nation of Oklahoma, Chad Smith insisted that the 2007 disenrollment of the Cherokee Freedmen had nothing to do with race. Rather, it was about the right of Cherokees to make their own laws governing membership and apply them equally to all.

MARK HIRSCH

RACE, CITIZENSHIP, AND SOVEREIGNTY IN THE CHEROKEE NATION

Chad Smith

Cherokees made headlines in 2007, when tribal members voted to make "Indian blood" a requirement for citizenship in the Cherokee Nation. The measure revoked tribal membership from some 2,800 descendants of African American slaves once owned by Cherokees, and quickly ignited a firestorm of controversy. Critics lambasted Cherokees for practicing racial discrimination, and the Congressional Black Caucus threatened to block the estimated $300 million in federal funds the Oklahoma-based tribe receives annually unless the ousted African Americans were reinstated. Cherokees, for their part, insisted that race had nothing to do with the amendment to their tribal constitution. "It has everything to do with who can be an Indian in an Indian tribe," explained Chad Smith, principal chief of the Cherokee Nation, the largest Indian tribe in the United States. "The right to define tribal membership lies at the core of tribal identity and self-governance."[1]

Turmoil in the Cherokee Nation was news for most Americans, but it was an old story for Cherokees. Tension over race and tribal citizenship flared after the Civil War, when the Cherokee Nation, like the United States as a whole, struggled to incorporate the former slaves, or Freedmen, into their social order.[2] Unlike the United States, whose sovereign power was secured through a bloody civil war, the Cherokee Nation faced withering challenges to sovereignty as tribal members simultaneously wrestled with the issue of citizenship. That confluence of events put Cherokees at loggerheads with people of African descent, and tribal self-government on a collision course with the citizenship claims of the Cherokee Freedmen.[3]

Cherokees first acquired African American slaves in the late 1700s, and by 1835, Cherokee planters owned 1,592 slaves. During Indian Removal, enslaved African Americans accompanied their Cherokee masters on the Trail of Tears to Indian Territory (modern-day Oklahoma), where the Cherokee Nation rebuilt its culture and institutions. By 1861, four thousand slaves lived among the Cherokees, who allied with the Confederacy during the Civil War.[4]

At war's end, the Cherokee Nation signed a treaty with the United States, granting the ex-slaves, or Freedmen, "all the rights of Native Cherokees." Under the Treaty of 1866, Freedmen who resided in Cherokee territory before the war, and who remained there in 1866, were to be considered citizens. Cherokee Freedmen living outside the nation were granted six months to return to claim tribal citizenship.[5]

Thousands of former slaves received citizenship in the Cherokee Nation after the Civil War. These citizen Freedmen enjoyed the right to farm tribal lands as well as vote in tribal elections and hold tribal office. Yet many Freedmen, including men and women of Afro-Cherokee ancestry, were not so lucky. These "too-lates"—ex-slaves who failed to return to Cherokee territory within six months after the Treaty of 1866—were denied citizenship in the Cherokee Nation, and struggled to claim their rights well into the twentieth century.[6]

The Freedmen staked their claim to citizenship at a time when the Cherokees faced a plethora of threats to their sovereignty and security. By mandating citizenship for Freedmen, the Treaty of 1866 had already usurped the Cherokee Nation's right to determine and enroll its own members. Now, powerful railroad corporations were demanding rights of way through tribal lands, industrialists were seeking to harvest timber and extract minerals, and ranchers were pressing for grazing land to fatten cattle. Worse still, homesteaders, including former slaves from the Deep South, were pouring into Indian Territory, intruding on Cherokee lands. If the trespassers were not removed, other settlers would follow, and before long, many believed, the squatters would outnumber the Cherokees. If that came to pass, the Cherokees feared, Congress could install a territorial government, which would dissolve the Cherokee Nation.[7]

To protect their security, Cherokees moved to assert control over the people living on tribal lands. Lobbyists were dispatched to Washington to press lawmakers for the expulsion of intruders. Stricter rules were also implemented for assessing tribal citizenship claims. A law authorizing the Cherokee Supreme Court to judge citizenship claims was passed in 1869, and a special court was created ten years later to screen citizenship applications on a case-by-case basis. If deemed noncitizens, Freedmen were evicted from tribal lands and expelled from the Cherokee Nation.[8]

Cherokees also sought to prevent adoptive citizens from harvesting the full fruits of tribal membership. In 1883, the tribal council passed legislation excluding the Freedmen—as well as Shawnees, Delawares, intermarried whites, and other adopted citizens—from sharing the proceeds from the sale of Cherokee lands. When Chief Dennis Wolf Bushyhead complained that the measure violated the Treaty of 1866, the tribal council authorized per-capita payments to "blood citizens" anyway.[9]

Undaunted, the Cherokee Freedmen mobilized to claim their rights as full citizens in the Cherokee Nation. In this, they received assistance from Congress and the U.S. courts, which upheld the Freedmen's claims to citizenship, property rights, and tribal assets.[10] Cherokees viewed Washington's interference in their nation's affairs as a deliberate effort to undermine tribal sovereignty—a conclusion that was reinforced in the 1890s, when Congress unveiled a new weapon to disempower Native nations.

In 1887, Congress passed the General Allotment Act (also known as the Dawes Act), which opened Indian lands to white settlement, dissolved tribalism, and promoted the assimilation of Native people. Under the act, communally held tribal lands were divided into parcels for distribution to individual tribal members. Surplus lands were sold to white settlers. To divide and assign the land, the Dawes Commission visited Cherokee Territory, where allotment agents collected and evaluated citizenship applications and added the names of verified tribal members to official enrollment lists, the Dawes Rolls. These rolls would become the basis for determining membership in the Cherokee Nation.[11]

The Dawes commissioners collected some 53,000 applications for citizenship in the Cherokee Nation. These were divided into three categories: "Cherokees by Blood" (which indicated an applicant's ratio of Cherokee "blood"), "Intermarried Whites," and "Freedmen." The category of "Freedmen" which did not record degree of Cherokee blood, included African Americans and Afro-Cherokees.[12] All individuals whose names were included on the Dawes Rolls of 1906 were entitled to allotments, and all enrolled members, including Freedmen and their descendants, were considered citizens of the Cherokee Nation.[13]

The Cherokee Nation lost some 6.5 million acres of tribal land as a result of allotment. But the tribe's travails did not end there. The final, devastating nail in the coffin of Cherokee self-government was driven in 1907, when the Indian and Oklahoma Territories were admitted to the Union as the state of Oklahoma. With statehood, the Cherokee Nation was dissolved as a political entity.[14]

The Treaty of 1866, controversy over tribal citizenship, allotment, detribalization, and statehood—these and other forces constituted a frontal assault on Cherokee sovereignty. Despite these challenges, and despite the temptation to turn inward to defend tribal sovereignty, the Cherokee Nation refrained from enacting rules that made "Indian blood" a requirement for tribal membership. Birth and adoption were the only criteria for tribal enrollment at the turn of the century. Neither blood nor skin color entered the calculus. Nor would blood measurement figure as a criteria for citizenship in the 1970s, when the Cherokee tribal government was reorganized. The new Cherokee Constitution declared that proof of descent from an ancestor listed on the Dawes Rolls was the only criteria for tribal citizenship.[15] But that would change.

In 1988, the Cherokee Nation passed legislation that transformed the criteria for tribal membership. Now, a Cherokee citizen had to prove descent from a person listed on the Dawes Commission "blood roll" of 1906. Since the Dawes Rolls recorded no blood measurement for Freedmen, the new law threatened to revoke citizenship for most African American tribal members.[16] Descendants of the Freedmen resorted to U.S. and tribal courts to retain their tribal citizenship, and in 2006 the Cherokee Nation Supreme Court upheld their citizenship rights. The only way the Cherokee Nation could abridge the Freedmen's citizenship rights, the court declared, was to amend the Cherokee tribal constitution to include a blood requirement for membership. The tribal council accordingly proposed an amendment requiring "Indian blood" for tribal citizenship, and

Marilyn Vann holding a photograph of her father, aunt, and sisters (shown at right), 2009. Vann's family members were registered as Cherokee Freedmen tribal members during the Dawes enrollment process. Vann and other descendants of the Cherokee Freedmen have filed a lawsuit to regain tribal citizenship.

a ratification election was held on March 3, 2007. The amendment, approved by two-thirds of the voters, put the citizenship rights of some 2,800 African American tribal members on the chopping block.[17]

Many Cherokees welcomed the outcome as a victory for tribal sovereignty. "Their voice is clear as to who should be citizens of the Cherokee Nation," declared Principal Chief Chad Smith. The right to define tribal membership, he noted, was a right of self-government that the Cherokee Nation "affirmed in 23 treaties with Great Britain and the United States and paid dearly with 4,000 lives on the Trail of Tears."[18] Jodie Fishinghawk, a pro-amendment Cherokee, put it bluntly: "We do not want non-Indians in the tribe; our Indian blood is what binds us together."[19]

Not everyone agreed. "This is a sad chapter in Cherokee history," observed Cherokee Tribal Council member Taylor Keen. "This is not my Cherokee Nation. My Cherokee Nation is one that honors all parts of her past."[20]

DAN AGENT

THE CHEROKEE NATION UNDER SIEGE

On March 3, 2007, Cherokee citizens voted to approve an amendment to the Cherokee Constitution that requires citizens to be Cherokee by blood. They exercised their sovereign right on the basis of the historic government-to-government relationship between the Cherokee Nation and the United States. That sovereign right is further founded on an ancient, cultural imperative by blood—the Cherokee clan system—that precedes first contact with the Europeans by thousands of years.

The amendment was approved by 77 percent of those who voted but has since been vigorously challenged by a vocal opposition. If this new attack on the rights of the Cherokee people is successful, the demise of Indian sovereignty will be imminent.

Indian citizenship based on blood has never been an issue for any federally recognized tribe other than the Cherokee. Every sovereign Indian nation has a blood requirement for citizenship. Unlike other tribes, however, the Cherokee Nation has been victimized by the Treaty of 1866, which recognized former slaves as "Native Cherokees."[1] The descendants of those slaves have contended for several years that they are entitled to Cherokee citizenship and benefits on the basis of Article 9 of the Treaty of 1866.

The March 3rd referendum followed a decision by the Cherokee Nation Judicial Appeals Tribunal in the case of *Allen v. Cherokee Nation Tribal Council* which made descendants of Freedmen eligible for citizenship.[2] The decision reversed the 2001 ruling in *Riggs v. Lela Ummersteskee*, which had stated otherwise.[3] Included in that ruling was the following statement:

> This Court sees no reason why the Cherokee Nation must be bound by a
> treaty . . . when that treaty has been broken by the other sovereign. How-
> ever, if the Cherokee Nation is going to make a decision not to abide by
> a previous treaty provision [Article 9 of 31], it must do so by clear actions
> which are consistent with the Cherokee Nation Constitution. . . . If the
> Cherokee people want to change the legal definition of Cherokee citizen-
> ship, they must do so expressly.[4]

The Cherokee people responded, collecting signatures as required by the
Cherokee Constitution for conducting a referendum.[5] After the results of the
referendum were announced, accusations of racism were leveled by descendants
of the Freedmen and their supporters. Media coverage of the issue was inflam-
matory and often inaccurate.

The Cherokee Nation is very likely the most ethnically diverse Indian tribe
in the country and includes citizens of European origin as well as Hispanic,
Asian American, and African American descent. Descendants of these mixed
unions, including descendants of former slaves and Freedmen who married
Cherokees, are citizens of the Cherokee Nation by virtue of one common blood
identity. Indeed, many African American Cherokees supported the March 3rd
amendment.[6]

Long before first contact with the Europeans or the treaties and ethnic blending that followed, Cherokee blood and bones became a part of the continent.
For thousands of years, the Cherokee people, or Ani-yunwi-ya (the Real People),
defined themselves based on the Cherokee clan system, which delineates a
relationship of consanguinity, specifically blood kinship of matrilineal descent.
Although clan inheritance has diminished owing to exogamy and miscegenation, the seven clans continue to function today.[7] And although children of
Cherokee men and non-Cherokee women cannot belong to a clan, blood heritage—no matter what the degree—remains the basis of being Cherokee. With
this in mind, the Treaty of 1866 and efforts to enforce it can be seen as direct
attacks on the heart and spirit of the Cherokee people.

It is important to understand details of the treaty and its historical context
to appreciate the current citizenship issue. Many feel that the Treaty of 1866
was forced upon the Cherokee Nation at the end of the Civil War as a punitive
measure because some Cherokee had sided with the Confederacy.[8] It is true that,
in the absence of Union forces and lacking protection guaranteed by the federal

government, some Cherokee allied with the Confederacy. However, it is also true that more Cherokee fought with the Union, and less than 2 percent of the Cherokees were slave owners.[9] Numerous publications—including two recently published books, *Way Down Yonder in the Indian Nation* (2007) by Michael Wallis and *The Cherokee Nation in the Civil War* (2007) by Clarissa Confer—have noted the punitive nature of the treaty. Moreover, in her research, Confer discovered that none of the states in the slave-holding South were required to "treat [their former slaves] as citizens." These histories are conveniently forgotten by proponents of Freedmen citizenship and the modern-day media. In fact, coverage of the issue has been anything but unbiased.

An analysis of press coverage of the March 2007 vote was conducted by the American Indian Policy and Media Initiative at Buffalo State University. The study reviewed coverage between February 27 and March 10, 2007, focusing on headlines, leads, quoted news sources, statistical information, and historical context. "In general, this was reported as a classic clash between oppressor and victim," stated Ron Smith, communication professor and principal author of the report. "Missing were nuance, historical perspective, and a context within which to understand the contemporary significance of the story. . . . Several headlines screamed 'racism,' such as one that read, 'Cherokees Accused of Racist Plot as Sons of Slaves Are Cast Out.'" The study further revealed that Freedmen sources were frequently the first quoted in the news reports, with two-thirds using the term "racism" in the lead or opening paragraphs. By contrast, although three-quarters of the articles implied the concept of sovereignty, only 12 percent used the term "sovereignty."[10]

Another attempt to challenge the amendment came from Representative Diane Watson, a Democrat from California, who introduced legislation to terminate the government-to-government relationship between the Cherokee Nation and the United States, including federal funding. H.R. 2824 called for compliance only with Article 9 of the Treaty of 1866.[11] Neither she nor anyone else in Congress addressed the article in the treaty that ensures all of what is northeastern Oklahoma shall remain the Cherokee Nation. Watson is not Cherokee by blood, but she made a trip to Oklahoma to conduct news conferences in support of the treaty and her legislation. When asked if she had discussed the issue with any of the eighty-six Cherokees who live in her home district in California, she said she did not have to do that.[12]

110th CONGRESS H. R. 2824

To sever United States' government relations with the Cherokee Nation of Oklahoma until such time as the Cherokee Nation of Oklahoma restores full tribal citizenship to the Cherokee Freedmen disenfranchised in the March 3, 2007, Cherokee Nation vote and fulfills all its treaty obligations with the Government of the United States, and for other purposes.

Courtesy Marty G. Two Bulls, Sr.

Conversely, Oklahoma State Representative Randy Shannon, a Republican and an African American, acknowledged the sovereignty of the Cherokee people and government in a press release dated March 27, 2007. "To me, this boils down to a fundamental, basic issue of recognizing the Cherokees' sovereignty. . . . The Cherokee Nation doesn't need me using my position as a state legislator to influence their decisions. . . . The Cherokee government preceded the government of this state and preceded the government of the United States. I am confident in their ability to determine their own tribal membership."[13]

Recognizing the threat to tribal sovereignty, the National Congress of American Indians, at its annual session in November 2007, unanimously approved a resolution opposing H.R. 2824. The resolution said H.R. 2824 "would break the promise of tribal self-government and threaten the right of all Indian tribes to determine, and thus preserve, our distinctively Indian identities; . . . [it is an] alarming, inappropriate and unacceptable overreach [that] undermines sovereign tribal governments and sets a dangerous precedent to all Indian tribes and nations."[14]

Another aspect of the Freedmen situation is that the leader of the federally recognized United Keetoowah Band of Cherokee Indians in Oklahoma (UKBCIO), also based in Tahlequah, has claimed that the tribe adheres to the 1866 treaty. That leader characterizes the UKBCIO as maintaining a more traditional Cherokee culture and he has been publicly critical of the Cherokee Nation for conducting the legal referendum to define citizenship requirements. Therefore, it would seem logical for the UKBCIO to invite the Freedmen to become citizens, and the Freedmen, who claim their primary desire in seeking Cherokee citizenship is to fulfill a cultural connection, petition to become citizens of a tribe that asserts adherence to the 1866 treaty. Neither has occurred.[15]

At this writing, it remains to be seen whether the Cherokee Nation will be the first tribe forced to accept non-Indians as citizens. Whatever course the rulings take, one fact will remain true and self-evident. Those without Cherokee blood, including the nearly 500,000 individuals from all ethnic groups that claimed Cherokee heritage on the 2000 census, will never be Cherokee.[16] When the basis for citizenship is blood kinship, it cannot be violated by a treaty, a court, or allegations of "racism." It is absolutely alien that blood no longer matters to a people whose very existence for thousands of years has been based on blood.

Cherokee blood powers the hearts and minds and sustains the culture of the Cherokee people. Eliminating the requirement of Cherokee blood to be Cherokee, in a treaty or otherwise, is as cruel and unusual a punishment as there can be.[17]

Nikki Lewis (left) and sister **Angel Goodrich** (right) celebrate a win with their mother and coach, Fayth Goodrich-Lewis, at the Native American Basketball Invitational in Phoenix, Arizona, 2008. Nikki and Angel are enrolled citizens of the Cherokee Nation in Oklahoma, since their mother is a tribal citizen by blood. Their father is African American.

The Goodrich-Lewis Family

The quality of a family can be defined by the direction parents give to their children toward a life of positive contributions to the community. Fayth Goodrich-Lewis and Jonathan Lewis of Tahlequah, Oklahoma, have devoted their lives to preparing their children for such a journey.

Fayth, who grew up in the Cherokee community of Stilwell, Oklahoma, and Jon, an African American from Fitchburg, Massachusetts, met when playing basketball and serving in the U.S. Air Force in Glendale, Arizona. After their military service ended, they settled in the Cherokee Nation in Oklahoma, continuing to play the game and teaching it to their children.

Zachery (Zak) Goodrich, 20, Angelisa (Angel) Goodrich, 19, and Nicollette (Nikki) Lewis, 17, are the extraordinary children of these loving parents. In the 2006–07 season they played on the Sequoyah High School basketball teams. Angel, then a junior, and Nikki, a freshman, were teammates on the state 3A championship girls' team. Zak, a senior point guard, helped lead his team to the state class 3A "Silver Ball" runner-up trophy. He now plays basketball

From left: Nikki Lewis, Angel Goodrich, Zak Goodrich, Fayth Goodrich-Lewis, and Jon Lewis. Photo by Dan Agent. Courtesy Goodrich-Lewis family.

at Sterling College in Kansas on partial athletic scholarship, and recently completed Christian mission service in Panama through the school.

In the summer of 2008, with Fayth as coach, Angel and Nikki were members of team "Anonymous," winning the championship of the Native American Basketball Invitational in Phoenix, Arizona. Angel was the tournament's most valuable player (MVP), adding to a trophy case that now includes three awards as state tournament and state MVP as well as many other awards. She now plays for the University of Kansas women's basketball team on an athletic scholarship. Nikki, junior point guard on the team in the 2008–09 season, led the state in assists, the team in steals, and was second in scoring.

All of the children play the game they love with great determination, but they are equally committed to achieving college degrees and contributing to their communities, honoring the teaching of their parents.

—Dan Agent

DANIEL LITTLEFIELD

THE CHEROKEE FREEDMEN
Cherokee Citizens by Treaty

Cherokee Freedmen are citizens of the Cherokee Nation today by virtue of Article 9 of the Treaty of 1866, between the United States and the Cherokee Nation, which says: "They further agree that all freedmen who have been liberated by voluntary act of their former owners or by law, as well as all free colored persons who were in the country at the commencement of the rebellion, and are now residents therein, or who may return within six months, and their descendants, shall have all the rights of native Cherokees."

The Cherokees executed the Treaty of 1866 admirably, given the racial climate in the adjoining states at the time. Soon after the treaty was signed, the Cherokee National Council amended the Cherokee Constitution to guarantee the Freedmen full citizenship rights. In the years that followed, Cherokee courts granted citizenship to large numbers of additional Freedmen applicants, especially to those who had not returned to the Cherokee Nation within the six-month limit set by the treaty. In their census reports, the Cherokee Nation listed two categories by which one could qualify for citizenship: blood or adoption. In the latter category, they identified four groups: Shawnees, Delawares, Freedmen, and intermarried whites. Any individual in one of these categories was considered a citizen of the Cherokee Nation. This was, in fact, a multiracial nation, whose citizenship was based not on blood or culture but on either birth or adoption.

Two Freedmen and two women, 1900. Muskogee County; Fort Gibson, Oklahoma. Photo by Frank C. Churchill. N27283

Over the years, like other citizens, Freedmen had access to land under the Cherokee improvement laws. Freedmen communities also had schools that were built and supported by the Cherokee Nation. They were subject to the courts of the Cherokee Nation and they sat on juries. They voted, ran for political office, and were elected and served in the National Council.

During the work of the Dawes Commission, the Cherokee Nation defended the rights of Freedmen citizens under the Treaty of 1866. When the commission began creating official tribal enrollment lists, the Cherokee Nation insisted that the commission use the nation's own census of 1880 as the basis for enrollment. The census listed five categories of citizens and included the adopted Freedmen. The Dawes Commission simply followed the Cherokee Nation's directions in making what became the final roll of citizens.

The Cherokee Nation's allotment agreement with the Dawes Commission was ratified by the Cherokee electorate—including the Freedmen—on August 7, 1902. Regarding the creation of tribal enrollment lists, the agreement stated, "The roll of citizens of the Cherokee Nation shall be made as of September first, nineteen hundred and two, and the names of all persons then living and entitled to enrollment on that date shall be placed on said roll by the Commission to the Five Civilized Tribes." It did not say "citizens by blood" or "citizens and Freedmen" or "citizens and others," but simply "citizens." The roll that the Dawes Commission made was a roll of Cherokees whose citizenship was acquired either by blood or adoption.

Thus, on September 1, 1902, the Freedmen were considered citizens of the Cherokee Nation, according to both the Cherokee Nation and the Dawes Commission. In subsequent elections, the Cherokee Freedmen, like other citizens of the Nation, voted for the offices of chief and National Council, just as they had done in decades past. The Dawes rolls had no impact on their status under the Treaty of 1866. Despite this fact, the focus of public debate in recent years has tended to deflect attention away from Freedmen rights to citizenship and toward the issues of blood quantum and race.

In its attempt in 2007 to oust the Freedmen, the Cherokee Nation pointed to the Freedmen's lack of blood quantum as noted on the Dawes Rolls. Blood quantum was used by Indian policy makers to lay the groundwork for the sale of allotted land. Rooted in the virulent racism of the late nineteenth century, it suggested that a person with whiter skin was more civilized than a person with darker skin. The policy laid the foundation for removal of restrictions on the sale of homestead allotments.

Mrs. Benson, a widely regarded healer, in a garden at the former home of Cherokee chief J.C. Bushyhead, 1900. Muskogee County; Fort Gibson, Oklahoma. Photo by Frank C. Churchill. N27287

The blood-quantum designation had no useful purpose in determining who was a Cherokee citizen or who received an allotment. It was, rather, a device to determine which Cherokee citizens would be the first to lose their land to white buyers. By the time the General Allotment Act of 1887 (Dawes Act) was passed, there was widespread public clamor for removal of restrictions on the sale of allotments in Indian Territory. First, restrictions were removed from the allotments of Freedmen and intermarried whites. Next, restrictions were lifted on allotments owned by Cherokee citizens listed as "half blood or less."

No action taken by the Cherokee Nation during the past three decades has nullified the Treaty of 1866 or the rights of the Freedmen to Cherokee citizenship under Article 9. The treaty remains a part of the Statutes at Large of the United States (Vol. 16). The United States has not delegated to the Cherokee Nation the authority to nullify or amend the supreme law of the land. By attempting to nullify Article 9 of the last treaty the Cherokee Nation made with the United States, the tribe places in jeopardy its trust relation with the federal government. In so doing, it jeopardizes the sovereignty it claims to be exercising in its attempts to nullify the Freedmen's rights to citizenship.

Phil Wilkes Fixico, 2009.

KEVIN MULROY

BEHIND THE ROLLS
Pompey Bruner Fixico

This is a story of identity and how inaccuracies written into the Dawes Rolls in the nineteenth century continue to affect families today. It is also a story about the transformative power of revelation and reconnection in the life of one individual.

Phil Wilkes Fixico (b. 1947), also known as Philip Vincent Wilkes and "Pompey" Bruner Fixico, is one-eighth Seminole Indian, one-quarter Seminole Freedman, one-eighth Creek Freedman, one-quarter Cherokee Freedman, and one-quarter mulatto. He is the grandson of Pompey Fixico, who was born in the late 1800s of an affair between Dinah Fixico, a Seminole woman, and Caesar Bruner, a respected Seminole maroon leader. The early deaths of Pompey's parents, however, and his subsequent guardianship by an adopted white citizen of the Seminole Nation with ties to the Seminole maroon Bruner family, severed his connection to his Seminole heritage. As a result, Pompey was raised as a member of Freedmen society and the Seminole heritage of his descendants was obscured. The story of Phil Wilkes Fixico and the Fixico-Bruner family sheds light on relations between Seminoles and Freedmen and on status and identity issues among individuals of mixed race within American society.

Seminole maroons descend from free blacks and fugitive slaves who had escaped to Florida, where they forged alliances with the Seminole Nation. Drawing upon both African and Seminole influences, they established their own autonomous communities and unique culture. Fearing re-enslavement by whites if forced to leave Florida, maroons fought against the U.S. military alongside

Katie M.W. Oliver, *Black Seminole Chief John Horse (Juan Caballo)*. The Seminoles were a union of southeastern Indian people who moved into Spanish-controlled Florida and were later joined by communities of escaped black slaves who became known as Black Seminoles. John Horse was a key figure in the war that the Seminoles waged with the United States between 1835 and 1842 to avoid forced removal to Oklahoma. Ultimately, Horse led a band of Black Seminoles to Mexico, where he died in 1882.

their Native allies during the Seminole Wars. With a promise of freedom from the U.S. government, Seminole maroons accompanied the Seminole Nation during their removal to Indian Territory in the mid-1800s. After the Civil War, the Seminoles incorporated maroon descendants into their nation, granting the Freedmen political representation, access to salaried offices, protection by the law, freedom of religion, equal education, and a share in the nation's land, annuities, and other monetary awards. The Freedmen enjoyed all the rights of Seminole Nation citizens and were able to control their own destinies free of interference. For forty years after Emancipation, Seminole Freedmen enjoyed rights and privileges equal to those of Indians—rights and privileges unknown to most African Americans at that time.

Seminoles distinguished between incorporating the Freedmen as citizens of their new nation (or polity) and including them as members of their tribe (culture and society). Freedmen typically were not part of Indian clans or bands, the mainstays of Seminole civilization, but because the Seminoles and Freedmen lived in close geographical proximity and had a partially shared history, some interaction naturally occurred.

A separate, vital, and clearly distinguishable Seminole Freedmen culture emerged after the Civil War. The Freedmen adopted certain Seminole cultural practices, such as food preferences and cooking and curing techniques. Like the Seminole, they organized into bands, determining band affiliation matrilineally. In 1951, anthropologist Art Gallaher suggested a number of other areas in which he perceived cultural transmission from the Seminole to the Freedmen, including spiritual beliefs and marriage and burial customs. But Freedmen society mostly reflected the group's African heritage and history of enslavement under both Europeans and Southern whites. Consequently, Freedmen culture differed substantially from that of the Seminoles.

Although intermarriage between Indians and Freedmen took place in the Seminole Nation during the late nineteenth century, it was uncommon. When intermarriage did occur, unions between Freedmen and Indian women were more common than between Indian men and black women. As the Seminole defined descent through the mother's line, an Indian marriage likely brought increased status for Freedmen males within the maroon community. Their children were included in Seminole clans and bands and considered Seminole by both Indian and Freedmen communities.

During the late 1800s, the U.S. government was pressured to open up lands in the West for white settlement. The Dawes Act of 1887 was passed in an effort to assimilate tribes in Indian Country and dispossess them of their tribally owned lands by creating individual allotments. To do this, the Dawes Commission was to create rolls listing the rightful members of tribal nations. The Seminoles historically had resisted white acculturative influences and were probably suspicious of the Dawes Commission's motives. Those with mixed ancestry likely were loath to acknowledge anything other than "full" Seminole citizenship. Although Pompey Fixico was the son of Seminole maroon leader Caesar Bruner, Pompey's census card listed Tolof Fixico—a full-blooded Seminole—as his biological father. Pompey was also listed on the Dawes Rolls as "fullblood," despite his mixed Seminole and Freedman heritage. Indians had reason to hide black admixture, most of which derived from a handful of earlier intermarriages. With massive white immigration, Oklahoma statehood, and institutionalized segregation rapidly approaching, the family probably sought to protect the child by claiming his "full" Indian rights and denying his African heritage. Other evidence also suggests that individuals with African and Indian admixture saw advantage in being enrolled as citizens "by blood" rather than as Freedmen. This has always been true for the Seminole Freedmen and is still true today. In the wake of the Dawes Act and with the approach of the Jim Crow era, people of African and Native American heritage realized that it was in their best interest to be considered Indian rather than black.

The convoluted heritage of race mixing and hidden paternity has followed the Bruner-Fixico family into contemporary times. Phil Wilkes Fixico was born out of wedlock to Dorothy Mae Rogers, the daughter of a Cherokee Freedman, and Pompey's son, Linwood Bruner Fixico. To avoid a potential family scandal, Dorothy hid the identity of Phil's biological father, just as Pompey's paternity had been hidden. In this way, Phil's paternal genealogy was lost to him; for more than a half century he knew only of his African American heritage and nothing of his mixed Seminole Freedmen and Indian background. Sensing he was "different" from his immediate family, young Phil grew alienated and fell into drugs and petty crime, but he eventually began to turn his life around. Finally, at age fifty-two, Phil Wilkes Fixico learned from other Bruner family members the identity of his biological father, "ending a lifelong identity crisis."

Having discovered his true identity, Phil is now proudly rooted in his Seminole Freedmen and Indian ancestry, history, and culture. He has embraced his mixed-race heritage, become a creative and energetic tribal historian, and connected with Seminole maroon communities in Oklahoma, Texas, and Mexico. In honor of Phil's grandfather, his cousin Frank "Buck" James gave him the nickname "Pompey." Nicknaming has a long history among the Seminole Freedmen and remains a common practice among maroon descendants in Oklahoma, west Texas, and northern Mexico.

A committed educator, Phil has given numerous presentations to school and civic groups. He designed a Seminole maroon peace belt as a teaching tool and coauthored "The Descendants' Creed" to help preserve the maroons' heritage and ground his people's lives in the community's past. The creed states, in part, "We descendants solemnly promise to study the history of our ancestors and to live our lives in a manner that gives honor to their memory."

Phil recently began combining the words "Seminole" and "maroon" to create a new identifier: "Semiroon." He believes the word offers "a paradigm for life in the now." He continues, "Metaphorically speaking, we are confronted daily with challenges that seek to enslave us, and as in the historical model, we must escape. More often than not, we will need help from others. We today must form alliances with people different from ourselves in race and culture. In these unions we can share and borrow from each others' successful and positive imperatives." Today, finally in tune with his identity and his community, Phil reflects contentedly, "My life now has a worthy passion and purpose. I am really blessed."

Constantino Brumidi, *The Boston Massacre, 1770* (detail). Crispus Attucks, the son of an enslaved African man and a Natick Indian woman, was the first martyr of the American Revolution. His death at the hands of British soldiers at the Boston Massacre of 1770 provided the impetus for the armed conflict that followed between the American colonies and British forces.

TIYA MILES

TAKING LEAVE, MAKING LIVES
Creative Quests for Freedom in Early Black and Native America

We also assume it as a first principle that slavery has been permitted and tolerated in all the colonies established in America by European powers, most clearly as relates to the blacks and Africans, and also in relation to Indians.

—Judge George Mathews of Louisiana, delivering the state Supreme Court's decision against the emancipation of an Indian man in *Seville v. Chretien*, 1817[1]

The colonial laws, down to the end of the colonial period, speak, in almost every statute relating to slavery, of "Negro and Indian slaves."

—A. Judd Northrup, *Slavery in New York*, 1900[2]

Throughout 2007, the settlement of Jamestown, Virginia, celebrated 400 years of history. Pomp, circumstance, and a visit from the Queen of England marked the series of special events. Founded in 1607, Jamestown was the first permanent English colony in what is now the United States. As such, it is also the birthplace of black slavery in America. Many of us are aware that African slaves and indentured servants were brought to Jamestown in 1619 and that a system of chattel slavery expanded into other colonies and hardened over time. We know that black slavery was gradually excised in the northern states in the aftermath of the American Revolutionary War and abolished throughout the country as a result of the Civil War. Scholars of American Indian history, colonial history, and ethnohistory, however, are illuminating the fact that this familiar chronology of U.S. slavery is in need of revision, as Spanish enslavement of indigenous people began in North America before Africans arrived. English, Dutch, and French colonists soon joined in the practice, holding Indians as slaves even as they imported Africans for the same purpose. Jamestown, the fledgling English settlement that barely survived, benefited from stolen labor of not only Africans but also Indians.

In 1981, historian J. Leitch Wright explored this topic in his book about southern Indians, writing: "From the time of European contact in the early sixteenth century until well into the nineteenth century, whites enslaved natives so long as it was profitable and sufficient numbers remained to be captured."[3] In 2002, historian Alan Gallay published a full-length study of Indians and the slave trade in which he discovered and documented the capture, sale, and enslavement of an estimated 30,000 to 50,000 southern Indians by English colonists alone, all before 1715.[4] The numbers, though high, are an incomplete estimate because they do not include Indians enslaved by the Spanish or French, or Indians enslaved throughout the eighteenth century and after.

At the same time that an African diaspora took shape through the dispersal of enslaved blacks, what anthropologist Jack Forbes has called an "American diaspora" was being formed through the sale of enslaved Native Americans.[5] Indian people became slaves of Euro-Americans as a result of being captives of war by members of other tribes and in the aftermath of major battles with European colonists, such as the Pequot War of 1637, King Philip's War of 1675–78, and the Yamasee War of 1715–17. Many of these Indian war captives and refugees—men, women, as well as children—were traded to the Caribbean, Europe, New England, or the upper South. The urban center of Charleston, South Carolina, was the main location for the sale of both African and Indian slaves. Many would have stood on the same auction blocks, traveled across the Atlantic on the same type of ships, and finally ended up in the same northern households or southern or Caribbean plantations. As historian Peter H. Wood observed in his classic study of blacks in South Carolina: "African newcomers found themselves in close proximity not only to Europeans but to Indians as well, for during the proprietary era several thousand Indian slaves still shared the same tasks and the same quarters with Africans from overseas."[6]

While the enslavement of Africans and their descendants in America increased in scale and intensity, the enslavement of Native people diminished and was gradually outlawed in the northern and southern colonies by the middle to late 1700s. But despite new laws forbidding wholesale Indian slavery,

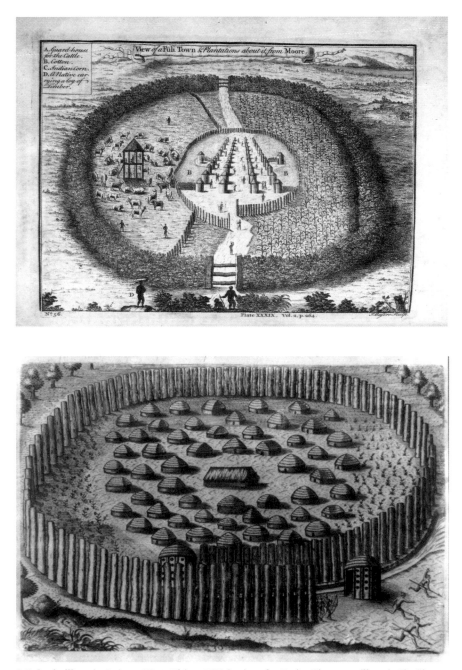

A Fulani village in Guinea, West Africa, 1738 (top), and a Native Timucua village in Florida, 1564. In these European views of two communities, the similarities between the two distinct peoples are compelling.

individual Native people could still be captured and held, and Native people who were descended from Indian and black unions were categorized as "Negro" and naturalized into the slavery system.

Making Lives: Creative Cultural Production

In the shared circumstance of enslavement in which many indigenous and African Americans found themselves for at least a century and a half, people came together to forge relationships and share cultural ways. Treated like beasts of burden and forced to labor for the profit of others, slaves faced an environment in which their humanity was degraded and their daily lives dimmed. But even as slavery and its perpetrators conspired to drain dignity from the slaves' existence, enslaved Indians and blacks maintained their unique cultural traditions and also blended those traditions to create new cultural forms. The impact of culture making in the lives of enslaved people cannot be underestimated. In lending their limited free time to cultural pursuits in evenings and on Sundays, in crafting objects of beauty and utility, and in recalling and enacting the practices of their ancestors, slaves renewed the dignity of their lives, sharpened traditional knowledge and skills, shaped spaces of pleasure and social connection, and infused their surroundings with flashes of beauty. Cultural production, then, was a form of freedom struggle that affirmed enslaved people's humanity and holistic worth.

Remnants of the myriad ways that African and Indian slaves shared and melded cultural knowledge have been traced by scholars of slave culture. The corn-based diet of southern Indian tribes left its mark on the recipes of African American "soul food," in dishes such as cornbread, grits, and hoecake.[7] Black women's basketweaving designs were probably augmented by Indian patterns and plant preferences.[8] Black southern men who built dugout canoes likely learned this skill from Native male relatives and plantation companions.[9] African American Brer Rabbit trickster stories, with their character, theme, and plot connections to West African stories and southeastern Native rabbit stories, suggest a cross-pollination of folkloric traditions.[10] Plants used as herbal medicines and gourds as containers combined West African and indigenous American knowledge with results that persisted for generations.[11] In the late 1930s, for example, Island Smith, an Afro-Creek Freedman and herbal doctor, would refer to his healing ability as deriving from those dual sources. Smith reported to anthropologist Sigmund Sameth: "Cross-blood means extra knowledge. I can

Island Smith at his desk, ca. 1935. Smith, an Afro-Creek herbal doctor who practiced in Oklahoma in the early 1900s, drew his spiritual power from both African and Native American traditions.

take my cane [a hollow reed used to apply medicines] and blow it twice and do the same as a Creek full-blood doctor does in four times. Two bloods makes two talents."[12]

Finally, in perhaps the best-known example of black and Indian cultural fusion, a pottery style known as Colono Ware, produced from the seventeenth through the mid-nineteenth-century, has been found in Indian towns as well as on Virginia and South Carolina plantations where black, Afro-Native, and Indian slaves worked. Archaeologists who study this pottery have identified both West African and American Indian influences, concluding that "a creolized culture, highly influenced by Native American beliefs, values, and practices, arose."[13] Archaeologist Leland Ferguson has discovered, further, that a subset of the Colono Ware bowls produced in the 1700s has been engraved with

Photo of a Montauk family, 1924. The Shinnecock and Montauk communities of Long Island, with their knowledge of ancestral land and the sea, prospered in the whaling industry of the mid-1600s and late 1700s. By the twentieth century, many Montauk joined other Native communities, and the Shinnecock have had to struggle to keep their land rights while they continue to celebrate their whaling heritage.

Oarsmen in bow of whaleboat, 1924. As sailors and laborers on whaleboats, and as captains and crew leaders on ships with mixed African and Indian crews, the Shinnecock and the Montauk prospered and retained land rights from the mid-1600s to the late 1700s. Ironically, their adaptability—and intermarriage with African Americans—obscured their Native identity in the eyes of the white population.

symbols derived from Kongo (West and Central African) religious traditions. The symbol series, distinguished by a cross enclosed within a circle, bears a striking resemblance to Native American medicine-wheel symbology, suggesting that "circle-and-cross symbols could be syncretic, incorporating Christian and Native American as well as African and newly created African American meanings."[14]

Sharing the experiences of race-based degradation and slavery in early American history led to the exchange and re-creation of cultural forms between Indians and Africans. Even as discrete indigenous traditions continued to be practiced within nationally specific contexts, Native people who had been parted from their home communities contributed to the formation of a creolized Afro-Native culture. What is more, historian Peter H. Wood and feminist theorist bell hooks have speculated that West African concepts of place and the environment, spirituality, respect for ancestors, and the oral tradition paralleled Native American concepts of the same, thereby facilitating the process of cultural synthesis.[15] In creating objects and enacting practices that derived from their multiple cultural traditions, African and Indian slaves improved the quality of their circumscribed lives and asserted their human rights to cultural self-determination and creative expression.

Taking Leave: Creative Escape and Rebellion

Pottery, cookery, dugout canoes—these are all material aspects of Native and black co-creativity during the long, dark night of shared racial slavery. But creativity—the work of imagining and bringing something into being—did not take place just in the realm of material culture. It also played a part in outright resistance to oppression. Written documentation, archaeology, and oral history tell us that enslaved people refused to be reduced to the status of property. Through everyday acts of defiance and plots long in the planning, slaves thwarted the power of owners to fully control and diminish their lives. Historians have mapped slave resistance along a number of axes: from an internal, psycho-social resolve to preserve their human dignity; to subtle external acts, such as negotiating with the master for greater autonomy, reducing work productivity, and briefly and frequently departing from the plantation; to outright attempts to poison the master, commit arson, or take full flight. All of these means of refusal were powered by a spirit of creativity. At a time when racial hierarchy was conceived as natural in Euro-American society and

Hallets Point, East River (Hell Gate) N. Y.

Lighthouse at Hell Gate on the East River in New York.

slavery was sanctioned by culture, church, and state, each deed of noncompliance began with an act of radical imagination. To engage in resistance or seek freedom was a creative endeavor for slaves, who had first to dream a free world and then attempt to reach it. Just as black and Native people blended their cultures in the forms of bowl and basket, they sometimes joined forces to find routes out of slavery.

The first recorded slave revolt in New York City is a dramatic case in point. Recent historical studies and museum exhibitions have illuminated the fallacy that slavery was solely a southern institution. In addition to being commercial partners with southern planters, northerners possessed both Indian and black slaves until the gradual emancipation that followed the American Revolutionary War. In the companion volume to the New York Historical Society's *Slavery in New York* exhibit of 2006, historian Jill Lepore points out that in the 1700s, "New York City was second only to Charleston, South Carolina, in its proportion of slaves in an urban population."[16] Indeed, as early as 1629, when New York (New Amsterdam) was occupied by the Dutch, colonists voiced a need for slave labor. They complained that their lack of productivity stemmed from the land's being "very difficult of cultivation, especially for our people who being unaccustomed to so hot a climate can with great difficulty betake themselves to agriculture; and being unprovided with slaves and not used to the employment of them cannot, like the Spaniards and Portuguese, supply through others their own inefficiency."[17] The West India Company, which had sponsored the colony, acknowledged that the Spaniards and Portuguese relied on "the labor of blacks and Indians," and suggested that the Dutch colonists follow suit.[18]

In 1664, the British crown won possession of New York, and King Charles II granted a charter to his brother, the Duke of York, to import African slaves from Guinea.[19] As the enslaved population increased, the New York Assembly passed slave codes that documented the presence of Native as well as black slaves and harshly regimented slave life. An act in 1706 proclaimed that "the baptizing of any Negro, Indian, or Mulatto Slave shall not be any cause or reason for setting them or any of them at liberty," and added: "All and every Negro, Indian, Mulatto, or Mestee shall follow the state and condition of the mother and be esteemed and reputed, taken and adjudged to be a Slave or Slaves to all intents and purposes whatsoever."[20] Slaves soon were forbidden to serve as witnesses in cases against free men, limited in the number of miles they could travel away from the city center, outlawed from buying or selling without their master's permission, and disallowed from assembling in groups of more than three slaves.[21]

In the aftermath of this curtailment of already-limited liberties, slaves in New York rebelled. The spectacular revolt of 1712 in which scores of slaves armed themselves and set fire to the outhouse of one of their owners has been well documented.[22] A fateful rebellion that took place four years earlier, however, remains largely unknown. The story of the slave revolt of 1708 begins on the East River, where Hell Gate, a natural passageway into Long Island Sound, rocked passing ships with terrible tides. Near this spot, an Englishman named William Hallett, Sr., received one of the earliest land grants in what would become Queens, New York, and named his haven Hallett's Cove. Hallett divided his land between his sons, one of whom, William Hallett, Jr., operated a farm there with the aid of at least two slaves—one African American, the other American Indian.

The slaves—a Native American man and an African American woman—chose to alter their circumstances, rejecting the yoke of their master by shockingly violent means. The plot they developed took planning and daring and must have arisen from a deep sense of desperation. In January 1708, the pair carried out their plan to kill their master's entire family. Two black slaves from outside the household were later charged as co-conspirators in the attack. A witness described the event as follows:

William Hallett Junior who labored at a place called Hellgate his wife and five children in a quarter of an hour were all murdered by one Indian slave whom he had up for 4 years. There was a Negro woman Slave in the house who was to him in counseling this bloody matter. . . . About seven at night Hallett and his wife returned home and went to bed. . . . The slaves were watching their opportunity for they had to do it that night.[23]

The Indian slave, called Sam in this testimony, was said to have killed his master, pregnant mistress, and all of their children with an axe. *The Boston News-Letter*, a regional newspaper, followed the case, reporting that "[o]n Saturday night last Mr. William Hallett junior of Newtown on Long-Island, his Wife who was big with Child, and five Children were all murdered by an Indian Man and a Negro Woman[,] their own slaves."[24] Without offering evidence, the newspaper claimed that "several other Families were designed for the like slaughter, had they succeeded in this without discovery."[25]

Retribution for the killings would be swift and final. Lord Governor Edward Hyde Cornbury reported on the incident in a letter to the Lords of Commissioners of Trade and Plantations in February 1708:

A most barbarous murder has been committed on the family of one Hallet by an Indian Man Slave, and a Negro Woman, who have murder'd their Master, Mistress, and five Children; The Slaves were taken, and I immediately issued a special commission for the Tryal of them, which was done, and the man sentenced to be hanged, and the woman burnt, and they have been executed; They Discovered two other Negros, their accomplices who have been tried, condemned & Executed.[26]

The couple at the center of the rebellion faced awful deaths. The Boston newspaper reported that they were "on Monday the 2d instant Executed at Jamaica [Queens] . . . and put to all the torment possible."[27] The woman, whose name is not recorded, was burned alive at the stake and taunted with a horn of water she could not reach, and Sam was hung to death on the gallows while being pierced by an iron spike.[28] The two accused African American men were also hanged. The punishments endured by these slaves were intended to be "a terror to others."[29] And soon after the executions were carried out, the New York Assembly passed an act threatening "the Pains of Death" to "all and every Negro, Indian, or other Slave or Slaves within this Colony who at any time after the execrable and barbarous Murther [*sic*] committed upon the Person and Family of William Hallett jun. late of New-Town . . . have has or shall Murder or otherwise Kill . . . or Conspire or Attempt the Death of his[,] her[,] or their Master or Mistriss."[30]

Beyond the evidence of increasingly harsh slave codes, the documentary record does not tell us who this Native man and black woman were as full individuals with life histories, what specific circumstances motivated their behavior, or why they chose to follow such a treacherous course of action in an attempt to be free. *The Boston News-Letter* asserts that the pair chose to rebel "because they were restrained from going abroad on the Sabbath days."[31] Whatever their motivations, their actions were undeniably violent and destructive. But their attempt to free themselves from the misery of their world was also without a doubt radical and resounding.[32]

A renaissance of scholarship on African American and Native American historical relations has examined the role of southern Indians as slaveholders,[33] and indeed, tracing the development and dynamics of Native adoption of black slavery is a necessary part of our broader historical understanding of race relations, colonialism, and power. Among the populations of the Choctaws, Chickasaws, Cherokees, and to a lesser extent, Creeks and Seminoles, nearly 10,000 black slaves were held in bondage between the late 1700s and the end of the Civil War.[34] After emancipation, those former slaves and their descendants faced racial prejudice within their Indian nations, as well as rampant Jim Crow discrimination across the state of Oklahoma.

At the same time that we must confront the reality of black slavery in Indian nations, it is equally important to recognize the much longer period that indigenous Americans and African Americans, as well as Afro-Indians, were enslaved together by European colonists and early Americans. Tens of thousands of Native people were held in bondage between the mid-sixteenth and the early-nineteenth-centuries. Nearly half a million enslaved Africans were transported to North America in the latter part of that same period, and their numbers would increase to approximately four million by 1865. Through the brutal shared experience of bondage, Native Americans and African Americans came into intimate contact, forging deep relationships that inspired collective cultural forms and emboldened creative quests for freedom.

BLACK HERITAGE

Charles W. Chesnutt

41
USA

Commemorative stamp honoring Charles W. Chesnutt, issued 2008. © 2007 USPS.
Used with permission. All rights reserved.

JUDY KERTÉSZ

CHARLES CHESNUTT'S MANDY OXENDINE

The late-nineteenth-century novel *Mandy Oxendine*, written by Charles Waddell Chesnutt (1858–1932), begins with the arrival of a well-dressed young man at a rural rail station. A sign that states Waiting Room for White People Only lets us know that we are in the South—specifically, North Carolina after the failure of Civil War era Reconstruction. The young man, Tom Lowrey, "not very highly colored, but sufficiently so," has come to find his former fiancée, Mandy Oxendine, after a two-year separation while he pursued his studies. Impatient, Mandy left the home they had shared and now "passes" as white. Theirs is a story of two fair-skinned young people of mixed-race ancestry who have chosen to live on opposite sides of the color line. The separation of the lovers—an ambitious young man and a young woman seeking security in marriage—is a familiar literary device that could easily provoke a maudlin romance, but Chesnutt enriches the plot of this novel, which remained unpublished until 1997, with the complexities of "passing" and the difficulties of making such a choice.

Chesnutt might have found his own contemporary identification as black or African American surprising. In almost every recent biography, Chesnutt is identified as an African American, but that reflects the changing perceptions of race and the means by which persons of African descent are classified in the United States more than Chesnutt's own sense of self. A man of his time, Chesnutt never described himself in those terms, choosing the contemporaneous "colored" most frequently. It is this particular identification that provided the foundation and resulting dilemmas to which he continually would return in his journals, letters, essays, and novels. Unfortunately, both the context and use of "colored" in large measure have become lost to us; that loss is reflected in much of the analysis of Chesnutt's life and work. Certainly, in his essays and fiction, Chesnutt tapped into the notion that interracial mixing placed the whole premise of racial differentiation in doubt. Critics to date, however, have yet to consider the possibility that Chesnutt was aware of, and had actual ties to, those who tenaciously held on to yet another identity. How does our understanding of the peculiar American phenomenon of passing change if Mandy Oxendine were neither white nor black but rather American Indian?

Almost all of Charles Chesnutt's work focuses on the personal predicaments and larger sociopolitical ramifications of mixed-race identity and passing, which he believed were "complex and difficult of treatment, in fiction as in life." With some exceptions, most readers and literary critics assume his first novel strictly addresses the significant, complicated problem of black/white passing. If every author's first novel invariably functions as autobiography, then *Mandy Oxendine* may well fall within that genre. Mandy appears to bear some relationship to Chesnutt's mother, Ann Maria Sampson, and given his education, dogged determination, and self-reflexive irony, Mandy's fiancé Tom Lowrey certainly bears great resemblance to Chesnutt himself.

While some critics define Chesnutt's family as free blacks or Negroes from Fayetteville, North Carolina, the Chesnutt family was also precariously situated "on the color line," or that "border line between the races." Literary critic Michael Flusche writes, "In their features and the lightness of their skin, they resembled whites more than they did blacks." Many scholars refer to John Hope Franklin's monumental work *The Free Negro of North Carolina* (1943) in their efforts to underscore the Chesnutt family's racial and social status. Franklin's history discusses miscegenation (the marriage or cohabitation between a man and woman of different races) as a phenomenon occurring primarily between white slaveholding men and enslaved black women from which, according to Franklin, 70 percent of North Carolina's Free Persons of Color would come. Unfortunately, no distinction is given to explain the classificatory terms Mustee, Mulatto, Indian, and Negro, so all are lumped under the rubric of Free Persons of Color. By claiming that "several of Chesnutt's uncles and aunts dropped their Negro identity and silently passed as whites," Flusche also implies that Chesnutt's relatives did in fact have a "Negro identity."

With this in mind, how is *Mandy Oxendine* a reflection of Charles Chesnutt's background? What was his background? His mother, Ann Maria Sampson, and father, Andrew Jackson Chesnutt, were from Fayetteville, and descendants of North Carolina's free colored population. In 1856, they left for Ohio, where they married and welcomed several children before returning to Fayetteville in 1867.

Historically, Fayetteville held one of the largest populations of free colored persons in the state. The earliest colonial records bemoan a city perilously perched north of what would eventually become "The County of Robeson [that] is cursed with a free-coloured population that migrated originally from the districts round about the Roanoke and Neuse Rivers." Significantly, these two rivers both map points of indigenous experience; they are the origin place of Indians, not Africans.

How would our understanding of miscegenation and passing change if Mandy Oxendine were descended not from the blacks of the region but rather from the Indians—Indians in their various racialized guises, constrained by a society that had legislated them out of existence? In the context of post-Reconstruction, with its increasing antimiscegenation legislation, arbitrary census enumerations, separate school systems, and bifurcated Southern racial hierarchy, in which all non-whites belonged to one undifferentiated racial group, Mandy "had left no near kindred behind to mourn [her] departure or be hurt by [her] desertion," thereby making a reasonable if uncomfortable choice. Perhaps the names and locations that color the novel's textual and geographic terrain provide fresh clues as to her origins and the reasons the ties that once bound her to them were broken.

It is arguable that Chesnutt failed to grasp the significance of Mandy's, and Tom's, surnames, and arbitrarily picked the names Oxendine and Lowrey for his characters without the knowledge that local persons with those names strongly identified as Indian. One could argue, furthermore, that Chesnutt arbitrarily situated his story in Sampson County and that the choice of this place bore no relationship to his own mother's maiden name. But like the town of Fayetteville and the county of Robeson, Sampson County was in Chesnutt's time and is today distinct for its Native populations, and the surname Sampson—like that of Lowrey, Oxendine, and Revels—marks those who then and now identify as American Indian.

What is certain is that at the very time Tom Lowrey and Mandy Oxendine would have deliberated the choices—or lack thereof—open to them, Robeson

Chief Buffalo Child Long Lance (1890–1932). The star of the film *The Silent Enemy* (1930), Long Lance claimed to be a Blackfoot chief. He was a darling of New York and European salon society until it was revealed he had been born to "Negro" parents (in fact, his mother and father were both of mixed black, white, and Indian heritage). Soon after, he killed himself.

George Applewhite, a former slave, joined the legendary Lumbee Indian gang of "Robin Hoods"—headed by Henry Berry Lowry—in their struggle against violent racist attacks committed by the Home Guard militia in North Carolina after the Civil War. Arrested and sentenced to be hanged, Applewhite escaped from prison in 1870 and was pardoned in 1873.

County was experiencing a violent and widespread resistance to the effects of U.S. Indian policy and state-legislated racial codes. The conflict's means of articulation were threefold: the violent confrontations of the Lowry War; politicization as a tribal entity; and the establishment of an aggressive tribal identity along separatist lines—far from the inclusive beliefs that Chesnutt espoused.

In the vitriolic contestation that marks this period in North Carolina's history, the names Lowrey and Oxendine are most prominent. By speaking through characters named Tom Lowrey and Mandy Oxendine, Chesnutt reveals his observations regarding the presence and place of origin of Oxendines, and his knowledge of the identities of those who would later be officially recognized as Lumbee and Coharie Indians. By 1885, as Chesnutt informs his readers, "These mixed Indians and Negroes were recognized by the North Carolina legislature as 'Croatan Indians.'" That Sandy Run, the setting of the novel, is inhabited by only one Revels family indicates how far Tom and Mandy had traveled from home, where "Indianness" makes sense and has a context. We come to know by the paucity of specific surnames just how far from their place of origin they had roamed—a place where identity is rooted in kinship, a construct that informs

Lumbee Indians
Charlie Warriax and Simeon Oxendine display the Ku Klux Klan (KKK) banner they had captured after a raid on a Klan rally in Lumberton, North Carolina, January 20, 1958.

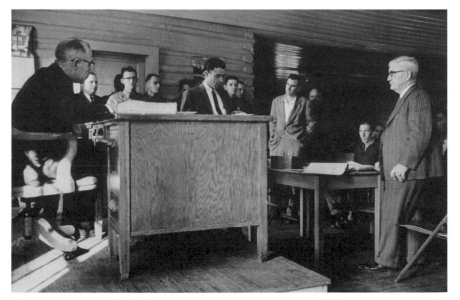

Klansman James G. Martin (hands in pockets) on trial, January 1, 1958, for organizing a rally against Native Americans. He is tried before Lumbee judge Lacy Maynor and Luther J. Britt (right), private prosecutor.

notions of tribe and nation, not necessarily race. Too far from the source of a kin-based tribal notion of identity, Tom and Mandy must negotiate the byways of a racialized construction of identity; for them, there are only two options from which to choose.

Chesnutt was aware that the famed Lowry gang—the "organized band of desperadoes" he described in an essay written in 1902—primarily comprised four Lowreys and two Oxendines. And we know for certain that Chesnutt appreciated the significance of their contestation with whites in Robeson County by his direct reference to Henry Berry Lowry, "one of these curiously mixed people [who] left his mark upon the history of the state—a bloody mark, too, for the Indian in him did not passively endure the things to which the Negro was rendered subject." As the center of a triracial group of farmers and skilled craftsmen that transformed into a guerilla army, Henry Berry Lowry challenged the inequities leveled at all oppressed groups in Reconstruction North Carolina.

Charles Chesnutt, engaging the conundrum of choice, grappled mightily and wrote with sagacity and humor, sensitivity and irony. He chose to shape his identity not according to arbitrarily defined codes of race, or the "one drop" rule, or relatedness rooted in biology, but according to the ties that bound him—that of mutual interest, personal ambition, and a shared rage at the reprehensible limitations placed on persons only recently defined as chattel—and to the vision of a contestable, negotiable future. A full decade before he set *Mandy Oxendine* to paper, in the spring of 1880, the twenty-two-year-old Chesnutt wrote:

> The object of my writings would not be so much the elevation of the colored people as the elevation of the whites—for I consider the unjust spirit of caste which is so insidious as to pervade a whole nation, and so powerful as to subject a whole race and all connected with it to scorn and social ostracism—I consider this a barrier to the moral progress of the American people: and I would be one of the first to head a determined, organized crusade against it. . . . It is the province of literature to open the way . . . to accustom the public mind to the idea; and while amusing them, to lead people out, imperceptibly, unconsciously, step by step, to the desired state of feeling. If I can do anything to further this work. . . . I would gladly devote my life to the work.

SAM DEVENNEY

TA-TEN-E-QUER FAMILY PHOTOGRAPH

Sam DeVenney is a Comanche Indian from Lawton, Oklahoma. In his sixty years, he has spent time visiting with elders and collecting stories and photographs that document Comanche and Kiowa history and contemporary family experience. Unofficially the Comanche tribal historian, he is sought out by his contemporaries for information and visual documentation. The following are his comments about this photograph.

This is Ta-Ten-e-quer (born ca. 1840–50) with his wife, Ta-Tat-ty, also known as Qu-vuh-tu. The woman in the center is Wife-per, or Frances E. Wright. Frances is a niece of Ta-Ten-e-quer, the daughter of his sister Tow-o-Ky. Tow-o-Ky was married to a black man, Henry Wright, who came to the Comanches around the Fletcher, Oklahoma, area. Research shows his father to be Sid Wright and his mother Fannie Wright. . . . I have heard he was a buffalo soldier who deserted and hid among the Comanches. . . . He was a farmhand and all-around handyman for a number of Comanches in these areas, and naturally some young good-looking Comanche woman would catch his eye. He stayed in the large barn built for Ta-Ten-e-quer by the department responsible for such needs through the Indian Agency at Anadarko. In this way, he got closer to this family.

Comanche family, early 1900s. Back row, from left: Ta-Tat-ty, also known as Qu-vuh-tu; Wife-per, or Frances E. Wright; Ta-Ten-e-quer. Front row: Henry (center) and Lorenzano, also called Moots. Courtesy Sam DeVenney.

Henry and Tow-o-Ky had only one child—Wife-per. Other blacks also hung around Henry, one by the name of Mr. McClain, who eventually married Wife-per. Two children were born to this marriage, both boys. First, Henry, then Lorenzano [also called Moots]. Henry was born in 1911 and Lorenzano in 1913. Lorenzano was married at one time to a Comanche woman. Both brothers moved to California and the last of the two recently died. I'm not for sure, but I think the last one to die was brought back to Oklahoma to be buried in the Little Washita cemetery east of Fletcher, where Ta-Ten-e-quer and his family are buried. Little Washita is a Methodist Indian church.

Ta-Ten-e-quer . . . was a very high official for the Comanches in the Fletcher-Cyril-Cement area. . . . [He and his wife] had several children, but they all died . . . so they helped Wife-per, whose children were actually three-quarters black and one-quarter Comanche. But back then it was not very common, and . . . blacks were kind of looked down upon because we didn't understand them, period. . . . I think that Comanches got along well with them, once they got to know them. . . . I think it depends on how you were raised. Some families were anti-black, very prejudiced. And then some families, they were people like we were. They didn't think anything of it.

Ann "Sole Sister" Johnson, *They Always Talk about Her Hair*. Intaglio, found objects, 12 x 12 in.

PHOEBE FARRIS

RED, BLACK, AND BROWN
Artists and the Aesthetics of Race

This essay explores the work of visual artists who reference race or identity in myriad ways, often juxtaposed with issues of gender. The profiled artists include women of mixed Native American, African American, or Latin American heritages whose identities are reflected in their art. They are artists who have been involved in cultural exchanges with indigenous peoples in the Caribbean, in Africa, and throughout the various diasporas, and whose work incorporates themes dealing with racism and social justice.

It is unintentional, but perhaps not surprising, that all of the artists discussed in this essay are women. Women are the culture bearers in many traditional indigenous communities, and their roles as culture bearers are evolving in the twenty-first-century exploration of aesthetics. The featured artists, Ann "Sole Sister" Johnson (African American), Darnella Davis (Muscogee Creek), Adrienne Hoard (African American and Blackfeet [Siksika] ancestry), Robin Chandler (who identifies as "multicultural"), and Regina Vater (Brazilian) work in varied styles and genres, including painting, sculpture, photography, printmaking, mixed media, performance art, and filmmaking.

These dynamic women artists of color have expanded the scope of politically significant art. Working with a complexity of media they fuse past and present, oppose racism and sexism, and deconstruct stereotypical mainstream representations of their hybrid identities. Whether working for tribal cultural institutions or grassroots arts organizations, or within the mainstream art establishment, Johnson, Davis, Hoard, Chandler, and Vater manage to maintain ties to their specific communities and also engage with national and international coalitions.

Ann "Sole Sister" Johnson

There is no single monolithic African American art, but the work of individual African American artists reveals what it means to be black or African American in all its complexities. For the purposes of this essay, "black" or "African American" refers to people of African descent whose lives have been affected by some or all of the following factors: the transatlantic slave trade, European colonialism, Western imperialism, racism, and global dispersion.

Johnson grew up in Cheyenne, Wyoming, the site of one of the largest rodeo events in the United States each summer. As a child, Johnson attended powwows and loved watching the women's hide dresses sway gracefully while they danced. The beading, jewelry, feathers, and cowrie shells of the regalia made a lasting impression on her and became prominent features in her artwork. Primarily a mixed-media artist, she demonstrates exquisite craftsmanship combining found

Ann "Sole Sister" Johnson, *Boxed History*. Intaglio, found objects, 12 x 12 in.

objects with fundamental art techniques such as printmaking to create socially conscious work.

Intertwined with slavery, colonialism, imperialism, racism, and global dispersion is interracial sexuality expressed through voluntary marriage, cohabitation, rape, or a combination of factors. Like many African American families, Ann Johnson has relatives who were legally classified as mulatto and could pass for white when economically necessary, as well as relatives with Native American ancestry. Johnson's interest in issues pertinent to the black community led her to create the series *It Is the Not Knowing That Burns My Soul: The Odyssey of Miss Emma Jean*, an "investigation of exploratory mixed-media works that examine the 'Black Indian'"[1] as well as pieces that ponder the life of her paternal great-grandmother, Emma Jean Henderson Coleman Hurt Mathis. *The Odyssey of Miss Emma Jean* explores the identity of this mixed-blood Native American woman who married three African American men while living in Alabama during the Jim Crow era.

Oral history places Emma Jean's birth around 1864. The daughter of a white man and a mother who may have been a Black Indian, she was kidnapped from her Indian community and raised by a white family. The artist's family does not know from which of the three local tribes in Alabama (Creek, Choctaw, or Cherokee) Emma Jean was descended. As an adult, she lived in African American communities and married African American men, the first of whom was Dick Coleman, a barber listed in the 1880 census as a mulatto and with whom she had two children. Coleman was lynched when it was discovered that he was trying to pass for white. Emma Jean's second husband, Isaiah Hurt, was the artist's paternal great-grandfather.

This history inspired Johnson's concept of a shadow-box quilt in which each of nine shadow boxes reflects a family story. In seven of the boxes, Emma's image has been transferred onto feathers and a corn husk. The last box bears phrases about lynching and segregation that are familiar to most African Americans. Johnson drew on her experience in fashion merchandising and fine art to create headdresses and garments that she felt embodied Emma's warrior spirit, and adorned them with Native American and African American objects. She researched regalia through the National Museum of the American Indian (NMAI) exhibition *Identity by Design* (2007–08) and studied Southwestern art to learn how artists sculpted and created headdresses using a variety of media. Not knowing Emma's tribal affiliation, Johnson took a pan-Indian approach in

Ann "Sole Sister" Johnson, *Herstory*. Handmade paper, intaglio, found objects, 60 x 60 in.

the design of this Native-inspired clothing. She states, "These works examine what I know about Emma Jean and emphasize what I do not know. It is the not knowing that has triggered my creativity. It is the not knowing that burns my soul. This is the story of Miss Emma Jean. This is the story of my identity."[2]

Darnella Davis

An artist, educator, and policy analyst, Darnella Davis is enrolled as Muscogee Creek with tribal roots in Oklahoma and Michigan. Davis exhibits her figurative watercolors, drawings, and oil paintings nationally and abroad. Together with the work of other contemporary Native American artists, Davis's work was seen throughout the United States in the College of Wooster Art Museum's two-year traveling exhibition *We the Human Beings: Twenty-Seven Contemporary Native American Artists* (1992–93), curated by Jaune Quick-to-See Smith (Salish/French Cree/Shoshone).

Davis explains, "Imagery in my work arises in part from my mixed heritage and in part from—and in reaction to—my Eurocentric training. . . . Across time, my genealogical research has unearthed words and pictures from my ancestors that reaffirm my place as the descendant of a long line of mixed-race peoples who struggled to keep their ways and their land. Although this personal information may provide some context for interpreting my paintings, the inspiration for this work springs from a source beyond personal history, where the color yellow signals a shift from the ordinary. In this visionary world, one can discern an America perceived not through the logic of the mind but sensed by the spirit and the heart—a place accessible, perhaps, to our children's children."[3]

The watercolor *Grace and Hope* was exhibited in the two-person show *Native Color* at the Parish Gallery in Washington, D.C. In this painting, two nude figures, one with lighter skin than the other, walk in a simple neutral-colored landscape with a deep yellow sky. The time period and the figures' race(s) are indeterminate. Are they an interracial couple, or people from the same tribe/ethnicity with varying skin tones? Is the nudity imposed, or a symbol of their bodies in their natural state? Is this scene in America, or a universal, primordial location? It is up to the viewer to determine specifics in this open-ended narrative.

Other works in the show were similar in palette and theme. The male figure in *Above the Ground* seems to be a child, his race indeterminate. He jumps high, a contrast to the child in *Yellow-Haired Brown Girl*, who stands stiffly on the ground, her legs pressed together and her arms held slightly behind her back.

Darnella Davis,
*Yellow-Haired
Brown Girl.*
Watercolor.

Her deep brown skin and facial features, those of a black person, are contrasted by her curly blonde hair. She looks down at her shadow with a sad, somber countenance. What connection do these figures have with one another? Why are all of them seemingly isolated?

The figures in Davis's work come from many sources. She talks of her ancestors' triumphs and losses related to Oklahoma Indian land claims, the names recorded on the Dawes Rolls, Native American interracial marriages and liaisons, family migrations from rural Oklahoma to urban Detroit, and the ever-present racial discrimination inflicted on her ancestors whether they identified as Muscogee Creek, African American, or mixed. In the gallery context, however, viewers are not privy to this information and they must form their own interpretations based on aesthetics, their knowledge of racial dynamics, and their own internalized biases about what constitutes a Native American, an African American, or a mixed-blood person.

Adrienne Hoard

Adrienne Hoard—a painter, photographer, and university professor—has exhibited and lectured internationally as a Fulbright Scholar and Ford Foundation Fellow. She is known for her shaped canvases, which progressed from hard-edged geometric perimeters to free-form organic shapes of brilliant color evoking African and Native American abstraction and universal spiritual cosmologies. Hoard's research into the psychology of the visual perception of color and shape, as well as the link between visual abstraction and various indigenous aesthetics, has had a profound impact on her development as an artist.

The summer of 1989 spent in Brazil and Peru (countries with significant indigenous populations) was the beginning of Hoard's *Cosmic Movements* series, works in oil and acrylic on heavy rag paper. During her travels in the late 1990s, Hoard encountered Bahían priestesses in Brazil and interacted with Ndebele women artists in Pretoria, South Africa. Both groups of women create abstract, colorful altar art forms that represent visual and spiritual traditions relevant to female deities and guardian spirits. Hoard's photo-documentation and watercolor studies of these Brazilian and South African altar forms were the

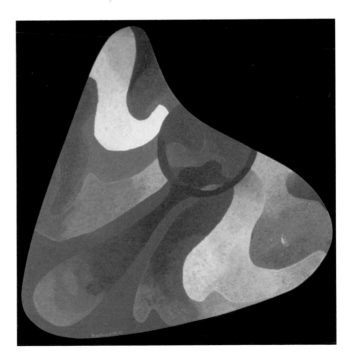

Adrienne Walker Hoard, *Etruscan II*, 1994. Florence, Italy. Oil on shaped linen, 48 x 45 in.

Adrienne Walker Hoard, *Cosmic Splash*, 1989. Oil on d'arches, 26 x 36 in.

inspiration for her *Gate Mothers* series, a tribute to divine guardian spirits and an offering to women healers/artists in Brazil, South Africa, and the diaspora.

Hoard's intuitive feel for color can be traced to early family experiences in which abundant color, ceramic figures, artifacts, and music dominated the atmosphere. Her paternal grandfather immigrated to the United States from the Caribbean in the 1890s. He and his wife, Hoard's paternal grandmother, who was Blackfeet (Siksika), shared an oral storytelling tradition in which inanimate objects became animate and animals could speak. Their spirituality also included her grandfather's Christianity and her grandmother's memories of Siksika rituals based on solar ceremonies and colorfully patterned spiritual paraphernalia—beliefs that later had an influence on Hoard's cosmological paintings. The origins of southern families claiming Blackfeet ancestry are complex, with varying histories based on oral traditions, historical documentation, and anthropological evidence. In Hoard's particular case, her Caribbean paternal grandfather met his Native American bride in the state of Mississippi, a location not usually associated with any of the three divisions of the Blackfeet Nation (the Piegan, the Siksika, and the Blood), which is located in Montana and Alberta, Canada.

Adrienne Walker Hoard, *Caiano Hills*, 1994. Florence, Italy. Acrylic, gouache, pastel on canvas paper, 26 x 38 in.

There are numerous competing origin theories with regard to the southeastern Blackfoot/Blackfeet peoples, and the subject is a source of great debate in the Native American community. Ultimately, however, Hoard and her family have the authority to determine who they are and what cultural legacies they choose to honor. In excerpts from a recent artist statement, she declared:

> I believe I came into being as an artist to translate visual stories. In photographs, on paper or shaped linen, in synthetic, glass, or stone, poems of myth and daily legends, all become my abstract colored forms. Abstraction allows my deeply personal expression to be interpreted freely from the viewer's own self-knowledge and experience. . . . For me the visual arts express the highest form of similarity among diverse people. My work is to foster communications of respect among all people, crossing perceived borders through knowledge of the "other."[4]

Robin Chandler

Robin Chandler is an artist, sociologist, educator, poet, and author of scholarly essays and books. She studied art and art history at the University of Massachusetts and obtained a PhD in sociology from Northeastern University in Boston, where she now works as a tenured professor. For more than twenty years, she has directed the Caravan for International Culture, a social and economic development organization that trains teachers and students to integrate the arts, culture, and diversity education into the classroom setting.

Chandler's poem "SIOUXJEWGERMANSCOTBLACK" describes her family's migrations and interracial and interfaith marriages. Below are excerpts from the work, published on her website.

Crossing four continents
my ancestors traveled over forty thousand years
    to make me
I am a Siouxjewgermanscotblack
   Of tribes
   And clans
  Among kin and
Courtiers I will never know.
   I do not come with directions.
So I must figure this identity thing out myself.[5]

Robin Chandler, *Taking Away the Medicine*, 1988. Mixed media collage, 20 x 30 in.

Chandler is interested in closing the boundaries that separate life, the arts, and social science, thus making twenty-first-century art more akin to indigenous cultural values. Chandler documents her travels in photographs and uses the resulting photos as collage elements in visual works, stand-alone examples of photography, and digital experiments. Chandler states, "For me art remains a sacred ritual; an attempt to create an aesthetic which inspires people. For art can and has healed, defended, and served humanity globally."[6]

Chandler's 2001 digital work *Four Nations* was shaped by her family's multicultural ancestry and her own international research initiatives. Another digital work from the same year, *Water*, consists of Chandler's self-portrait in a water-based medium within a small centered rectangle. The image calls to mind these lines from her autobiographical poem "SIOUXJEWGERMANSCOTBLACK":

Running in the summer woods, I am enfolded by greensong.
On the water I am gunwalling in the canoe, humming
        Indiansong
And the pines and greenwood and birch voices all sing with
        me.[7]

A more recent work, *Taking Away the Medicine*, is dedicated to the three generations of women from the maternal Sioux side of Chandler's family. The figure at the top is her Sioux grandmother, the early-twentieth-century photo at the bottom is Chandler's mother, and the abstract central figure is Chandler.

Chandler's research on six continents is rooted in her belief in the innate nobility of humankind; the need for the eradication of prejudice, poverty, and extreme wealth; and the need for spiritual solutions to social-justice inequities. Her ancestry is formed from a rich tapestry of Sioux, Scottish, Jewish, German, and African American heritage. This, along with her faith as a Baha'i, guides her on her journey toward the oneness of humanity.

Regina Vater

Like many Latin American artists, Brazilian-born Regina Vater incorporates religious rituals from Santería, Candomblé, and indigenous pre-Christian beliefs into her installations, earthworks, and body art. Vater emphasizes in her writings and multimedia art that the African spirit is everywhere in Brazil—in the foods, the words, the sensorial spirituality, the endurance under adverse conditions, the music, the freedom of bodily movement, and so on. She states, "For the African culture, the body acts as a stage for our emotions, or connection to the life energy, our creativity and the primordial tool for our spirituality."[8]

Working in the United States and her native Brazil, Vater is proficient in fusing both African and Native American spiritual symbols. Her installations and videos embrace the hybridization of African, American Indian, and European beliefs with an emphasis on nature's sacred forces. Although well educated in Western traditions, she feels that as an artist she has much to learn from ancient societies and their natural understanding of nature and cosmologies;

Regina Vater, *VerVê*, 1997. Corn, rice, black beans, 12 x 8 ft.

cosmologies that she thinks establish a system of sacredness permeating every-thing, everywhere. She is particularly disturbed with the way African cultural heritage is despised and/or patronized by Europeans, including Latin Americans of European descent who wield power over the majority indigenous groups, mestizos like herself, and black populations.

Since the late 1990s and continuing into the twenty-first century, Vater has been influenced by both North and South American indigenous customs, Asian practices, and her consistent connections to African spirituality. In *VerVê*, an installation inspired by African ground paintings and Navajo and Tibetan sand-paintings, she used corn, black beans, and rice to create a large spiral combined with the image of the jaguar's eye, a symbol of Afro-Brazilian healing. The daughter of a Brazilian doctor and granddaughter of great-grandparents who were poets and doctors, Vater is carrying on their healing arts, although with a

Regina Vater, *Oxalá's Path*, 1993. White feathers, fishing line, wood, bamboo, popcorn, glitter, 10 x 5 x 4.5 ft.

return to more primordial traditions. In excerpts from an artist statement, she explains, "I am compelled to be faithful to the sources of my energy and those sources still are in the place of my birth. I think that our roots have a lot to contribute in terms of connections with the sources of life and understandings about life itself."[9]

Ann "Sole Sister" Johnson, Darnella Davis, Adrienne Hoard, Robin Chandler, and Regina Vater are artists with various overlapping identities—Native American, African American, and Latin American—who have much in common. Within their artistic and scholarly pursuits, their involvement in social justice, and their lived experiences is a synthesis of cultural traditions manifested in visual expressions of feminism, the environment, spirituality, and identity. Their work is often considered in terms of race and gender because they have chosen to explore their roles as artists on these topics. They write critically about their art, devote a great deal of time to educating people about the diversity of their respective cultures, and reclaim their own subjectivity.

As prominent Native American scholar Jack Forbes notes, unraveling misconceptions is almost as important as new conceptions. One must clear away mistakes arising out of the very nature of discourse in a racist-colonial environment. Forbes states, "The ancestry of modern-day Americans is often quite complex. . . . Persons have been forced by racism into arbitrary categories which tend to render their ethnic heritage simple rather than complex."[10] In counteracting stereotypes and preconceived notions about their racial and ethnic identities, Johnson, Davis, Hoard, Chandler, and Vater promote understanding about the complexities of lives such as theirs, and in the process confirm that there is no monolithic Native American, African American, or Latin American experience.

Sarann Knight Preddy, ca. 1934.

TIFFINI BOWERS

SARANN KNIGHT PREDDY

Sarann Knight Preddy bears the distinction of being the first woman of color to own both a non-restricted gaming license and a major hotel in the United States. She was born in Eufaula, Oklahoma, in 1920 to a wealthy family with a deep appreciation for their richly mixed culture. Her mother was a member of the Muskogee (Creek) Nation and was of more Muskogee descent than black; her father was a businessman, musician, and professional baseball player of black, Spanish, and European heritage. Her family owned several successful businesses, and because they viewed their abundance with a cultural perspective that did not permit boasting or selfishness, they did not succumb to the pitfalls sometimes associated with wealth in mainstream America. Sarann's major influences growing up were her parents, who created a caring home that always had a heart for others in the community.

From a young age, Sarann was interested in business and showed a resilient spirit that served her well when she left her family to attend school in various communities throughout Oklahoma. Sarann married her first husband shortly before graduating from Dunbar High School in Okmulgee, Oklahoma, where her favorite subject was science. In these early years, Sarann encountered some racism as a result of her mixed Native American and African American background:

Back in the day, I grew up in what I call an Indian village. There was some prejudice between blacks and Indians, but it wasn't like it is today; it was more like an overtone. I lived in a small town, where my grandfather had a lot of influence, so I think that we didn't experience some of the things that happened in bigger towns. It wasn't like what was happening in the Deep South where you had lynching and people being hosed with water. It was segregated in Oklahoma, but there weren't a lot of problems going on.

Sarann's introduction to commercial gaming began when she moved with her husband and parents to Las Vegas, Nevada, in 1942. It was a time when the business district of Las Vegas was segregated, the "Vegas Strip" was in its infancy, and organized crime had not yet taken hold of the city. Sarann took her first job at the Cotton Club as a Keno writer and later became a dealer. In 1951, she moved to Hawthorne, Nevada, where she seized the opportunity to purchase her own gambling establishment. For $600, which she borrowed from her father, she bought Hawthorne's one club for blacks, renamed it the Tonga Club, and operated it for seven years. With this move, Sarann became the first woman of color to have a nonrestricted gaming license in the United States.

The Tonga Club was a great success, and Sarann operated it until her return to Las Vegas in 1957. It was an era of glamour and celebrity, when she mingled with the likes of Sammy Davis, Jr., Pearl Bailey, Nat King Cole, Eartha Kitt, and Joe Lewis. She worked as a casino dealer until a new city ordinance prohibited women from being employed as dealers. Compelled by her ever-resourceful nature and the need to support four children, Sarann owned and operated well-known gaming establishments such as the Playhouse Lounge and The People's Choice, along with numerous other businesses, including a dry cleaner and a clothing store. With the ordinance repealed and facing new challenges, she returned to work as a dealer and was the first woman of color to work at Jerry's Nugget.

In 1985, Sarann embarked on her most famous venture: the reopening of the Moulin Rouge, which was the first racially integrated hotel-casino in Las Vegas. This was the first time the Moulin Rouge had been fully operational since its debut in 1955, when it had played host to some of the biggest names in Las Vegas for just five short months. Working with her third husband, William Scruggs, Sarann operated the Moulin Rouge for twelve years and eventually succeeded in having the property declared a historic landmark before cost concerns and logistics in obtaining another gaming license led to its close in the late 1990s.

Over the years, as Sarann established an impressive record of entrepreneurial accomplishments, she also actively participated in the community, serving as president of the NAACP in Hawthorne, organizing the Las Vegas area's first NAACP Women's Club, and again making history by becoming the first woman to win the primary and proceed to the general election for the Las Vegas City Council. Without a doubt, she holds an important place in Nevada's political, business, and cultural history. When asked about her Native heritage, Sarann explained:

> My Native heritage means a great deal. Knowing the history of my Native ancestors made me more interested in my mother, the tribe, and what they went through. It made me more concerned. Out of respect, I wanted to continue to carry on the things that I learned. All of my ancestry has contributed to making me a unique person; I am proud of that and I would like to know even more about my heritage. People today are looking up their heritage and finding things out, and I think that's great. As for me, I have always known; it's something that's built in.

A woman shaped by both Native and black cultures, Sarann Knight Preddy drew on her innate talents and inner strength to become a pioneer in an industry that has become a significant economic resource for communities throughout the U.S. and Indian Country. These days, Sarann is raising a grandson with great promise in the performing arts and encouraging him to join her as an enrolled member in the Muskogee Nation. When asked what she would tell young people today, she shared the following words of wisdom: "Tell them to go to school, get an education, be honest, and try to help other people as people help them. . . . Keep focused. . . . If you try hard you can do anything you want to do."

ROBERT KEITH COLLINS

WHAT IS A BLACK INDIAN?
Misplaced Expectations and Lived Realities

"We must recognize that one of the fundamental human rights of individuals and of groups includes the right to self-identification and self-definition."

—Jack Forbes[1]

Dr. Jack Forbes (Powhatan-Renape/Delaware-Lenape) is a central figure in scholarship concerning the intersections between African Americans and Native Americans.

William Katz's book *Black Indians* (1997) illuminated the existence of individuals of blended Native American and African American cultural and racial heritage.[2] However, since the publication of the book and with recent attention brought to the potential expulsion of the Cherokee Freedmen, backed by a rationale that suggests they possess "no Cherokee blood,"[3] questions have arisen about whether individuals of mixed Native American and African American heritage are "wannabe Indians." In the quote above, Jack Forbes—a noted authority on the relationship between the political manipulation of ancestry and the racial classification of African Americans, Native Americans, and "red-black" people—alludes to a less entertained idea, particularly that the right to self-determination and definition is the right of not only groups but also

Crop-ear Charley (Seminole), Florida, 1908. Photo by M. R. Harrington. L00321

individuals. This essay engages two infrequently addressed questions: what is a Black Indian and what motivates some African Americans to claim Native American heritage? Without answers from the people themselves, the definition of a Black Indian remains unclear and the diversity of what it means to be a Black Indian elusive.[4]

Supported by a person-centered ethnographic approach,[5] this essay begins by addressing some general racial expectations of individuals with blended African American and Native American heritage. Next is a discussion of the primary attributes of Afro-Native American identities—"blooded" Indians, Freedmen, and reclaimers (i.e., those seeking to reconnect with their Native American heritage). Although many other attributes of Black Indian identity are recognized in the anthropological, historical, and social-scientific literatures (e.g., linguistic competence, knowledge of foods, ceremonial participation, etc.), these three illustrate exactly when, where, and in which contexts federal Indian policy and/or cultural-specific American Indian lifeways are salient in the lives of individuals of blended African American and Native American heritage.[6] The goal here is to examine the answer to a perennial question surrounding this group: are Black Indians really American Indians, or just black people pretending to be Indian?

Racial Expectation and Black Indians

What motivates people who look "black" to claim to be Indian? When answered in a manner divorced from lived experience, this question produces many misplaced expectations about black and Indian mixed-bloods and demonstrates the fixity with which American race-making practices ascribe blackness. The question is central because it engages the problematic American cultural practice of assessing and assuming identity from skin color. It also lies at the intersection of what Americans—including other Native Americans—expect of people who look "black," and how Afro-Natives are raised and socialized within their families to understand themselves. Racial expectations have affected how black and Indian mixed-bloods have been understood and why some are motivated to forcefully assert their culturally specific or generic Native American heritage despite their "black" appearance.[7]

One set of expectations urges black and Indian mixed-bloods to accept that they are black and stop "pretending" to be Indian. This scenario requires individuals to forget that they have Indian relatives and remember that it is skin

Foxx family (Mashpee Wampanoag), 2008. From left: Anne, Monét, Majai (baby), Aisha, and Maurice Foxx.

color that determines who they are. Other expectations suggest that African American and Native American mixed-bloods are only trying to claim that they are Indian based on a remote ancestor, since some Native Americans were historically known for providing sanctuary for runaway slaves.[8] These expectations about African and Native American mixed-bloods create several misconceptions: that 1) assessments of heritage from skin color are viable and accurate; 2) family composition and lived cultural practices can be determined from an individual's skin color; and 3) skin color may indicate personal motivational forces.[9]

Anthony Wallace and Raymond D. Fogelson[10] allude to the importance of understanding the types of identities Americans create to cope with inconsistencies between self-understanding and racial recognition. They suggest that individuals are simultaneously themselves and extensions of groups, and the combination may create "an ideal identity, an image of oneself that one wishes to realize; a feared identity, which one values negatively and wishes to avoid; a 'real' identity, which an individual thinks closely approximates an accurate representation of the self or reference group; and a claimed identity that is presented to others for confirmation, challenge, or negotiation in an effort to move the 'real' identity closer to the ideal and further from the feared identity."[11]

Thus, while navigating the racial expectations of others—particularly from peers invested in the maintenance of "real Indianness" and "real blackness"—within the contexts of everyday interpersonal interactions, a black and Indian individual with a real identity as one-eighth Cherokee, for example, may assert an ideal identity as three-quarter Cherokee when around Native Americans or Caucasians who do not like black people or believe "real" Indians have high blood quanta. This individual might also claim to be a half-blood Cherokee raised traditionally in Tahlequah, Oklahoma, out of fear of being seen as a black "wannabe Indian" when surrounded by other African Americans or Native Americans who believe black people cannot also be Indians and do not look "Indian enough." Despite a thorough illustration by Wallace and Fogelson[12] of the dynamic nature of identity struggles among Native Americans, serious misunderstandings regarding whether or not individuals of blended African American and Native American heritage are really "Indian" continue in academics and society.[13]

The Indian Part of Being a Black Indian

Using examples from ethnographic research with African American and Choctaw mixed-bloods, three primary categories of Afro-Native American identity—"blooded" Indians, Freedmen, and reclaimers—illustrate the salience of American Indian blood-quantum policies and the importance of kinship in the lives of African American and Native American mixed-bloods.[14]

No other group better demonstrates the misplaced expectation that black and Indian mixed-bloods should just be regarded as black than those who were tribally enrolled by their families at birth, possess a Certificate of Degree of Indian Blood (CDIB) card, or both. This group consists of individuals with varying degrees of Native American blood above and below the one-quarter blood marker: the degree commonly used by the Bureau of Indian Affairs and many tribal nations to recognize an individual as Native American. This means that some black and Indian individuals may be of one-quarter or more Native American blood (verified by a CDIB card) and enrolled in a federally recognized nation (verified by a citizenship enrollment card). Others may possess CDIB cards reflecting blood quanta less than one-quarter Indian, which may make them nonstatus Indians and ineligible for services in the eyes of the Bureau of Indian Affairs. In a similar vein, individuals with blood quanta below one-quarter may find themselves ineligible for enrollment—even though they have a CDIB card—in nations that require a blood quantum of one-half. Among the Oklahoma Choctaw and Cherokee, tribal members trace their lineage through descent from one or more enrollees from the Dawes Roll of 1906 to prove citizenship eligibility. This means that any degree of Indian blood can be possessed by descendants from the final Dawes Rolls.[15]

"Blooded" individuals are often raised with a broader sense of self and consider their blackness part of their Native American history. Self-understanding as an "Indian" may be more associated with immediate, extended, and adopted family ties—such as mother, father, beloved friends of family, clan, and moiety kin[16]—than with their tribe or blood-quantum card. My own recent studies of black Choctaw life experiences, conducted in southeastern Oklahoma and the San Francisco Bay Area, have revealed that knowledge of what one's skin color represents to social peers is usually acquired during interpersonal interactions with nonfamilial peers.[17] Consequently, parents and grandparents (even those without black blood) raised black Choctaw children with a variety of life strategies needed to cope with the prejudices of others. One example can be found in the life history of Mr. Mark, a farmworker in his thirties.[18]

Mr. Mark has always lived in Foi Tamaha, a community in southeastern Oklahoma. The second eldest of four children, Mr. Mark grew up with both English and Choctaw spoken in the home, as both of his parents are half Choctaw and half African American. According to Mark, his parents often reinforced both Choctaw and African American cultural practices at home (i.e., attending local Juneteenth celebrations and Stomp Dances, going to an English-speaking Pentecostal church, singing Christian hymns at home in Choctaw). Only after working on local farms with different employers in Texas and Oklahoma did he begin to experience what he calls "other peoples' ideas about who I am supposed to be."

> Mr. Mark: Like this one time, I was working alongside my cousin, and I guess we were not picking fast enough, when this supervisor come up and say, "Why don't you boys act like other blacks do?" So, I just looked [at] him and asked, "How are we supposed to act, sir?" He made a sly remark, so I turned to my cousin and say, "Katimih o hattvk tohbi anumpa o?

Huklo tvk o̱?" (Why is this white man talking? Were you listening?) He
said, "Kiyoh. Hvklo o̱? Katimih o huklo o̱? Anumpa momah?" (No. Listen?
Why listen? Is he still talking?) That man got all bent out of shape and say,
"Get out of here with all that mumbo jumbo." All you can do is laugh, but
it makes me sad to see our own people acting like this. Grandma always
said, "If your mom or dad is Choctaw, then you are Choctaw."[19]

A second type of Black Indian is the Indian Freedman, or Freedmen descendant.
Most commonly found among the Five Civilized Tribes—Cherokee, Chickasaw,
Choctaw, Creek, and Seminole—these individuals were slaves, or descendants
of slaves, owned by Native American masters. Freedmen possess varying degrees
of Indian blood; the amount is often below one-quarter and they are usually
not recognized with CDIB cards. Their slave status and visible African American heritage (as determined by Dawes enrollment agents) originally relegated
them to the Freedmen rolls, regardless of their degree of Indian blood.[20] Some
nations, such as the Choctaw and Creek, have nonetheless allowed movement
from the Freedmen rolls to the blooded rolls for those disenfranchised during
an enrollment process that did not recognize the children of Indian men and
slave women. Chickasaws, on the other hand, outright expelled their Freedmen
in the late 1800s and subsequently refused to recognize them.[21]

Freedmen descendants have recently been the source of great media controversy, particularly because the Cherokee and Seminole nations have sought
legislation to expel their Freedmen descendants and dissolve their Freedmen
rolls, claiming these people possess no Indian blood and no longer practice
Cherokee or Seminole culture.[22] The works of Daniel Littlefield on Cherokee
Freedmen and his book, *Africans and Seminoles,* encourage us to contemplate
the potential racism embedded in such opinions by examining the lived experiences of Freedmen and their descendants.[23] The life history of Spence Johnson,
obtained in Waco, Texas, by Works Progress Administration (WPA) fieldworker
Ada Davis in June 1937, illustrates the limitation of contemporary assumptions
about Freedmen having no Indian blood:

"De nigger stealers done stole me and my mammy out'n de Choctaw
Nation, up in de Indian Territory, when I was 'bout three years old. Brud-
der Knex, Sis Hannah, and my mammy, and her two step-chillun was
down on de river washin'. De nigger stealers drive up in a big carriage,

Spence Johnson, as a black Choctaw child, was kidnapped from Indian Territory with his mother and sisters and sold into slavery.

and Mammy jus' thought nothin', 'cause the ford was near dere, and people goin' on de road stopped to water de horses and res' awhile in de shade. By and by, a man coaxes de two bigges' chillun to de carriage, and give dem some kind-a candy. Other chillun sees dis and goes, too. Two other men was walkin' 'round smoking and gettin' closer to Mammy all de time. When he kin, de man in de carriage get de two big step-chillun in with him, and me and sis' climb in, too, to see how come. Den de man haller, "Git de ole one, and let's get from here." With dat de two big men grab Mammy, and she fought, and screeched, and bit, and cry, but dey hit her on de head with something, and drug her in, and threwed her on the floor. De big chilluns begin to fight for Mammy, but one of de men hit 'em hard, and off dey drive, with de horses under whip.

Dis was near a place called Boggy Depot. Dey went down de Red Ribber, 'cross de ribber, and on down in Louisiana to Shreveport. Down in Louisiana, us was put on what dey call de block and sol' to de highes' bidder. My mammy and her three chillun brung $3,000 flat. De step chillun was sol' to somebody else, but us was bought by Marse Riley Surratt. He was de daddy of Judge Marshall Surratt, he's who get to be judge here in Waco. Marse Riley Surratt has a big plantation; don't know how many acres, but dere was a factory, and gins, and big houses, and lots of nigger quarters. De houses was right on de Tex-Louisiana line. Mammy cooked for 'em. When Marse Riley bought her, she couldn' speak nothin' but de Choctaw words. I was a baby when us lef' de Choctaw country. My sister looked like a full-blooded Choctaw Indian and she could pass for a real full-blooded Indian. Mammy's folks was all Choctaw Indians. Her sisters was Polly Hogan and Sookey Hogan, and she had a brudder, Nelan Tubby. Dey was all known in de Territory in de ole days. Near as Marse Riley's books can come to it, I mus' of been born 1859, up in de Territory."[24]

In a time before contemporary blood-quantum rules, Johnson, his mother, and his siblings were abducted and sold into slavery, a condition unrelated to their family heritage and which would take precedence over who they were. These types of WPA narratives have propelled some Freedmen descendants and others to question their lack of Indian blood, as well as the absolute blackness of slaves in the Unites States.

The reclaimers represent individuals of varying degrees of Native American blood who are seeking to reclaim this ancestry by asserting a cultural-specific (sometimes several) or generic Native American identity. The cultural-specific Native American background for many of these individuals is as elusive as their cultural-specific African background; many know only that "grandmother was an Indian." On the other hand, some individuals know their cultural-specific Native American heritage but simply are not enrolled, while others are members of state-recognized tribes that are not recognized by the federal government.[25]

An example of the reclaimer experience can be found in the narrative of a black and Choctaw woman called Madame Iber. The following excerpt provides an example of the lived experience of a nonstatus black and Indian mixed-blood.

Heriberto Dixon at the Tutelo Homecoming Festival near Ithaca, New York, 2006. Dr. Dixon was instrumental in reclaiming the history of his community. The Tutelo were once a powerful people in contact-era Virginia, but by the early eighteenth century, they had been uprooted and dispersed in colonial wars. Many surviving Tutelos were adopted by and then assimilated into the Haudenosaunee (Six Nations) located in upstate New York and Canada.

Madame Iber: When I was little, I had blonde hair. And, I can remember, as told by my mother something that someone said. "Johnny come here! Come and looks at this. I have never seen a nigger with blue eyes." And I have never ever forgotten that. So there were issues. I had issues. Kids had issues with me when I was growing up, because I did not fit the pattern of what it was to be black. (Note: Respondent began to cry.)

Q: So how did your Choctaw ancestry factor into all of this?

Madame Iber (crying): You know, it did not factor in at all. I grew up very middle class, and probably not very black except politically. . . . So it was very, very middle class, except for there was literature that made reference to the black experience, a black experience to us. When I came to California, we would go to family gatherings when my parents would come out; otherwise, I had nothing to do with my relatives.

And we would always talk about that we were supposed to get a loan, and Chubee or Tubee signed the Dancing Rabbit Creek treaty, and it was never clear what they were saying. For years, I just thought that we were Cherokee. One day, I decided that I was going to do some research, and I found the Dancing Rabbit Creek treaty. I thought, my god, all these years I have been telling people that I am Cherokee and yet I am Choctaw. I got a copy of the treaty and of course everyone is Chubee and Tubee on there. It was part of my oral tradition, and I simply accepted that. I had often been involved with Indians. It was all in the back of my mind. So I think it was more of a political identity, certainly not cultural. There was nothing really cultural in my family. I met another Choctaw and she had gotten deeply involved in her Oklahoma roots and has kind of pulled me along, so we got regalia and have gone to some of the gatherings. I am not sure where I want to go with that. I am not interested in learning the language. I am simply interested in claiming that heritage. And I guess that is it. I guess say "this is who I am" also.

Q: What does it mean for you to be able to claim the ancestry, as far as who you are?

Madame Iber (crying): I think it means . . . does this have a reference to me or for me? I think it has a reference for me intellectually. I get real emotional about it. In terms of the history of our culture, our country, and the evils that have been perpetrated and continue to go on, the issue of people not being able to claim who they are. That is in the sense what I struggle for and fight for.

Q: What kind of meanings do you think this will have for your family?

Madame Iber (crying): It has no meaning for my son. He just asks that he is not going to be anything, he is just going to be a film producer. My sister is maybe where she can run away from the whole racial issue. She finds it a burden to be black, much less Indian. My nieces have begun to claim Choctaw; in fact, on the census they wrote down Choctaw along with everything else. They had never really acknowledged it before; they heard it, but never voiced it. My son says when I go to Scottish festivals—because we are also Scottish, Irish, and French—"What are you going to be today?" I tell him that I am going to claim it all. I am going to claim it and embrace it all, although being Choctaw is remote for me.

Another example of reclamation can be found among one of the least-discussed populations of Native America: the ever-growing number of Native American individuals and families who are refusing to enroll their children or seek CDIB cards because they disagree with enrollment and/or blood-quantum assessment procedures. These concerns are voiced in the account of Ms. Tuchina[26] ("three" in Chahta, or Choctaw) and her mother.

Tuchina: Most people never look at me and think Indian, let alone Choctaw. Maybe it is because I am dark, my hair nappy, and my face is round. But I look like my grandmother, whose mother is the only enrolled member of our family. My mom does not think that enrollment is right and wants me to wait and decide.

Tuchina's mother: It ain't right! And, if she enrolls, I have to. And I dare anyone to tell me that this is not my mother right here or that I am not Choctaw. Chahta is the language of this house and this woman (pointing toward her full-blood mother). Make sure you put that in your recorder, sir!

Q: What do you think that she means?

Tuchina: Well, you see, it seems that every time my friends, and now co-workers, ask me about my family, I get into an argument. I work with whites, blacks, and Indians from up north and down here. But, it seems every time I mention anything about being Choctaw, they say, "Here we go with the Indian stuff again." Even the Indians ask where is my card. When I tell them that my family does not want to enroll, they tell me that (we) are not Indian. Maybe this is a good thing. One lady making a *comment* (emphasized) says, "Why can't you people just be black?" You people? I almost got fired that day. I got too much of my grandmother in me.

Conclusion

The narratives presented here examine some lived experiences of black and Indian mixed-bloods, helping to explain—in their own voices—the dynamics of what a black Indian is and why these individuals put so much effort into claiming their Native heritage. Lived realities such as these are important to anthropological studies of U.S. race-making culture because they highlight the limitations of assessing self-understanding and heritage based on skin color. Most important, these narratives illuminate the racial variation that exists among those that have an understanding of self as American Indian.

Today, as in the past, black and Indian mixed-bloods are under heavy suspicion. The accounts of Mr. Mark, Mr. Johnson, Ms. Tuchina, and Madame Iber reveal details of interpersonal interactions with nonfamilial others who expected these individuals' skin colors and self-understandings to be consistent; when they were not consistent, these others felt free to challenge the narrators' assertions of Native heritage. This practice of identity negation helped motivate these individuals to challenge the misplaced assumption that they should "just be black."[27]

Mr. Mark's resistance is based on how he was raised and on his grandmother's words: "If your mom or dad is Choctaw, then you are Choctaw." Ms. Tuchina's motivations can be heard in family disagreements about enrollment and blood-quantum policies, and how they reduce knowledge of kin to what Ms. Tuchina's grandmother calls "blood math." Mr. Johnson's testimony is seldom seen or questioned in the literature on American Indians, African Americans, or slavery: that Native Americans were made slaves and sold as such.[28] What implication does this hold for understanding the variations in race and culture that exists among these two groups? Similarly, Mr. Johnson's narrative addresses how people project a particular identity onto others based on their actions or occupations.[29] Expectations that Mr. Johnson should "just be black" say more about the misplaced efforts of others in forcing an individual to fit their social constructs—such as those of Mr. Johnson's slave traders—than pointing out some falsehood in his answer to the question: who am I?

Finally, for Madame Iber, the motivational forces behind her assertion of her Choctaw heritage lie in another issue seldom addressed in scholarly literature on American Indian, African American, or Afro-Native identities: how class aspirations influence the way a mother chooses to raise her children, the advantages that she may seek for them, and how the children translate these desires into their own lives. Parents do not always qualify and label what they are teaching their children in a manner consistent with public identities (i.e., this is Indian, this is American, and so on). When the desire is for a comfortable life, social mobility, and a better future for their child, parents may suppress certain cultural practices (i.e., Choctaw culture, the need for validation through enrollment and blood-quantum certification, etc.) for the sake of giving their children advantages in life. One might argue, as Madame Iber does, that Choctaw culture then becomes remote. But how remote is it? Psychologist Erik Erikson, who introduced the term *identity* to the social sciences, alluded to the significance of these questions in *Identity and the Life Cycle* (1959). He suggested that "students of history continue to ignore the simple fact that all individuals are borne by mothers."[30] These mothers will have an understanding of self that is oriented toward a group and an "ego" that encompasses their own understanding of who they are within this culturally constructed group that is then passed on to their children. If this is true, then one can attribute Madame Iber's claim of Choctaw heritage to a desire to explain why her family required her to remember that her ancestor signed the Treaty of Dancing Rabbit Creek.[31]

In this paper, being a Black Indian is examined in terms of three defining conditions: "blooded" Indians, Freedmen, and reclaimers. These conditions demonstrate a range of personal experiences of black and Indian mixed-bloods and reveal how these experiences motivate individuals to assert their American Indian heritage despite social forces that encourage them to "just be black." The motivational forces behind self-understanding and identity should be an area of central importance to scholars investigating Native American and African American identities and interactions. The experience near (i.e., as close to lived experience as possible) understandings of African-Native American lives revealed through person-centered investigations offer scholars a window into the salience of ethnoracial categories to heritage and self-understanding; illuminating why it is important to challenge the misplaced expectations of those who seek to make identity based on skin color consistent with family-based understandings of self.[32]

Fernando Medina and his wife are the patrons of the Dorado Chico celebration in honor of the patron saint San Benito. Fernando, originally from Dorado Chico, works in La Paz as a driver for a major industrialist and political leader.

PETER MCFARREN

AFRO-BOLIVIANS REVITALIZE THEIR CULTURAL IDENTITY

Dorado Chico is a small farming community located on the eastern slopes of the Andes in the Yungas subtropical region of Bolivia, where Afro-Bolivians and Aymara farmers live side by side. Dorado Chico is reached after a five-hour journey across the Andes from the highland city of La Paz. Much of the trip is along a dilapidated, winding road bordered by tropical foliage, coca leaf, and orange and coffee plantations. The hillsides are patterned with terraces of coca plants, the main crop in the region.

Every year, in honor of the town's patron saint, San Benito, hundreds of locals and La Paz city residents of mixed Aymara and African origin visit Dorado Chico to perform the traditional Saya, a rhythmic dance that is part of the cultural revitalization of the estimated 20,000 Afro-Bolivians living in La Paz and the Yungas region. The dozens of Afro-descendant communities in this area still bear the names given by their ancestors: Mururata, Chijchipa, Chulumani, Kala Kala, Colpar, Coroico, and so on.

The Afro-Bolivian communities maintain their own cultural traditions, but the links with the Aymaras of the Bolivian highlands remain strong, a legacy of the colonial period when both were indentured by Spanish landowners. African slaves arrived in Bolivia more than 450 years ago to work in the silver mines of Potosi. Unable to adapt to the harsh and rarefied air, thousands of slaves were sent to work in the coca leaf and coffee plantations of the Yungas. Although slavery was abolished in 1851, it was not until the 1952 revolution, followed by the passing of the Agrarian Reform Law, that Afro-Bolivians and indigenous peoples were freed from indentured servitude and allowed to be landowners.

La Saya was revived in the 1980s by the Saya Afro-Bolivian Movement, which was founded by young city residents to assert the identity of Afro-Bolivian communities. Today, young Afro-Bolivians are spearheading the social, cultural, and political participation of the community.

Afro-Bolivian residents in Dorado Chico wear the same bowler hat and *cholitas* (multilayered pleated skirt) worn by Aymara city and rural residents.

Beatriz Torrez represents a new generation of Afro-Bolivians who are asserting their cultural heritage. Her mother is Aymara, a Bolivian indigenous community, and her father Afro-Bolivian. Torrez is part of the Afro-Bolivian cultural movement that is strengthening the cultural identity of the community through the Saya dance and music group.

Beatriz and other members of the cultural movement dance La Saya, a form of dance and music unique to Afro-Bolivians and heavily influenced by the rhythms of Africa.

"After the abolishment of slavery, Afro-Bolivians formed stable communities and adopted a lifestyle very similar to that of Aymara peasants," says Korey Capozza, an expert on the Afro-Bolivian communities.[1] Afro-Bolivian women wear the same dress and braid their hair in the same style as the Aymaras; some even speak Aymara. "We can no longer talk about 'cultural purity,' because a cultural syncretism is what we actually have," states Monica Rey, a leader of the Afro-Bolivian community.

In 1932, Bonifacio Pinedo, a descendant of the Senegalese, was crowned king of the Afro-Bolivians. He held sway over many of the communities where Afro-Bolivians and Aymaras lived among each other in adobe homes covered with sheets of tin or straw. His son, Julio Pinedo, was sworn in as king in 2007 by the Prefect of La Paz. According to Sara Busdiecker, an authority on the Afro-Bolivian community, the monarchy is an Afro-Bolivian tradition dating from the seventeenth century, when a slave of royal Kikongo Senegalese origin was brought to the hacienda of Mururata.

RON WELBURN

NATIVE AMERICANS IN JAZZ, BLUES, AND POPULAR MUSIC

Jazz, blues, and popular music performers are very often storytellers. It is hardly surprising, then, that many accomplished jazz musicians of the twentieth century were of Native American origin. Less surprising, perhaps, is the fact that Native musicians are rarely acknowledged in orthodox histories for their impressive contributions to these vernacular forms. Native musicians had an uncanny ability to display both technical facility and imagination while improvising on a composition's melodic, harmonic, and rhythmic properties—skills that are fundamental to providing the swinging performances that jazz audiences loved. While the involvement of indigenous Americans in this quintessentially American music is extensive, the Native identity of musicians commonly believed to be black or white still provokes wonder and contention. As to verifying Indian identity, from the Removal Era of the 1830s until Wounded Knee in 1973, many Indians in the East and Southeast navigated social pressures to assimilate to a black, colored, or white identity just to survive. Native entertainers felt surreptitious camaraderie wherever they encountered one another; they played in Midwestern "territory bands" and on the ubiquitous "chitlin' circuit," and they settled in large cities. Remarkable individuals, they gained sophistication on and off the bandstand in a profession that brought opportunities to tour the United States and the world, along the way meeting dignitaries and adoring fans alike. Native people continue to play a role in the world of jazz, blues, and popular music. Now is the time for this story to be told.

Doc Cheatham joins trombonist Vic Dickinson (not pictured) and alto saxophonist Earle Warren during an appearance at the Overseas Press Club in New York.

Native Musical Elements

Certain beats, rhythms, and lyrical and syncopation qualities in jazz have been attributed as American Indian in origin rather than strictly African American. Given the orthodox history of jazz musicology, much debate surrounds how these elements are heard—and felt. The proudly Native bassist and composer Oscar Pettiford vigorously maintained to jazz critic George Hoefer that "4/4, the basic time of jazz, came directly from the American Indian, and though 4/4 existed in European music, it was not used in the same way, and African rhythms, supposedly the important ingredient in jazz, were of a very different rhythmic nature." Indeed, the four-to-the-bar beat on the bass drum typifying the standard jazz rhythm heard on innumerable recordings of the 1920s closely resembles several Native drumming styles. Count Basie Band alumni drummer Jo Jones and trumpeter Buck Clayton privately believed that drummer Jesse Price innovated the "chinga-ching" beat on the high-hat cymbal based on Native rhythms he heard in the Midwest; perhaps coincidentally, Price was part Mohawk.

The call-and-response song pattern (antiphony) distinguishes much African American singing, but in Native American musical styles the delineation of phrases differs. This unique phrasing can be found in social dance songs of indigenous southeastern tribes and is not restricted to stomp dancing. Call and response characterizes innumerable jazz and popular-music orchestrations; a remarkably close example to the southeastern style is "Shotgun" (1965) by Junior Walker & the All Stars. Comparisons of Native call-and-response cadences and rhythmic inflections with African American work and prison songs suggest a syncretism of indigenous and African-derived style, yet reveal differences in how Indian response patterns melodically repeat or slightly vary the line of the caller or are expressed in shorter lengths. "Goin' Down to Muskogee" (1983), recorded by saxophonist Jim Pepper, follows a Stomp Dance form. Another musical quality is the "war whoop" effect, characterized by a dramatic, sharply ascending glissando. Frankie Trumbauer, a Texas Cherokee, exhibited this affectation playing C-melody saxophone during the 1920s, but its most influential exponent was another Texan, Count Basie tenor saxophonist Herschel Evans (of unknown tribal heritage), in his "One O'Clock Jump" solo (1938). The ascending "whoop" became a signature lick in the big sound of the Texas tenor and southwestern soloists.

"Cherokee" and Other Popular "Indian" Musical Themes

Romanticizing Native culture and trivializing Native experience and lifeways affects Indian Country, and offensive recordings parallel the Indian mascot issue. Mainstream music plays a dubious though interesting role in this history. Of more than one hundred musical works by non-Indians invoking Indians, three are titled "Mohawk"; others include "Apaches," "Big Wig in the Wigwam," a light classical piece named "Indian Love Call," and "Please, Mr. Custer." Indians, meanwhile, composed "Walking by the River" (Una Mae Carlisle), "Lakota Song" (Jim Pepper), "Come and Get Your Love" (Redbone), and two culturally reflective rock songs, "Halfbreed" (Cher, of Cherokee heritage), and "Indian Reservation (The Lament of the Cherokee Reservation Indian)," written by John Loudermilk and performed by Paul Revere and the Raiders. By far the most famous song in jazz history with an Indian theme is "Cherokee," composed by British songwriter Ray Noble as part of his *Indian Suite* and first recorded in 1939 by Count Basie's Orchestra; Billy May's orchestration later that year for Charlie Barnet's Orchestra remains the favorite. Most Americans probably did not realize that the infectious arrangement imaginatively captured the call-and-response structure of southeastern social dance songs, resulting in a catchy style that appealed to many listeners. Bebop-era musicians established "Cherokee" as a modern jazz standard and also executed its intricate chord structure at breakneck tempos; combos led by Oscar Pettiford and others did so to chase untalented musicians off the jam-session bandstand.

Mardi Gras Indians

New Orleans, with its extraordinarily complex cultural history, is the most important city in early jazz history. The Mardi Gras Indians are part of a large cultural phenomenon that—viewed in the historical crosscurrents of indigenous and African cultures in the Caribbean, the Atlantic Islands, and Latin America (and mumming traditions of Ireland and Europe)—bears a significant though controversial counter to surface presumptions about stereotyping Indians. During pre-Lenten carnivals and other holidays, blacks and Creoles (which came to signify Indian, French, or Spanish mixtures) in and around New Orleans gathered at the famous Congo Square, where Houmas, Chitimachas, and other tribes traditionally gathered for festivities. When New Orleans hosted Buffalo Bill's Wild West Show in 1884 and 1885, local blacks, Creoles, and Indians socialized with the Plains Indians in Buffalo Bill's extravaganzas and observed their parades. This

Mardi Gras Indians, New Orleans, Louisiana, 2004. Photo by Steven M. Cummings. Courtesy Anacostia Community Museum, Smithsonian Institution.

led to the first acknowledged Mardi Gras Indian group, the Creole Wild West of the late 1880s, organized by Becate Batiste who was part Choctaw.

Segregation laws preventing non-white revelers from participating in Mardi Gras compelled them to make their own festivities. According to Michael P. Smith, historically (and to a lesser degree today), local Indians were among these Mardi Gras Indians. With their tremendous headdresses, elaborate costumes consisting of painstakingly beaded and sequined patterns, parades, and names such as the Yellow Pocahantas and the Golden Star Hunters, members of today's Mardi Gras "tribes" continue to take seriously identities that are steeped in the history of New Orleans secret societies. Each Mardi Gras tribe has its "big chief," its "wild man" (a medicine-man figure), and scouts called "spy boys" (one of whom was Jelly Roll Morton as a youth), and all members feign and gesticulate in an "Indian" way. The Mardi Gras Indian subculture, unlike ordinary Indian mascot performers, is a handed-down survival strategy against colonialism and slavery. As in Trinidad during Carnival, to "masque," or "mask," in New Orleans means to dress up for a festive occasion, and by masking as Indians, the Mardi

Gras revelers acknowledge Indians for their assistance during tough times. One Mardi Gras Indian utterance, "kogma-feena," has been traced by linguist Emanuel J. Drechsel to the Choctaw-based Mobilian trade jargon that developed among Gulf-region Natives as a form of language interchange. "To-way-pa-ka-way," a common refrain in their call and responses, is in the rhythm-and-blues song "Don't You Know Yockomo," recorded in 1958 by the New Orleans group Huey Smith & the Clowns. Drechsel and Joseph Roach believe this phrase may have filtered through Mobilian from African and Creole sources.

Native American Orchestras and Small Groups

Listening to and playing music recreationally, Indians became exposed to European music forms and African American vernacular music. During the controversial and often painful years in reservation and boarding schools, students developed the skills to perform in school orchestras and parade bands. Born from that experience were three generations of the Idaho band The Nezpercians, who played ragtime, jazz, and jazz fusion; the 1930s Lollipop Six also hailed from Idaho. Other Indian dance bands that enjoyed popularity during the early jazz years were the All-American Jazz Band, led by Chief Joe Shunatona (Osage)—who performed at the presidential inauguration for Herbert Hoover and his Kaw vice president, Charles Curtis—and Pawnee musician Dan Bayhylle and his Ten Little Indians. While none of these bands seem to have recorded, they are musical ancestors of today's smaller bands such as Redbone, Xit, Blues Nation, and Brulé. Other groups include Afro-Algonquin, led by Mahican-Mohawk reed player and percussionist Mixashawn (Lee Rozie) and occasionally accompanied by his brother, bassist Rick Rozie; the Redhouse Family (Navajo/Filipino); and the Plateros (Navajo), who perform gospel-flavored blues rock. The Chavis Brothers (North Carolina Tuscarora) sang and recorded R&B and other genres. Like mainstream performers, current Native artists such as Litefoot and Pamyua utilize jazz and R&B nuances to enhance the particular eclecticism of their hip-hop or a cappella foundations. As they have for decades, indigenous musicians from the U.S., Canada, and Latin America add their own flavor to mainstream contemporary music, which they continue to appreciate and be inspired by today.

SOME OUTSTANDING NATIVE JAZZ PERFORMERS

From a potentially exhaustive list of Native performers in jazz, blues, and popular music, the following represent major and innovative contributors to the collective genres.

Mildred Bailey (Couer d'Alene, 1903–1951) became the first popular female jazz vocalist when she recorded "Rocking Chair" in 1929. Born in Idaho, she admired the timing of Bessie Smith but refused to imitate her. Her brother, Al Rinker, sang in a trio with Bing Crosby in the 1920s.

Jimmy Blanton (Cherokee, 1918–1942) from Chattanooga, Tennessee, died of tuberculosis at age twenty-four, yet he played the string bass with sturdy yet supple guitarlike lines that left an indelible mark on modern jazz. He joined the Duke Ellington Orchestra in 1940, recording legendary duets with the maestro.

Oscar Pettiford (Cherokee and Choctaw, 1922–1960) and Jimmy Blanton "woodshedded" (played jam sessions) together, and Pettiford eventually succeeded Blanton with Ellington. Pettiford evolved into the principal innovator of modern jazz bass. He was a superlative instrumentalist and a key bebop artist and composer.

Adolphus "Doc" Cheatham (Cherokee and Choctaw, 1905–1997) was a journeyman trumpeter and vocalist who received numerous lifetime achievement awards in recognition of his remarkably long and respected career. He toured Europe with Sam Wooding in 1928, then played with Cab Calloway, Teddy Wilson, Claude Hopkins, and Sam Price, and in the 1940s with Machito and other Latin bandleaders.

Off the bandstand, bassist Oscar Pettiford and his wife Jackie had their hands full with their children, Little Cello, Cellina, and Celeste in this undated photograph.

Lee Wiley in the studio for Columbia Records, ca. 1951.

Russell "Big Chief" Moore (Akimel O'odham, 1912–1983) left the reservation as a teenager to join his uncle in Chicago, where, from outside a nightclub, he listened, enthralled, to the young Louis Armstrong. He went on to play trombone with his childhood idol from 1944 to 1947 and 1964 to 1965. He toured for more than three decades with the Lester Lanin Society Orchestra and encouraged O'odham youth to continue their education.

Lee Wiley (Cherokee, 1915–1975) was born in Fort Gibson, Oklahoma, to a family listed on the Dawes and Guion Miller Cherokee rolls. Critically acclaimed for her singing, her musical sophistication never brought her widespread fame, although Columbia Records producer and bandleader Mitch Miller described her as possessing "individuality and excellence."

Jim Pepper (Creek and Kaw, 1941–1992) is fondly remembered for his 1969 recording "Witchi-Tai-To," based on a peyote road-man song, which became a West Coast underground favorite. Pepper toured internationally with Carla Bley's Orchestra and performed in Europe with pianist Mal Waldron and the assertive part-Choctaw pocket trumpeter Don Cherry.

ADDITIONAL NATIVE MUSICIANS

Drummers and Percussionists: Ray Mantilla (Taino), Lewis McMillan, and Lionel Hampton (Cherokee)

Guitar and Banjo Players: Scrapper Blackwell (Eastern Cherokee), Lowell Fulson (Choctaw), Gil Roberts (Narragansett/Montaukett), Bill Jonasee (Comanche), Cliff Shenandoah (Oneida), Jimi Hendrix (Cherokee), Joe Barrick (Choctaw), Link Wray (Shawnee), and Charley Patton (Choctaw)

Bassists: Joe Mondragon (Apache) and Hugh Wyatt (Cherokee)

Pianists: Paul Seminole (Seminole)

Trombonists: Charlie "Big" Green, Dick Burrell (Ojibwe), Leon "Snub" Moseley, Steve Turre (Aztec), and Cherokee musicians Kid Ory, Jean Travis, Jimmy Cleveland, and Jack Teagarden.

Trumpeters: Benny Harris (San Blas) and Nova Lee McGee (Native Hawaiian)

Vocalists: Clea Bradford (Choctaw), Cher, Eartha Kitt, Frieda Payne, Keely Smith, and Clarence Collins of Little Anthony & the Imperials (all of whom claimed Cherokee ancestry), Lena Horne (Iroquois), "Tiny" Joe Eleazer (Mashantucket Pequot), Andrea Menard (Métis), Wayne Newton (Chickahominy), Pete J. Peter (Gwich'in), Pura Fé (Tuscarora), Martha Redbone (Shawnee/Choctaw/Cherokee/Blackfeet), Robbie Robertson (Mohawk), Janice Marie [Robinson] (Stockbridge-Munsee), Kay Starr (Cherokee/Choctaw), Una Mae Carlisle, and Princess White.

Saxophones/Reeds: Nina De La Cruz (Pueblo), Joy Harjo (Muscogee Creek), Charles Harmon (Chickasaw), Charlie Parker, Margie Pettiford (Choctaw/Cherokee), Paul Quinnichette (Saponi), Joe Salzano (Choctaw), Chief White Eagle, and Richard Yellow Hawk and Fred White Face (both Lakota).

Composer-Performers: Carlos Nakai (Navajo), Brent Michael Davids (Stockbridge Mahican), Don Patrick Martin (Kahnawake Mohawk), Brulé (Lakota), and Lee Johnson and Ron Warren (both Cherokee).

Members of Pamyua (left to right): Stephen Blanchett, Phillip Blanchett, Ossie Kariaiuak, and Karina Moeller, 2003.

THE BAMBOULA.

African slaves performing the bamboula dance in Congo Square, New Orleans. Engraving by E.W. Kemble illustrating "The Dance in Place Congo" published in *Century Magazine*, February 1886.

MWALIM (MORGAN JAMES PETERS)

WE HEARD IT IN THE FIELDS
The Native American Roots of the Blues

Some say, it began with a word;

Some say, it began with light;

Some say, it began with an explosion.

But I know, it began with a thump.

A thump

A pulse

A vibration, creating a sound

And for every action

there's an equal and opposite reaction

and it probably sounded like a hand-clap

—EXCERPT FROM THE PERFORMANCE PIECE
"THEY NEVER TOOK OUR DRUMS" BY MWALIM

The roots of American music are firmly planted in African American culture, a combination of West African, Native American, and European traditions. Blues and jazz were the first forms of music to originate in post-colonial America—born in the rice, tobacco, and cotton fields of the rural South and eventually fusing with the chants and drum sessions of Congo Square in urban New Orleans. While jazz is rooted in a mix of cultures, including Yoruba, Ibo, Senegalese (West

Yup'ik one-string banjo, ca. 1900–1930. Kuskokwim River; Calista Native Corporation, Doyon Native Corporation; Alaska; USA. 20/9342

African), and French, blues had little European influence. After a careful study of both West African (particularly the cultures of Ghana and Nigeria) and traditional eastern Native American songs, a logical conclusion is that blues merges African and Native American music, played on European instruments. It should be noted, however, that the banjo was created by African slaves.

West African slaves were imported to the East Coast during the transatlantic slave trade. Africans belonging to specific cultures were preferred in certain regions of the Americas based on their skills. People from coastal Nigeria, for example, came with an understanding of metalwork and blacksmithing and were preferred in the northern states, along with the Senegalese, who served primarily as house servants and skilled laborers. On the other hand, the agricultural southern states preferred Africans from farming regions such as Ghana, inland Nigeria, and Angola. The people of the Akan and Ashanti cultures, experienced rice growers, were favored in places such as South Carolina and Georgia.

In 1963, critic, poet, theorist, and playwright Amiri Baraka (Leroi Jones) published a groundbreaking collection of essays titled *Blues People*. He theorized that the social, cultural, and political conditions of enslaved Africans and their descendants gave birth to the blues, citing it as the most influential musical form in American culture and, subsequently, world music. Likewise, contemporary Ghanaian guitarist Ali Farka Touré also described the rudiments of the blues as derived from African music. Musicologists, however, have been unable to trace certain aspects of the blues, such as melodic components, to Africa or Europe. Those who have studied the melodies found in the traditional Stomp Dance and Round Dance songs of eastern Native American tribes have discovered that they are almost identical to the melodic flow of many blues songs recorded by Robert Johnson, Bessie Smith, and Lead Belly. Many of these songs cross linguistic lines and are shared by tribal nations along the East Coast. Wampanoag oral tradition teaches that the Mohawks shared songs sung by the Tuscarora and the Seminole with both the Wampanoag and the Oneidas; these songs predate Native contact with Africans. The syncopation on the beats of the songs from southeastern nations is more pronounced and similar to the backbeat found in some blues and contemporary funk. This includes the heavy "one" beat, found in the music of James Brown and Muddy Waters, as well as the drumming of West African drum master Babatunde Olatunje and his many protégés. The blues are African rhythms and harmonies, mixed with Native melodies.

Common to many West African and eastern Native American cultures is the work song, used to pass the time and coordinate the work in the fields. Of particular note are the rhythms of these songs, such as those found in the eastern Native American Round Dances performed to soften the earth after a long winter to prepare it for clearing and planting. Likewise, the rhythms in the planting songs of several West African cultures are used to coordinate the work of preparing soil and sowing seeds. A central similarity in the work-song rhythms of these cultures is the backbeat emulation of a heartbeat. Another related element is "call and response," in which a lead singer's lines are repeated or responded to by a chorus; the practicality of this technique was imperative in communicating and coordinating work in sprawling plantation fields.

The experiences of African-Native American artists with African American styles of music allow them to engage their traditional Native music from a different angle. Charlie Parker's recording of "Cherokee," for example, melodically explored the fusion of Native music with jazz, incorporating solos and harmonic extensions.

Pappy Johns Band performing at one of the grand opening celebrations for the National Museum of the American Indian, 2004. Courtesy FotoBriceno.

Blues is the music of the storyteller. The blues crosses cultural and social boundaries and is the root of most popular twentieth-century music. It has resonated with Native American musicians, giving birth to a blues-based tradition of Native blues artists. Mixashawn, Cornbread, Redbone (with the 1970s hit, "Come and Get Your Love"), Brock Stonefish, Jimi Hendrix, Charlie Parker, and Jim Pepper are all examples of Native and Black Indian jazz and blues artists.

While I was a junior at Boston University majoring in music composition and history, my cousin Robert took me to see his friend Mixashawn (Lee Rozie) perform during *The Nameless Coffeehouse* series in Cambridge. In those days, I was still struggling with my identity: Was I black or was I Wampanoag? Judging from the African medallion I wore around my neck and the kufi on my head (lovingly made by my maternal grandmother), I had made a decision. I rarely referred to my Native heritage and if somebody else mentioned it publicly, I felt outed. Robert is the one who introduced me to the concept of being a "Black Indian," which intrigued me, but of which I was still skeptical.

With Mixashawn's long, flowing black hair and obviously mixed-heritage features, I realized why Robert felt it was important for me to see him. Mixashawn referred to his instrument as a berimbau [berimbow] and expounded on its origins as an instrument found in both Africa and South America. He also talked about the link between Native and African American music. He tapped the string with a stick and began singing what sounded like Native American music; he then suddenly transitioned into songs by Chuck Berry and Bo Diddley. After the show, I met Mixashawn to talk with him about his presentation. Looking back, this formative moment started my journey toward self-identity as a Black Indian and understanding the roots of African American culture.

—Mwalim (Morgan James Peters)

Reies Lopez Tijerina speaking at the Poor People's Campaign March on Washington, D.C., 1968. People standing behind him include Hank Adams and Ralph Abernathy.
Item # 2000-008-0130.

PENNY GAMBLE-WILLIAMS

RED POWER/BLACK POWER
The People, the Land, and the Movement

Racial hatred and violence, segregation, voter suppression, and poverty were a way of life for African Americans who lived under the Jim Crow laws of the South. American Indians were contending with broken treaties, termination of federal recognition and relocation to urban areas, and the abject poverty of reservations. Such oppressive practices gave rise to various movements. The civil rights era spawned the black power and red power movements. The Black Panther Party and the American Indian Movement (AIM) were formed as a result of the deplorable conditions American Indians, African Americans, and poor people were forced to endure. For African Americans, the thrust of the issue was civil and equal rights; for American Indians, the overarching issue was sovereignty. This confluence of events between the 1950s and the late 1970s had a profound impact on me and propelled me to get involved.

As a person carrying the blood of the Chappaquiddick Wampanoag, African American, and European, my political consciousness was heightened not only by the firestorm of racial violence in the news and the trauma blacks and Indians suffered in my native New England, but also by my own personal experiences. My father, Otis Gamble, who was African American and Creek, would often remember painful experiences of growing up in Alabama—the lynching of blacks and Indians, the bombing of black churches, and his performances as a jazz musician in hotels and clubs where he could not sleep or have a meal. Those events forced me to question my own identity.

"Vivan los Indios," Poor People's Campaign March, Washington D.C., 1968.
Item # 2000-008-0075.

Unidentified member of AIM with Reies López Tijerina and Father Luís Jaramillo of the
Alianza Federal de Mercedes at the Poor People's Campaign March in Washington D.C., 1968.
Item # 2000-008-0070.

The education system of the 1950s and 1960s perpetuated the myth that New England Indians had vanished. Self-identity was further complicated if you were Indian and African American. No one, including many African Americans, believed that you were Indian. That crisis of identity—differences in the perceptions of others versus the perceptions of self—caused pain and sometimes shame for people like me. Fortunately, the community in which I was raised and my family ties gave me a sense of belonging. My community was diverse yet shared a sense of connection to cultural ways. Stories were told at family gatherings that centered on how our people came to be and how they lived. The elders stressed the importance of knowing our history. A consistent recital of our Wampanoag roots by my mother, Adele Gamble, imprinted my indigenous heritage on my psyche and motivated me to keep close connections with relatives and people who shared the same history. My mother was well-respected in many communities in Providence, Rhode Island, for her activism in civil rights issues, and she enjoyed dispelling the myth that all of the New England Indians had disappeared. Adele Gamble left a legacy of righteous indignation that I carry to this day.

For thousands of years, the cosmology of the Chappaquiddick people remained unadulterated while they lived harmoniously as one with the land. Their spirituality guided their everyday lives and they enjoyed a bountiful existence. In 1620, European settlers arrived and eventually made their way to the island of Chappaquiddick. They created land disputes and eventually removed the Chappaquiddick people from the heart of the land to an area located on the northern neck of the island they called "the place of the barren soil." This became the reservation land of the Chappaquiddick. Forced conversion to Christianity, economic hardship, imposed citizenship, and taxes changed life dramatically for my people. Our cultural ways ended traumatically, our cosmology was obfuscated, and our spiritual practices and ceremonies on the land were forever compromised.

The struggles and pain caused by the suppression of traditional ways and the loss of land didn't resonate with me until my early twenties. In 1972, I relocated from Providence to Washington, D.C. I arrived in November, just before the Trail of Broken Treaties and the takeover of the Bureau of Indian Affairs by AIM. In February 1973, the Indian occupation of Wounded Knee occurred. I met and interacted with many activists involved in the civil rights movement who shared solidarity with AIM. Lively, heated discussions took place when the

The Longest Walk, 1978. Solidarity between African Americans and Native Americans grew with the black power movement of the 1970s, the goals of which were closer to the nationalism espoused by American Indian Movement activists. Pictured here (left to right) are Muhammad Ali, Buffy Sainte-Marie, Floyd Red Crow Westerman, Harold Smith, Stevie Wonder, Marlon Brando, Max Gail, Dick Gregory, Richie Havens, and David Amram at a concert at the end of the Longest Walk, a 3,600-mile protest march from San Francisco to Washington, D.C., in the name of Native rights.

subjects of racial identity and Indian blood came up. Some knew of their Indian heritage but would state that they were black and that there was no reason to mention any other part of their ancestry. One person said to me, "You have to make a choice. So I have Indian blood. So what's that going to get me?" His point was that anyone who looked at him would see only a black man, not an Indian, so it was therefore easier to say that he was black, end of story. I had a different point of view, which grew stronger as events taking place in Indian Country escalated. I was not going to compromise. I knew myself, my people, and our story, and nothing was going to change that.

In July 1978, the Longest Walk caravan arrived in Washington, D.C. This was a historic event that brought to light the pressing issues of American Indian people. I put on my shoes, got my backpack, and walked the six miles from my house in Maryland to Malcolm X Park in the District. I arrived in time to see the Lakota elders enter the park with the sacred pipe. For me, it was a deeply spiritual experience. Thousands of people had assembled. I saw banners that said Mashpee and Narragansett. Actors and dynamic speakers from black liberation organizations spoke, and black people who were in the crowd expressed their support for Indian demands. I remained directly involved in the movement as a volunteer working at the Longest Walk office. I met many Indian activists, elders, and youth from various nations who would come to the office, where we would talk and share stories. Many Native people had never met a person with a combination of red and black blood. We talked about East Coast and Plains Indian history and experiences and saw a common struggle.

I joined AIM and Women of All Red Nations and met people from Maryland's Piscataway Indian Nation. They were spiritually and culturally centered and involved in indigenous issues. We grappled with solutions for

Luci Murphy is a long-time social justice activist in Washington, D.C. Of African American and Native heritage, she has worked for peace for several decades—often coordinating events and bringing her beautiful voice to enliven protests, demonstrations, and rallies.

serious problems, such as protecting sacred sites; preserving water, hunting, and fishing rights; and gaining religious freedom to conduct sacred ceremonies. Attention was focused on events dealing with the Black Hills in South Dakota, strip mining on the land of the Diné people in Arizona, and the desecration of sacred sites at Point Conception in California. These and other important issues—such as the religious freedom of Indians in Maryland and other parts of the East Coast, as well as American Indian women and men who were incarcerated in federal prisons—were addressed.

Tribes with federal status, urban Natives with ties to tribal nations, and those who were nonfederally recognized were reevaluating their sovereignty and challenging in state and federal courts the denial of treaty rights, removal from lands, theft of resources, and protection of sacred sites. Embracing our cultural ways and honoring the ancestors helped us remain anchored to our spirituality and survive our ordeals. The purification lodge and Sun Dance ceremonies that I participated in strengthened my spiritual knowledge and caused me to center

Penny Gamble-Williams, 2001, stands next to the gravestone of William A. Martin and her great-great-grandmother's sister Sarah Brown Martin (Chappaquiddick Wampanoag). William Martin was the first documented African American whaling captain on Martha's Vineyard.

Chappaquiddick Island, 2001. Members of the Chappaquiddick Wampanoag tribe have not lived on their ancestral island in Massachusetts for nearly a century, yet tribal members gather annually in honor of their ancestors on the island.

on challenges the Chappaquiddick Wampanoag faced. During the early 1980s and 1990s, I spent time reconnecting with elders who knew my mother as a child and had not seen me in years. I visited Mashpee, Narragansett, and Aquinnah. It was clear to me that the civil rights and American Indian movements made an impact on the Mashpee and other New England tribes. The Mashpee and Aquinnah were dealing with major land issues. The Narragansett were dealing with hunting rights. All were working on the federal recognition process. The Passamaquoddy and Penobscot had won major land cases in Maine and received federal acknowledgment.

The Chappaquiddick became focused on how we could return to the land and become a federally recognized tribe. Since the 1950s, my family had been facing harassment from lawyers who represented non-Native people who had settled on reservation lands held in common with us on Chappaquiddick Island. We realized that we had to get back to the land, the place where the bones of our ancestors were buried. Chappaquiddick families would meet to go over family documents and land and census records and share family stories. In 1979, we litigated land claims in federal district court cases such as *Epps v. Andrus*. I was a plaintiff in the case of *Smith v. Jenora Trust*, which was litigated for thirteen years in the Massachusetts state courts to restore my family's land claim.

The resurgence of Indian identity and sovereignty awakened in Indian people the need to preserve ceremonies and traditions. Our vision became clear as we revisited our history and reflected on the power and strength of our ancestors. As we talked about our history, we were reminded that by 1900 only seven Chappa-quiddick families were living on the island. The others had moved to places where they could earn a living, but in their hearts, they wanted to return to the land. Those who left understood their connection to Kiehtan, the Creator. Whether they settled on Martha's Vineyard or Cape Cod, in New Bedford, Fall River, Plymouth, Providence, Nantucket, or Boston, they knew one day they would return. We understood as the children, grandchildren, and great-grandchildren that we had to take a stand as a cohesive body and continue the ceremonies on the land.

For the Chappaquiddick people, the red power movement became a catalyst for change, enlightenment, and unity. It was a personal and collective journey that brought the Chappaquiddick people back to the ceremonial grounds and thus began a new chapter that kept the threads connected and the flame alive for the elders and future generations. The black power and red power movements unlocked the doors, empowering New England tribes. The history books could no longer dismiss us as the "so-called" Indians. We were on the rise and taking action. We pledged never to let our story die. I am forever grateful for the ancestors who directed me to places where I never thought I would go and for meeting strong, dedicated people along the "red road" of life. We are still here. The Chappaquiddick did not vanish.

Maceo Leatherwood, *Mo'Pak*, 1990. Acrylic on canvas, 36 x 48 in. A native of Washington, D.C., and the former art director for NASA's Goddard Space Flight Center, Mr. Leatherwood considers himself an artist-traveler who enjoys cross-cultural experiences. His love of horses came from childhood visits with his African-Algonquian maternal grandparents on their farm in Maryland. His paternal grandparents were African-Iroquoian from North Carolina.

Bones and Drums
For Lewis McMillan

Generations unfold from our faces.
We have found Kwanzaa celebrants
and bearers of Yoruba, Ibo, and Muslim
names with connections among the Chickasaw:
a hoop broken like the faces, mouths,
a few brows native to Apalachicola, Catawba,
Creek, and the Ramapos.

Has America ever noticed
how some of these voices match
the trombone? The big horn of
"Big Chief" Russell Moore,
Fletcher's Charlie "Big" Green,
Snub Mosley,
the Jack Teagarden we speak of.
Does America recall Chief Shunatona
at the '28 Inaugural?
What does it know of Willie Colon, Steve Turre,
and so many salseros in this bull eagle's
timbre of speaking?

Have they listened to the bass,
a tree of rhythm smooth as a Jimmy Blanton,
sinewy as Oscar Pettiford, thickset as Mingus,
supple as Rick Rozie?

Or the drums; Baby Lovett to Sunny Murray,
for a basic two-step,
a round dance grass dance beat on the stretched
snare hide of Ponca City, Tishomingo, Okmulgee, Tahlequah.
The rolling piano of Muskogee.
Sock cymbals and hi-hats of seed beats, patterned and flowing
like leaves in a river
in the split rhythm accents of 4/4.

—Ron Welburn

AUTHORS' NOTES AND WORKS CITED

RACE AND POLICY

Theda Perdue

1   For Louisiana, see Daniel H. Usner, Jr., *Indians, Settlers, and Slaves in a Frontier Exchange Economy: The Lower Mississippi Valley before 1783* (Chapel Hill: University of North Carolina Press, 1992).

2   Alan Gallay, *The Indian Slave Trade: The Rise of the English Empire in the American South, 1670–1717* (New Haven: Yale University Press, 2002).

3   J. Leitch Wright, Jr., *The Only Land They Knew: The Tragic Story of American Indians in the Old South* (New York: Free Press, 1981), 248–78.

4   William S. Willis, Jr., "Divide and Rule: Red, White, and Black in the Southeast," *Journal of Negro History* 48 (1963): 157–76; James H. Merrell, "The Racial Education of the Catawba Indians," *Journal of Southern History* 50 (1984): 363–84.

5   William G. McLoughlin, "Red Indians, Black Slavery, and White Racism: America's Slaveholding Indians," *American Quarterly* 26 (1974): 367–85; Theda Perdue, *Slavery and the Evolution of Cherokee Society, 1540–1866* (Knoxville: University of Tennessee Press, 1979); Kathryn E. Holland, "The Creek Indians, Blacks, and Slavery," *Journal of Southern History* 57 (1991): 601–36; Claudio Saunt, *A New Order of Things: Property, Power,* *and the Transformation of the Creek Indians, 1733–1816* (New York: Cambridge University Press, 1999); Saunt, *Black, White, and Indian: Race and the Unmaking of an American Family* (New York: Oxford University Press, 2005); Tiya Miles, *Ties that Bind: The Story of an Afro-Cherokee Family in Slavery and Freedom* (Berkeley: University of California Press, 2005).

6   Susan A. Miller, *Coacoochee's Bones: A Seminole Saga* (Lawrence: University of Kansas Press, 2003).

7   Howard N. Martin, "Texas Redskins in Confederate Gray," *Southwestern Historical Quarterly* 70 (April 1967); Douglas Summers Brown, *The Catawba Indians: The People of the River* (Columbia: University of South Carolina Press, 1966); Clara Sue Kidwell, *Choctaws and Missionaries in Mississippi, 1818–1918* (Norman: University of Oklahoma Press), 170; E. Stanly Godbold and Mattie U. Russell, *Confederate Colonel and Cherokee Chief: The Life of William Holland Thomas* (Knoxville: University of Tennessee Press, 1990).

8   William McKee Evans, *To Die Game: The Story of the Lowry Band, Indian Guerillas of Reconstruction* (Baton Rouge: Louisiana State University Press, 1971).

9   Constitution of the State of Florida, Adopted February 25, 1868, Article 16, section 7; Jerrell H. Shofner, "The Constitution of 1868," *Florida Historical*

Quarterly 41(1962–63): 356–74; Lorenzo D. Creel, "Investigation of the Seminole Indians in Florida, 1911," Central Classified Files, 1907–1939, Seminole, Record Group (hereafter, RG) 75: Records of the Bureau of Indian Affairs, National Archives and Records Administration (hereafter, NARA), Washington, D.C.

10 Pauli Murray, ed., *States' Laws on Race and Color* (1951; reprint, Athens: University of Georgia Press, 1997), 82.

11 Irving G. Tragen, "Statutory Prohibitions against Interracial Marriage," *California Law Review* 32 (1944): 271 n12. Arizona and Nevada also prohibited intermarriage between Indians and whites.

12 George Brown Tindall, *South Carolina Negroes, 1877–1900* (Columbia: University of South Carolina Press, 1952), 296–97.

13 Karen I. Blu, *The Lumbee Problem: The Making of an American Indian People* (Cambridge and New York: Cambridge University Press, 1980), 73.

14 John Garland Pollard, "The Pamunkey Indians of Virginia," *Bureau of American Ethnology Bulletin* 17 (Washington, D.C.: Government Printing Office, 1894): 342; Murray, *States' Laws*, 462–478; Helen C. Rountree, *Pocahontas's People: The Powhatan People of Virginia Through Four Centuries* (Norman: University of Oklahoma Press, 1990), 219–42. Indians who lived on Virginia state reservations were considered Indian even if they had African ancestry, but the "one drop rule" made Indians with African ancestry living off-reservation "colored."

15 *States' Laws*, 173.

16 Ibid., 238, 330; Adolph L. Dial and David K. Eliades, *The Only Land I Know: A History of the Lumbee Indians* (1975; reprint, Syracuse: Syracuse University Press, 1996), 89–106; Kidwell, *Choctaws and Missionaries*, 182–83; John Holbrook Peterson, "The Mississippi Band of Choctaw Indians: Their Recent History and Current Social Relations" (Ph.D. diss., University of Georgia, 1970), 84, 101–2. The state closed Indian schools in anticipation of the removal of all Mississippi Choctaws to Oklahoma in 1903, an effort that failed. After the establishment of a federal Choctaw

agency in Mississippi in 1918, the state insisted that the education of Indians was the responsibility of the United States.

17 M. R. Harrington, "Grievances of the Chitimacha Indians living near Charenton, St. Mary Parish, Louisiana" [May 19, 1908], Central Classified Files, 1907–1939, General Service, RG 75, NARA, Washington, D.C.

18 National Association for the Advancement of Colored People, *Thirty Years of Lynching in the United States, 1889–1918* (New York: National Association for the Advancement of Colored People, 1919).

19 Frank Kyselka to Commissioner of Indian Affairs, Nov. 2, 1911, Superintendent's Letterbooks, 1892–1914 (Chronological Correspondence Files), Records of the Cherokee Indian Agency, 1892–1914, RG 75, NARA, Morrow, Ga.; Malinda M. Maynor [Lowery], "People and Place: Croatan Indians in Jim Crow Georgia" (M.A. thesis, University of North Carolina, 2002).

20 Theda Perdue and Michael D. Green, *The Columbia Guide to American Indians of the Southeast* (New York: Columbia University Press, 2001), Chapter 7; Frank E. Brandon to Commissioner of Indian Affairs, Jan. 12, 1920, Central Classified Files, 1907–1939, General Service, RG 75, NARA, Washington D.C.

21 George E. Butler, *The Croatan Indians of Sampson County, North Carolina: Their Origin and Racial Status; A Plea for Separate Schools* (Durham, N.C.: Seeman Printery, 1916), 44. http://docsouth.unc.edu/nc/butler/butler.html, Jan. 12, 2008.

22 L. A. Weathers, "Indian Missions in Southern Alabama," n. d. [1931], Una Lawrence Papers AR 631, Southern Baptist Archives, Nashville, Tenn.

23 E. P. Bradby to John Collier, April 25, 1934, Central Classified Files, 1907–1939, General Service, RG 75, NARA, Washington, D.C.

24 *State School Facts* 17 (Sept. 1944), Central Classified Files, 1907–1939, General Service, RG 75, NARA, Washington, D.C.

25 Pollard, "Pamunkey Indians," 10–11.

26 Forest Hazel, "The Dimery Settlement: Indian Descendants in the

South Carolina Low Country," *Independent Republic Quarterly* 29 (1995): 32–36, http://www.hchsonline.org/places/dimery.html, Jan. 12, 2008.

27   Frank Kyselka to Commissioner of Indian Affairs, Superintendent's Letterbooks, 1892–1914 (Chronological Correspondence Files), Records of the Cherokee Indian Agency, 1892–1914, RG 75, NARA, Morrow, Ga.

28   Donal F. Lindsey, *Indians at Hampton Institute, 1877–1923* (Urbana: University of Illinois Press, 1995).

29   R. W. Averitt, "South Ala. Mission Field," n.d. [1935], Una Lawrence Papers, AR 631, 11–14, Southern Baptist Archives, Nashville, Tenn.

30   Butler, *Croatan Indians*, 42.

31   Blu, *Lumbee Problem*, 81.

32   James Henderson to Commissioner of Indian Affairs, Sept. 25, 1923, Central Classified Files, 1907–1939, General Service, RG 75, NARA, Washington, D.C.

33   Peyton Carter to H. B. Peairs, June 12, 1924 Central Classified Files, 1907–1939, RG 75, NARA, Washington D.C.

34   Escambia School Board Minutes, Feb. 26, 1954 (Appendix 117), Petition for Federal Recognition Submitted by the Poarch Band of Creeks to the United States Department of Interior, January 10, 1980 (Prepared by Main Office of NARF), Bureau of Acknowledgement and Research, Bureau of Indian Affairs, Washington, D.C.

35   "Report of the Special Called Meeting of the Mississippi Band of Choctaw Indians Held December 11, 1962, at Philadelphia, Mississippi," Five Civilized Tribes Agency, Office of Tribal Operations, Mississippi Choctaw, RG 75, NARA, Ft. Worth, Texas.

36   Butler, *Croatan Indians*, 34.

37   Betty Mae Tiger Jumper and Patsy West, *A Seminole Legend: The Life of Betty Mae Tiger Jumper* (Gainesville: University Press of Florida, 2001), 13–16.

38   "Announcing… All Choctaw Indian Fair, Aug. 31, Sept. 1, 2, 1955 Pearl River Indian School," Program, n.d., Five Civilized Tribes Agency, Office of

Tribal Operations, Mississippi Choctaw, RG 75, NARA, Ft. Worth, Texas; Interview with W. Stanley Hanson, Jr., June 25, 1975, Samuel Proctor Oral History Program, University of Florida, http://www.uflib.ufl.edu/UFDC/UFDC.aspx?g=oral, Jan. 12, 2008.

39   The Historical Census Browser, available in the digitized collections of many libraries, is an easy way to total and map populations. The one at the University of Virginia can be accessed at http://fisher.lib.virginia.edu/collections/stats/histcensus/.

40   Sarah Avery McIlhenny to Charles E. Dagenette, Jan. 31, 1914, Central Classified Files, 1907–1939, General Service, RG 75, NARA, Washington, D.C.

41   Myron Jones, Report on Marksville Meeting, Dec. 30, 1969, Records of the National Congress of American Indians, Tribal Records, Box 111, Smithsonian Institution, National Anthropological Archives (hereafter, NAA), Suitland, Md.

42   Jack Thorne [D.B. Fulton], *"Eagle Clippings" by Jack Thorne, Newspaper Correspondent and Story Teller, A Collection of His Writings to Various Newspapers* (Brooklyn, NY: D. B. Fulton, 1907), 65–71, Documenting the American South, http://docsouth.unc.edu/nc/thorneeagle/thorneeagle.html (Sept. 22, 2007).

43   Ed. Charles Hackenberry (Urbana, Il.: University of Chicago Press, 1997).

44   "The Free Colored People of North Carolina," *Southern Workman*, March 1902, reprinted in *Charles W. Chesnutt: Essays and Speeches*, ed. Joseph R. McElrath, Jr., Robert C. Leitz III, and Jesse S. Crisler (Stanford: Stanford University Press, 1999), 175.

45   Clyde Pulley, *Blacks Who Pass for Indians and Whites* (Chicago: Adams Press, 1978).

46   Brewton Berry, *Almost White* (New York: Macmillan Company, 1963), 63–72. Berry's book is useful, but his condescending style and use of pejoratives such as "Red Bones" and "Brass Ankles" are problematic.

47   Myron Jones, Marksville Meeting, Dec. 30, 1969, Records of the National Congress of American Indi-

ans, Tribal Records, Smithsonian Institution, NAA, Suitland, Md.

48 "Report of the Special Called Meeting of the Mississippi Band of Choctaw Indians Held December 11, 1962, at Philadelphia, Mississippi," Five Civilized Tribes Agency, Office of Tribal Operations, Mississippi Choctaw, RG 75, NARA, Ft. Worth, Texas.

49 Vine Deloria, Jr., *Custer Died for Your Sins: An Indian Manifesto* (1969; Norman: University of Oklahoma Press, 1988), 168–96.

50 Gerald Sider, *Living Indian Histories: Lumbee and Tuscarora People in North Carolina* (1993; Chapel Hill: University of North Carolina Press, 2003), *69–72*; "Indians of Two States Organize; Support Voluntary Segregation," *Montgomery Register* Feb. 2 [?] 1958 (Appendix 135), [petition for Federal Recognition of the] Principal Creek Indian Nation (The Wind Clan Creek Nation East of the Mississippi River), BAR.

José Barreiro

1 Maximilian Christian Forte, ed., *Indigenous Resurgence in the Contemporary Caribbean: Amerindian Survival and Revival* (New York: Peter Lang, 2006) and kacike.org online journal.

2 José Barreiro, *Panchito cacique de montaña: Testimonio guajiro-taíno de Francisco Ramírez Rojas* (Santiago de Cuba: Ediciones Catedral, 2001); Manuel Rivero de la Calle, "Supervivencia de descendientes de indoamericanos en la zona de Yateras, Oriente" (Santiago de Cuba: Cuba Arqueológica, Editorial Oriente, 1978). Rivero amply documents the long-standing existence of the aboriginal population of the Yateras Mountains.

3 Juan C. Martinez Cruzado, "The Use of Mitochondrial DNA to Discover Pre-Columbian Migrations to the Caribbean: Results for Puerto Rico and Expectations for the Dominican Republic" [39 paragraphs], *KACIKE: The Journal of Caribbean Amerindian History and Anthropology, 2002* [Online Journal], Special Issue, Lynne Guitar, ed. Available at: http://www.kacike.org/MartinezEnglish.html.

4 Gabriel Haslip-Viera, *Taino Revival: Critical Perspectives on Puerto Rican Identity and Cultural Politics* (Princeton, NJ: Markus Wiener, 2001).

5 Ibid., 57.

6 Jorge Duany, *Puerto Rican Nation on the Move: Identities on the Island and in the United States* (Chapel Hill: University of North Carolina Press, 2002), 262.

Bethany Montagano

1 A. M. Gibson, *Kickapoos: Lords of the Middle Border* (Oklahoma: University of Oklahoma Press, 1976), 200.

2 Committee on Indian Affairs, *Affairs of the Mexican Kickapoo v. 3, Appendix: Hearings Before The Subcommittee of The Committee on Indian Affairs United States Senate (1908)* (Montana: Kessinger, 2008), 1886.

3 Gibson, *Kickapoos*, 201.

4 Ibid., 202.

5 Ibid., 204–6.

6 Christian Oppriesnig, "Kickapoos at the Emperor's Court: Photographs, Engravings, Paintings," *European Review of Native American Studies* 7, no. 2 (1993): 31–37, 32.

7 Ibid., 33.

8 Dolores L. Latorre, *The Mexican Kickapoo Indians* (New York: Dover, 1991), 5.

9 Gibson, *Kickapoos*, 202.

10 Oppriesnig, "Emperor's Court," 33.

11 Kevin Mulroy, *The Seminole Freedmen: A History* (Oklahoma: University of Oklahoma Press, 2007), 3–8.

12 Ibid., 57.

13 Kevin Mulroy, *Freedom on the Border: The Seminole Maroons in Florida, the Indian Territory, Coahuila, and Texas* (Texas: Texas Tech University Press, 2003), 108–9.

14 Oppriesnig, "Emperor's Court," 33.

15 Raymond D. Fogelson and William Sturtevant, eds., *Handbook of North American Indians*, vol. 14. (Washington, D.C.: Smithsonian Institution, 2004).

16 Mulroy, *Freedom on the Border*, 108.

17 Oppriesnig, "Emperor's Court," 36.

18   Ibid., 31.

19   Ibid.

20   Kartar Singh Duggal, *Maharaja Ranjit Singh: The Last to Lay Arms* (New Delhi: Abhinav Publications, 2001), 116.

21   Michael A. Gomez, "Of Dubois and Diaspora: The Challenge of African Studies," *Journal of Black Studies* 35, no. 2 (2004): 175–94.

Herman J. Viola

William H. Leckie, *The Buffalo Soldiers: A Narrative of the Negro Cavalry in the West* (Norman: University of Oklahoma Press, 1967).

William Loren Katz, *Black Indians: A Hidden Heritage* (New York: Simon and Schuster, Simon Pulse, 1986).

William Loren Katz, *Black West* (New York: Random House, Harlem Moon, 2005).

Angela A. Gonzales

Deloria, Vine, Jr. and Clifford Lytle. *The Nations Within: The Past and Future American Indian Sovereignty.* New York: Pantheon Books, 1984.

Drees, Ann L. *The Enumeration of the Indian Population in the Censuses of the United States, 1790–1960.* Report prepared for the History Division, Bureau of the Census, Washington, D.C., 1968.

1   U.S. Bureau of the Census. *Two Hundred Years of Census Taking: Population and Housing Questions, 1790–1990.* Washington, D.C.: U.S. Government Printing Office, 1989.

2   Ibid., 22.

3   Unlike the biological mechanisms for inheritance based on the contributing genes of both parents, Galton's notion of fractional inheritance not only failed to define what "characteristics" would be inherited from parents, grandparents, and so on, but also was deeply subjective and reflective of cultural values disguised as science. For an analysis of Galton's notion of fractional inheritance and a thorough investigation into the development of science and the rise of eugenics, see Daniel J. Kevles, *In the Name of Eugenics: Genetics and the Uses of Human Heredity* (Cambridge, MA: Harvard University Press, 1995). Margaret T. Hodgen investigates the early modern transition to biologically rooted understandings of race in *Early Anthropology in the Sixteenth and Seventeenth Centuries* (Philadelphia: University of Pennsylvania Press, 1964); see also Stephen Jay Gould, *The Mismeasure of Man* (New York: Norton, 1981); Pat Shipman, *The Evolution of Racism: Human Differences and the Use and Abuse of Science* (New York: Simon and Schuster, 1994); and Ivan Hannaford, *Race: The History of an Idea in the West* (Baltimore: Johns Hopkins University Press, 1996).

4   Angela A. Gonzales, Judy Kertész, and Gabrielle Tayac, "Eugenics as Indian Removal: Sociohistorical Processes and the (De)Construction of American Indians in the Southeast," *Public Historian* 29 (2007): 53–67.

5   F. James Davis, *Who Is Black? One Nation's Definition* (University Park: Pennsylvania State University Press, 1991).

6   Russell Thornton, *American Indian Holocaust and Survival: A Population History Since 1492* (Norman: University of Oklahoma Press, 1987).

7   Claudio Esteva-Fabregat, *Mestizaje in Ibero-America*, translated by John Wheat (Tucson: University of Arizona Press, 1995); see also Magnus Morner, *Race Mixture in the History of Latin America* (Boston: Little Brown, 1967); Carl Degler, *Neither Black nor White: Slavery and Race Relations in Brazil and the United States* (New York: MacMillan, 1971); and Jack D. Forbes, *Africans and Native Americans: The Language of Race and the Evolution of Red-Black Peoples* (Champaign, IL: University of Illinois Press, 1993).

8   U.S. Bureau of the Census. *Report on Indians Taxed and Not Taxed in the United States (except Alaska) at the Eleventh Census: 1890.* Washington, D.C.: U.S. Government Printing Office, 1894.

9   U.S. Bureau of the Census. *Indian Population in the United States and Alaska, 1910.* Washington, D.C.: U.S. Government Printing Office, 1915.

10 James C. Scott, *Seeing Like A State: How Certain Schemes to Improve the Human Condition Have Failed.* (New Haven, CT: Yale University Press, 1998).

Kimberly TallBear

1 Deborah A. Bolnick et al., "The Science and Business of Genetic Ancestry," *Science* 318, no. 5849 (October 19, 2007): 399–400; Howard Wolinsky, "Genetic Genealogy Goes Global," *European Molecular Biology Organization EMBO Reports* 7, no. 11 (2006): 1072–74.

2 Sheila Jasanoff, *Designs on Nature: Science and Democracy in Europe and the United States* (Princeton and Oxford: Princeton University Press, 2005).

3 Carole Goldberg, "Members Only? Designing Citizenship Requirements for Indian Nations," *University of Kansas Law Review* 50 (2002): 437–71.

4 David Schneider, *American Kinship: A Cultural Account* (Englewood Cliffs, N.J.: Prentice-Hall, 1980).

Angela Walton-Raji

For Further Study: Documents, Websites, and Research Facilities

The Final Rolls of Citizens and Freedmen of the Five Civilized Tribes (National Archives Microfilm Publications, Microcopy T529).

Enrollment Cards for the Five Civilized Tribes, 1898–1914 (National Archives Microfilm Publications, Microcopy M1186).

Application Jackets for the Five Civilized Tribes (National Archives Microfilm Publications, Microcopy M1301).

Special Indian Census 1910 (Documents reflecting black and Indian families in the following states: Virginia, New York, Massachusetts, North Carolina, Mississippi, Louisiana, and Oklahoma).

Ancestry: www.ancestry.com

African-Native American Genealogy: www.african-nativeamerican.com

AfriGeneas: www.afrigeneas.com

Footnote: www.footnote.com

National Archives and Records Administration (Washington, D.C.)

Brian Klopotek

Portions of this work appear in Brian Klopotek, "Dangerous Decolonizing: Indigenous Methodologies, White Supremacy, and Black-Indian Relations," *Narrating Native Histories in the Americas*, ed. Florencia Mallon (Durham: Duke University Press, 2008).

1 James. H. Merrell, "The Racial Education of the Catawba Indians," *Journal of Southern History* 50, no. 3 (August 1984): 374.

2 Arica L. Coleman, "'Tell the Court I Love My [Indian] Wife': Interrogating Race and Self-Identity in *Loving v. Virginia,*" *Souls* 8, no. 1 (2006): 75.

3 Any Indian person there with more than one-quarter African "blood" (later one-sixteenth) would be classified as "colored," and thus have access to fewer rights and resources than those classified as Indians, who were those of more than one-quarter Indian blood (later one-sixteenth). Helen C. Rountree, *Pocahontas's People: The Powhatan Indians of Virginia Through Four Centuries,* (Norman: University of Oklahoma Press, 1990), 200, 211.

4 While typically the term "white supremacy" conjures images of Klan robes and neo-Nazi skinheads, the term as it is used in contemporary ethnic studies also refers to the everyday ideology of white racial superiority and domination carried out even by people who do not consider themselves racist, including people of color. For a general discussion of white racial ideology and material advantages in the United States, see P. S. Rothenberg, ed., *White Privilege: Essential Readings on the Other Side of Racism* (New York: Worth Publishers, 2002); and George Lipsitz, *The Possessive Investment in Whiteness: How White People Profit from Identity Politics* (Philadelphia: Temple University Press, 1998; revised and expanded, 2006).

5 Claudio Saunt, *Black, White, and Indian: Race and the Unmaking of an American Family* (New York: Oxford University Press, 2005); Saunt, *A New Order of Things: Property, Power, and the Transformation of the Creek Indians, 1733–1816* (Cambridge: Cambridge University Press, 1999); Miles, 2004; Theda Perdue,

Slavery and the Evolution of Cherokee Society, 1540–1866 (Knoxville: University of Tennessee Press, 1979); Theda Perdue, *Cherokee Women: Gender and Culture Change, 1700–1835* (Lincoln: University of Nebraska Press, 1999); and Daniel F. Littlefield, *Africans and Seminoles: From Removal to Emancipation* (Westport, CT: Greenwood Press, 1977).

6   See Brian Klopotek, "The Long Out-waiting: Federal Recognition Policy in Three Louisiana Indian Communities," Ph.D., University of Minnesota, 2004; Mark Miller, *Forgotten Tribes: Unacknowledged Indians and the Federal Acknowledgment Process* (Lincoln: University of Nebraska Press, 2004); Bruce G. Miller, *Invisible Indigenes: The Politics of Non-Recognition* (Lincoln: University of Nebraska Press, 2003).

7   Susan Greenbaum adeptly and precisely addresses this matter, even though others have addressed it elsewhere. Susan Greenbaum, "What's in a Label? Identity Problems of Southern Indian Tribes," *Journal of Ethnic Studies* 19, no. 2 (Summer 1991): 107–26; Rachael Paschal, "The Imprimatur of Recognition: American Indian Tribes and the Federal Acknowledgment Process," *Washington Law Review* 66 (1991): 209–28; William Starna, "'We'll All be Together Again,': The Federal Acknowledgment of the Wampanoag Tribe of Gay Head," *Northeast Anthropology* 51 (1996): 3–12; Jack Campisi, *The Mashpee Indians: Tribe on Trial* (Syracuse, NY: Syracuse University Press, 1991); James Clifford, "Identity in Mashpee," in *The Predicament of Culture: Twentieth-Century Ethnography, Literature, and Art,* (Cambridge, MA: Harvard University, 1988), 277–346. A number of significant contributions can be found in Tiya Miles and Sharon Holland, eds., and James F. Brooks, ed.

8   Circe Sturm discusses this issue in the article "Cherokee Nation of Oklahoma," Circe Sturm, *American Indian Quarterly*, 1998.

9   *Measuring America: The Decennial Censuses From 1790 to 2000*, United States Census Bureau, September 2002, 55.

10   *Measuring America*, 56.

11   The racial epithet, "Redbone," suggests that the person so called was racially impure, akin to a mongrel. Various undocumented theories explain its origin, ranging from folk tales about people actually having red bones to the assertion that it came from red ibo, a West Indian term applied to any group of mixed ancestry. Pronounced "reddy bone," it eventually became "red bone," according to J. L. Dillard, an authority on Black English in the United States. Cited in Kniffen, et al., 92, though Kniffen, et al., do not cite the exact work where Dillard makes this argument. See also W. L. Williams, "Patterns in the History of the Remaining Southeastern Indians, 1840–1975," in *Southeastern Indians Since the Removal Era* (Athens: University of Georgia, 1979), 193–210.

12   Ruth M. Underhill, "Report on a visit to Indian groups in Louisiana, Oct. 15–25, 1938," 20. File 68776–1931–800, Part 2, National Archives, RG 75. Certainly they had mixed much with other Indians and some whites, but little with blacks at the time of her report.

13   A. C. Hector to W. Carson Ryan, Jr., September 12, 1934, File 68776–1931–800, Part I, National Archives RG 75.

COMMUNITY

Joseph O. Palacio, Sr.

I read the paper "A Reconsideration of the Native American and African American Roots of Garifuna Identity" in 2000. For more comprehensive publications on the Garifuna, see Gonzalez (1988), Gullick (1985), and Palacio (2005). The following are the sources for my essay:

Cayetano, Marion, and Roy Cayetano. "Garifuna Language, Dance, and Music: A Masterpiece of the Oral and Intangible Heritage of Humanity. How Did It Happen?" In *The Garifuna, A Nation Across Borders: Essays in Social Anthropology*, ed. Joseph O. Palacio. Belize: Cubola Productions, 2005.

Gonzalez, Nancie. *Sojourners of the Caribbean: Ethnogenesis and Ethnohistory of the Garifuna*. Chicago: University of Illinois Press, 1988.

Gullick, C.J. *Myths of a Minority: The Changing Traditions of the Vincentian Caribs.* The Netherlands: Van Gorcum, 1985.

Palacio, Joseph O. "Looking at Ourselves in the Mirror: The Caribbean Organization of Indigenous Peoples (COIP)." In *Indigenous Resurgence in the Contemporary Caribbean,* ed. Maximilian C. Forte. New York: Peter Lang, 2006.

Palacio, Joseph O., ed. *The Garifuna, A Nation Across Borders: Essays in Social Anthropology.* Belize: Cubola Productions, 2005.

Palacio, Joseph O. "A Reconsideration of the Native American and African Roots of Garifuna Identity." Paper delivered at the Professional Agricultural Workers Conference (PAWC) 58th Session, Tuskegee University, 2000.

Van Sertima, Ivan. *They Came Before Columbus: The African Presence in Ancient America.* New York: Random House, 1976.

Richard W. Hill, Sr.

1   Pennsylvania Colonial Records, 5: 402, 409.

2   Cadwallader Colden, ed. *History of the Five Indian Nations Depending on the Province of New York in America* (London, 1747). Facsimile edition reprinted by Coles Publishing Co., Toronto, 1972.

3   Louis Hennepin, *A New Discovery of a Vast Country in America,* vol. 2 (London, 1698), 92.

4   "Journey of Dollier and Galinee," in *Early Narratives of the Northwest, 1634–1699,* ed. Louise Phelps Kellogg (New York: Charles Scribner's Sons, 1917), 167–209.

5   Elizabeth Eggleston Seelye with Edward Eggleston, *Brant and Red Jacket* (New York: Dodd, Mead), 1879.

6   Jeromus Johnson, New York, to William L. Stone, Esq., December 1, 1837.

Gabrielle Tayac

Archives of Maryland, volumes 27, 75, and 426.

Davidson, Thomas E. and Helen Rountree. *Eastern Shore Indians of Virginia and Maryland.* (Charlottesville: University of Virginia Press, 1997).

Rountree, Helen. *Pocahontas's People: The Powhatan Indians of Virginia Through Four Centuries.* (Norman: University of Oklahoma Press, 1996).

Gabrielle Tayac, "To Speak with One Voice." Ph.D. diss., Harvard University, 1999.

Mark Hirsch

1   Jeninne Lee-St. John, "The Cherokee Nation's New Battle," *Time,* June 21, 2007, www.time.com; Smith quoted in "Federal District Court Judge Greenlights Cherokee Nation's June 23 Election to Go Forward," *Cherokee Nation News Release,* June 13, 2007, 2.

2   Eric Foner, *Reconstruction: America's Unfinished Revolution, 1863–1877* (New York: Harper, 1988), 251–80.

3   Daniel F. Littlefield, Jr., *The Cherokee Freedmen: From Emancipation to American Citizenship* (Westport, CT: Greenwood Press, 1978), 249–56.

4   William G. McLoughlin, "Red Indians, Black Slavery, and White Racism: America's Slaveholding Indians," *American Indian Quarterly* 26 (October 1974), 380–81; Circe Sturm, "Blood Politics, Racial Classification, and Cherokee National Identity: The Trials and Tribulations of the Cherokee Freedmen," *American Indian Quarterly* 22 (Winter-Spring 1998), 249; Tiya Miles, *Ties That Bind: The Story of an Afro-Cherokee Family in Slavery and Freedom* (Berkeley: University of California Press, 2005), 185, 203; Claudio Saunt, et al., "Remaking Race and Culture in the Early South," *Ethnohistory* 53 (Summer 2006), 401–2; Tiya Miles and Cecelia Naylor-Ojurongbe, "African-Americans in Indian Societies," in Raymond D. Fogelson and William Sturtevant, eds., *Handbook of North American Indians,* vol. 14 (Washington, D.C.: Smithsonian Institution, 2004), 756.

5   Donald A. Grinde, Sr., and Quintard Taylor, "Red vs. Black: Conflict and Accommodation in the Post Civil War

Indian Territory, 1865–1907," *American Indian Quarterly* 8, no. 3 (Summer 1984): 212; Linda W. Reese, "Cherokee Freedwomen in Indian Territory, 1863–1890," *Western Historical Quarterly* 33 (Autumn 2002): 22–23.

6   Circe Sturm, "Blood Politics, Racial Classification, and Cherokee National Identity: The Trials and Tribulations of the Cherokee Freedmen," in James F. Brooks, *Confounding the Color Line: The Indian-Black Experience in North America* (Lincoln: University of Nebraska Press, 2002), 227; Miles, *Ties That Bind*, 193–94.

7   Fear of invasion was no figment of the Cherokee imagination. In 1870, Native Americans constituted 87% of the population of Indian Territory, blacks 10%, and whites 3%. By 1890, whites comprised 61% of the population, blacks 11%, and American Indians just 28%. See Grinde and Taylor, "Red vs. Black," 217–18.

8   Miles, *Ties That Bind*, 193–94; McLoughlin, *After the Trail of Tears*, 359.

9   Circe Sturm, *Blood Politics: Race, Culture, and Identity in the Cherokee Nation of Oklahoma* (Berkeley: University of California Press, 2002), 76–77.

10 Littlefield, Jr., *Cherokee Freedmen*, 250–51; Sturm, *Blood Politics*, 77–78. In 1888, Congress enacted a law requiring the Cherokee Nation to share its assets with the Freedmen and other adopted tribal members. Two years later, lawmakers authorized the U.S. Court of Claims to hear suits brought by the Freedmen against the Cherokee Nation for recovery of proceeds that were denied to them, and in 1895 the Court of Claims held that the Freedmen were entitled to share in the tribe's proceeds. Finally, in 1906, the U.S. Supreme Court confirmed that the Freedmen were citizens of the Cherokee Nation, entitled to the same property rights as other tribal members. See *Vann v. Kempthorne*, U.S. District Court for the District of Columbia, Memorandum Opinion and Order, Dec. 19, 2006, 3–4.

11 Duane H. King, "Cherokee in the West: History Since 1776," in Fogelson and Sturtevant, eds., *Handbook of North American Indians*, 367.

12 The final Dawes Rolls showed that 41,824 people were entitled to land through tribal membership. Of these, 36,619 (87.5%) were identified as Cherokees, 4,919 (11.8%) were Freedmen, and 286 (0.7%) were whites. See Kent Carter, "Deciding Who Can Be Cherokee: Enrollment Records of the Dawes Commission," *Chronicles of Oklahoma* Vol. LXIX (Summer 1991): 201; Miles, *Ties That Bind*, 194–95; Grinde and Taylor, 217–18.

13 The Dawes Commission's blood quantum measurements were used to establish restrictions on the sale of land allotments. The restrictions were based on early-twentieth-century notions of racial competency, which was governed by racial mixture. Allottees who were one-half Indian were initially disallowed from selling their parcels. Instead, the property was held in federal trust and exempted from taxation. Allottees who were less than one-half Indian—such as Freedmen and intermarried whites—were required to pay taxes and were free to sell their lands. See Theda Perdue, "Race and Culture: Writing the Ethnohistory of the Early South," *Ethnohistory* 51, no. 4 (Fall 2004): 719; Sturm, "Blood Politics," 233–34.

14 See William McLoughlin, *After the Trail of Tears: Cherokees' Struggle for Sovereignty, 1839–1880* (Chapel Hill: University of North Carolina Press, 1994), xiv; Miles and Naylor-Ojurongbe, "African-Americans in Indian Societies," 758; Littlefield, Jr., *Cherokee Freedmen*, 251; Miles, *Ties That Bind*, 192; King, "Cherokee in the West," 367; McLoughlin, "Red Indians," 359, 381.

15 Duane H. King, "Cherokee," in Frederick E. Hoxie, ed., *Encyclopedia of North American Indians: Native American History, Culture, and Life from Paleo-Indians to the Present* (Boston: Houghton Mifflin, 1996), 105–6; Cherokee Constitution, Article III, at http://thorpe.ou.edu/constitution/cherokee/index.html.

16 Cherokee Nation Judicial Appeals Tribunal, *Allen v. Cherokee Nation Tribal Council*, JAT–04–09, March 7, 2006, 3–4, 9–10; Sturm, "Blood Politics," 232–34. The Dawes Rolls identified 4,208 adult Cherokee Freedmen, of whom some 300 had Cherokee blood. Nonethe-

less, Afro-Cherokees and African Americans were lumped together as "Freedmen" on the basis of skin color. See Sturm, "Blood Politics," 240.

17 Ronald Smith, "The Cherokee-Freedmen Story: What the Media Saw," *American Indian Policy and Media Initiative Research Report* (March 2007): 2; Cherokee Nation Judicial Appeals Tribunal, *Allen v. Cherokee Nation Tribal Council*, JAT–04–09, March 7, 2006, 3–4, 9–10.

18 Smith quoted in "Future Unclear for 'Freedmen Descendants,'" Associated Press, March 4, 2007, www.msnbc.com.

19 Fishinghawk quoted in Frank Morris, "Cherokee Tribe Faces Decision on Freedmen," National Public Radio (hereafter, NPR), September 18, 2007, www.npr.org.

20 Keen quoted in "Cherokees Eject Slave Descendants," BBC News, March 4, 2007, http://news.bbc.co.uk.

Dan Agent

1 Cherokee Treaty of July 19, 1866, in Charles J. Kappler, ed., *Indian Affairs: Laws and Treaties* (Washington, D.C.: Government Printing Office, 1904), Treaties, vol. 2, 942–50, at http://digital.library.okstate.edu/kappler/Vol2/treaties/che0942.htm.

2 Cherokee Nation Judicial Appeals Tribunal, *Allen vs. Cherokee Nation*, JAT–04–09.

3 Cherokee Nation Judicial Appeals Tribunal, *Riggs vs. Cherokee Nation*, JAT–97–03.

4 *Allen vs. Cherokee Nation*, JAT–04–09.

5 Cherokee Constitution of 1975, at www.cherokee.org/Government/238/Page/Default.aspx; Cherokee Constitution of 2003, at www.cherokee.org/Government/CCC/Default.aspx.

6 LeeAnn Dreadfulwater, Mike Miller, and Sammye Rusco, *We Are Cherokee* (Tahlequah, OK: Cherokee Nation, 2007).

7 Richard L. Allen, *Indians Not Taxed and the 1866 Cherokee Treaty* (unpub. essay), February 27, 2008.

8 Michael Wallis, *Way Down Yonder in the Indian Nation* (Norman, OK: University of Oklahoma Press, 2007); Clarissa W. Confer, *The Cherokee Na-*

tion in the Civil War (Norman, OK: University of Oklahoma Press, 2007).

9 First Peoples Human Rights Coalition, *The Cherokee Nation, the United States and the Rule of Law, Part I and II*, (Cherokee and Federal) Timeline 1798–1975, November 1, 2007.

10 "American Indian Policy and Media Initiative at Buffalo State University," American Indian Initiative, March 22, 2007, www.buffalostate.edu/communication.

11 H.R. 2824 (110th): "To sever United States' government relations with the Cherokee Nation of Oklahoma until such time as the Cherokee Nation of Oklahoma restores full tribal citizenship to the Cherokee Freedmen disenfranchised in the March 3, 2007, Cherokee Nation vote and fulfills all its treaty obligations with the Government of the United States, and for other purposes."

12 Tony Cox and Diane Watson. Interview on National Public Radio (NPR), June 22, 2007, www.npr.org.

13 Randy Shannon, Press Release, March 27, 2007, www.okhouse.gov/OkhouseMedia/pressroom.

14 National Congress of American Indians, November 2007, NCAI Resolution #DEN–07–071, at www.ncai.org.

15 S.E. Ruckman, "Keetoowahs to Push Enrollment," *Tulsa World*, March 5, 2005.

16 A *USA Today* Snapshot, June 5, 2002, noted that 729,533 people had declared they had Cherokee "racial origins" in the 2000 census. In fact, at the time, the total of Cherokees by blood registered with the three federally recognized Cherokee tribes was approximately 250,000.

17 First Peoples Human Rights Coalition.

CREATIVE RESISTANCE

Tiya Miles

I owe a debt of gratitude to the School of Advanced Research in Santa Fe, New Mexico, where a residential fellowship in 2007–2008 supported the research and writing of this essay.

1 William Goodell, *The American Slave Code in Theory and Practice: Its Distinctive*

Features Shown by Its Statutes, Judicial Decisions, and Illustrative Facts (New York: American and Foreign Anti-Slavery Society, 1853), Part 1, Chapter 23, HTML by Dinsmore Documentation, 266–69. Judge Mathews, a slaveholder, delivered the court's opinion of the case, reproduced in Judge Francois-Xavier Martin, *Louisiana Term Reports, or Cases Argued and Determined in the Supreme Court of the State of Louisiana*, vol. 3 (New Orleans: Benjamin Hanna, 1819), 275–91.

2   A. Judd Northrup, *Slavery in New York: A Historical Sketch* (New York: State Library Bulletin, 1900), 310.

3   J. Leitch Wright, *The Only Land They Knew: The Tragic Story of the American Indians in the Old South* (New York: Free Press, 1981), 126. See also, Almon Wheeler Lauber, *Indian Slavery in Colonial Times within the Present Limits of the United States* (1913; reprint, Williamstown, MA: Corner House, 1970).

4   Alan Gallay, *The Indian Slave Trade: The Rise of the English Empire in the American South 1670–1717* (New Haven: Yale University Press, 2002).

5   Jack D. Forbes, *Africans and Native Americans: The Language of Race and the Evolution of Red-Black Peoples* (Urbana: University of Illinois Press, 1993), 47, 64.

6   Peter H. Wood, *Black Majority: Negroes in Colonial South Carolina from 1670 through the Stono Rebellion* (New York: Norton, 1974), 115.

7   Wright, *Only Land They Knew*, 264.

8   Wood, *Black Majority*, 122; Wright, *Only Land They Knew*, 263.

9   Wood, *Black Majority*, 124; Wright, *Only Land They Knew*, 263.

10   Wright, *Only Land They Knew*, 266–67; see also Jonathan Brennan, "Introduction: Recognition of the African-Native Literary Tradition," in Brennan, ed., *When Brer Rabbit Meets Coyote: African-Native American Literature* (Urbana-Champaign: University of Illinois Press, 2003), 17–21.

11   Wood, *Black Majority*, 121; Wright, *Only Land They Knew*, 265.

12   Sigmund Sameth, "Creek Negroes: A Study of Race Relations," M.A. thesis, University of Oklahoma, Norman, OK, 1940, 62. Island Smith's comment is also quoted in Gary Zellar, *African Creeks: Estelvste and the Creek Nation* (Norman: University of Oklahoma Press, 2007), 257. Celia Naylor discusses cooking and medicinal herb use as described in WPA narratives of slaves formerly owned by Indians in Celia E. Naylor-Ojurongbe, "'Born and Raised Among These People, I Don't Want to Know Any Other': Slaves' Acculturation in Nineteenth-Century Indian Territory," in James F. Brooks, ed., *Confounding the Color Line: The Indian-Black Experience in North America* (Lincoln: University of Nebraska Press, 2002), 161–91.

13   L. Daniel Mouer, et al., "Colonoware Pottery, Chesapeake Pipes, and 'Uncritical Assumptions,'" in Theresa A. Singleton, ed., *"I, Too, Am America": Archaeological Studies of African-American Life* (Charlottesville: University Press of Virginia, 1999), 83–115, 113. Colono Ware pottery also has European influences, especially regarding "vessel forms" (84). Wright, *Only Land They Knew*, 264.

14   Leland G. Ferguson, "'The Cross is a Magic Sign': Marks on Eighteenth-Century Bowls from South Carolina," in Singleton, ed., *"I, Too, Am America,"* 116–131, 124.

15   Wood, *Black Majority*, 116; bell hooks, "Revolutionary 'Renegades': Native Americans, African Americans, and Black Indians," in *Black Looks: Race and Representation* (London: Turnaround, 1992): 180–81.

16   Jill Lepore, "The Tightening Vise: Slavery and Freedom in British New York," in Ira Berlin and Leslie M. Harris, eds., *Slavery in New York* (New York: New Press, 2005): 60.

17   Quoted in William Renwick Riddell, "The Slave in Early New York," *Journal of Negro History* 13, no. 1 (Jan. 1928): 54–55.

18   Quoted in ibid., 55.

19   Ibid., 64.

20   Quoted in ibid., 66. Also quoted in Northrup, *Slavery in New York*, 264–65. For more on the early slave statutes, see Edwin Olson, "The Slave Code in

Colonial New York," *Journal of Negro History* 29, no. 2 (April 1944): 147–65.

21 Riddell, "The Slave in Early New York," 66–8.

22 Lepore, "Tightening Vise," 78–83; Leslie M. Harris, *In the Shadow of Slavery: African Americans in New York City, 1626–1863* (Chicago: University of Chicago Press, 2003), 37; Herbert Aptheker, *American Negro Slave Revolts* (1943; reprint, New York: International, 1963), 173.

23 "An Eyewitness Report of a Slave Revolt," *New York and Slavery: Complicity and Resistance*, New York State Council for the Social Studies, Documents, http://www.nyscss.org/resources/publications/NYandSlavery.cfm; also quoted in Graham Russell Hodges, *Root and Branch: African Americans in New York and East Jersey* (Chapel Hill: University of North Carolina Press, 1999), 64. Herbert Aptheker has pointed out that the date of this revolt has confounded researchers. While some have concluded that it occurred in 1708, others have attributed it to 1707. The confusion arises from the original report of Lord Cornbury, which is dated February 10, 1707–08. In addition, the newspaper account of the event is dated February 1707. However, other primary accounts note the year as 1708, and the law in response to the rebellion was passed in 1708; Aptheker, *Slave Revolts*, 169, n. 24.

24 *The Boston News-Letter*, February 2–9, 1707.

25 *The Boston News-Letter*, February 16–23, 1707.

26 "Lord Cornbury to the Board of Trade," February 10, 1707–08, New York State Council for the Social Studies, *New York and Slavery: Complicity and Resistance*, Documents, http://www.nyscss.org/resources/publications/NYandSlavery.cfm; also quoted in Northrup, *Slavery in New York*, 306.

27 *The Boston News-Letter*, February 16–23, 1707.

28 Olson, "The Slave Code," 162; Hodges, 64; *History of Queens County, New York with Illustrations, Portraits, and Sketches of Prominent Families and Individuals* (New York: W. W. Munsell, 1882), 51.

29 *The Boston News-Letter*, February 16–23, 1707. Quoted in Olson, "The Slave Code," 162.

30 Quoted in Riddell, "The Slave in Early New York," 69; also quoted in Northrup, *Slavery In New York*, 265.

31 *The Boston News-Letter*, February 2–9, 1707.

32 The 1708 revolt is mentioned in Kenneth W. Porter, "Relations Between Negroes and Indians Within the Present Limits of the United States," *Journal of Negro History* 17, no. 3 (July 1932): 287–367, 296. Also see the companion piece to this article: Kenneth W. Porter, "Notes Supplementary To 'Relations Between Negroes and Indians,'" *Journal of Negro History* vol. 18, no. 3 (July 1933): 282–321.

33 For a sampling of work in this area since 2000, see, for instance, James F. Brooks, ed., *Confounding the Color Line*; Patrick Minges, *Slavery in the Cherokee Nation: The Keetoowah Society and the Defining of a People 1855–1867* (London: Routledge, 2003); Claudio Saunt, *Black, White, and Indian: Race and the Unmaking of an American Family* (New York: Oxford University Press, 2005); Tiya Miles, *Ties That Bind: The Story of an Afro-Cherokee Family in Slavery and Freedom* (Berkeley: University of California Press, 2005); Gary Zellar, *Africans and Creeks*; Celia E. Naylor, *African Cherokees in Indian Country: From Chattel to Citizens* (Chapel Hill: University of North Carolina Press, 2008); Fay A. Yarbrough, *Race in the Cherokee Nation: Sovereignty in the Nineteenth Century* (Philadelphia: University of Pennsylvania Press, forthcoming 2007). For a review essay of classic and new works on African American and Native American interrelated histories, inclusive of links, see Barbara Krauthamer, "Africans and Native Americans," Black Studies Center, Schomburg Studies on the Black Experience (an online resource), Proquest Information and Learning Company, http://bsc.chadwyck.com. For a full overview of primary and secondary sources in this subject area, see Lisa Bier, *American Indian and African American People, Communities, and Interactions: An Annotated Bibliography* (Westport, CT: Praeger, 2004).

34 Barbara Krauthamer, "Ar'n't I A Woman? Native Americans, Gender, and Slavery," *Journal of Women's History*, 19, no. 2 (Summer 2007): 157.

Phoebe Farris

1   Ann "Sole Sister" Johnson, *Artist/Bio Statement*, www.solesisterart.com, 1.

2   Ibid., 1.

3   Darnella Davis, *Artist Statement*, Curriculum Vitae, 2008.

4   Adrienne Hoard, *Artist Statement*, www.homegirlinc.com, 1.

5   Robin Chandler, "SIOUXJEWGER-MANSCOTBLACK," 2002 poetry, www.robin-chandler.com.

6   Chandler, *Artist/Bio Statement*, www.robin-chandler.com.

7   Chandler, "SIOUXJEWGER-MANSCOTBLACK," 2002.

8   Regina Vater, "The Continent of Ashe" in Phoebe Farris, ed., *Voices of Color: Art and Society in the Americas* (Long Island, NY: Prometheus-Humanity Books, 1997), 72.

9   Vater, *Artist Statement*, Curriculum Vitae, 2008.

10 Jack D. Forbes, *Africans and Native Americans: The Language of Race and the Evolution of Red-Black Peoples* (Urbana-Champaign: University of Illinois Press, 1993), 271.

LIFEWAYS

Robert Keith Collins

1   Jack D. Forbes, "The Manipulation of Race, Caste, and Identity: Classifying Afro-Americans, Native Americans, and Red-Black People," *Journal of Ethnic Studies* 17, no. 4 (1990): 48–49.

2   William Loren Katz, *Black Indians: A Hidden Heritage* (New York: Simon and Schuster, Atheneum, 1986).

3   Donna Hale, "Cherokees Vote Out Freedmen," *Muskogee Phoenix*, March 4, 2007; "Freedmen Issue on Today's Ballot," *Muskogee Phoenix*, March 3, 2007.

4   Forbes, "Manipulation of Race," 1–51.

5   This approach differs from other ethnographic approaches in that it accepts the individual as an active agent in his or her own lived experiences and culture. Each individual is interviewed at least fifteen times, as opposed to one time in one setting (as with standard ethnography). This approach affords the ethnographer a chance to hear a respondent's experience near (i.e., as close to lived experience as possible) and evolving understandings of self and lived experiences, as well as enabling respondents to reexamine and provide further explanation of statements previously given during the interview process. V. Crapanzano, "The Life History in Anthropological Field Work," *Anthropology and Humanism Quarterly* 2 (1977): 3–7; Robert Levy and Douglas Hollan, "Person Centered Interviewing and Observation in Anthropology," *Handbook of Research Methods in Anthropology*, ed. Russell Bernard (Walnut Creek, CA: Altamira Press, 1998).

6   Brewton Berry, *Almost White* (New York: Macmillan, 1969); Karen Blu, *The Lumbee Problem: The Making of an American Indian People* (Cambridge and New York: Cambridge University Press, 1990); Forbes, *Africans and Native Americans*; Laurence Foster, *Negro-Indian Relationships in the Southeast* (Philadelphia, 1935); Alan Gallay, *The Indian Slave Trade: The Rise of the English Empire in the American South, 1670–1717* (New Haven: Yale University Press, 2002); Bonita Lawrence, *"Real" Indians and Others: Mixed Blood Urban Native Peoples and Indigenous Nationhood* (Lincoln: University of Nebraska Press, 2004); Daniel F. Littlefield, *Africans and Seminoles: From Removal to Emancipation* (Jackson: University of Mississippi Press, 2001); Tiya Miles, *Ties That Bind: The Story of an Afro-Cherokee Family in Slavery and Freedom* (Berkeley and Los Angeles: University of California Press, 2005); Celia Naylor, *African Cherokees in Indian Territory: From Chattel to Citizens* (Chapel Hill: University of North Carolina Press, 2008); Claudio Saunt, *Black, White, and Indian: Race and the Unmaking of an American Family* (New York: Oxford University Press, 2005); Gerald Sider, *Lumbee Indian Histories: Race, Ethnicity, and Indian Identity in the Southern United States* (Cambridge and New York: Cambridge University Press, 1993); David Usner, *Indians, Settlers, and Slaves in a Frontier Exchange Economy: The Lower Mississippi Valley Before 1783* (Chapel Hill: University of North Carolina Press, 1992); Fay Yarbrough,

Race and the Cherokee Nation: Sovereignty in the Nineteenth Century (Philadelphia: University of Pennsylvania Press, 2007).

7   James F. Davis, *Who Is Black?: One Nation's Definition* (University Park: Pennsylvania State University Press, 2001); Laura L. Lovett, "African and Cherokee by Choice: Race and Resistance Under Legalized Segregation," *American Indian Quarterly* 22 (1998); Patrick Minges, *Black Indian Slave Narratives* (Winston-Salem: John F. Blair, 2004); Robert I. Rotberg, *The Mixing of Peoples: Problems of Identity and Ethnicity* (Stamford, CT: Greylock, 1990); Audrey Smedley, *Race in North America: Origin and Evolution of a Worldview* (Boulder: Westview Press, 1993); Hilary N. Weaver, "Indigenous Identity: What Is It and Who Really Has It," *American Indian Quarterly* 25, no. 2 (2001).

8   Forbes, *African and Native Americans*; Littlefield, *Africans and Seminoles*; Theda Perdue, *Slavery and the Evolution of Cherokee Society, 1540–1866* (Knoxville: University of Tennessee Press, 1979).

9   Dorothy Holland, "How Cultural Systems Become Desire: A Case Study of American Romance," in *Human Motives and Cultural Models*, ed. Roy D'Andrade and Claudia Strauss (New York: Cambridge University Press, 1992); idem, *History in Person: Enduring Struggles, Contentious Practice, Intimate Identities* (Santa Fe: School of Advanced Research Press, 2001).

10 F. C. Wallace and Raymond D. Fogelson, "The Identity Struggle," in *Intensive Family Therapy: Theoretical and Practical Aspects*, ed. Ivan Boszomenyi-Nagy and James L. Framo (New York: Harper and Row, 1965), 365–406.

11 Raymond D. Fogelson, "Perspectives on Native American Identity," in *Studying Native America: Problems and Prospects*, ed. Russell Thornton (Madison: University of Wisconsin Press, 1998), 40–59.

12 Wallace and Fogelson, "The Identity Struggle," in *Intensive Family Therapy: Theoretical and Practical Aspects*.

13 Ibid.

14 Robert Keith Collins, "When Playing Indian Is a Misplaced Assumption: Evidence from Black Choctaw Lived Experi-

ences," *Race, Roots, and Relations: Native and African Americans*, ed. Terry Strauss and Denine Dequintal (Brooklyn: Albatross Press, 2005); idem, "Katimih o Sa Chata Kiyou? (Why Am I Not Choctaw?): Race in the Lived Experiences of Two Black Choctaw Mixed Bloods," *Crossing Waters, Crossing Worlds*, ed. Sharon P. Holland and Tiya Miles (Durham: Duke University Press, 2006); Raymond D. Fogelson, "Perspectives on Native American Identity"; Melissa Meyers, *Thicker Than Water: The Origins of Blood As Symbol and Ritual* (New York and Oxford: Routledge, 2005); Circe Sturm, "Blood Politics, Racial Classification, and Cherokee National Identity: The Trials and Tribulations of the Cherokee Freedmen," *American Indian Quarterly* 22 (Winter-Spring 1998); Russell Thornton, "The Demography of Colonialism and 'Old' and 'New' Native Americans," in *Studying Native America: Problems and Prospects* (Madison: University of Wisconsin Press, 1998), 17–39.

15 Kent Carter, *The Dawes Commission: And the Allotment of the Five Civilized Tribes, 1893–1914* (Orem, UT: Ancestry Publishing, 1999); Angie Debo, *The Rise and Fall of the Choctaw Republic* (Norman: University of Oklahoma Press, 1972); Raymond J. DeMallie, "Kinship: The Foundation of Native American Society," in *Studying Native America: Problems and Prospects*, ed. Russell Thornton (Madison: University of Wisconsin Press, 1998), 305–56; Forbes, *African and Native Americans*; Thornton, "The Demography of Colonialism and 'Old' and 'New' Native Americans"; Theda Perdue, *Mixed Blood Indians? Racial Construction in the Early South* (Atlanta: University of Georgia Press, 2005); Sturm, "Blood Politics."

16 Moiety here refers to one of two major divisions into which some tribal nations divide based on unilineal descent. See Elsie Clews Parsons, "Tewa Kin, Clan, and Moiety," *American Anthropologist*, 26 (1924), 333–39.

17 Collins, "When Playing Indian"; idem, "Katimih o Sa Chata Kiyou?"

18 This narrative is merely one example of more than twenty-five that were given during my dissertation fieldwork conducted 1998–2000 in Foi Tamaha (Bee Town). This fictitiously named

town—done so to protect the anonymity of the respondents—is located in southeastern Oklahoma along the Red River on the northeastern Texas border.

19   Collins, "When Playing Indian"; idem, "Katimih o Sa Chata Kiyou?".

20   Carter, *Dawes Commission*; Littlefield, *Africans and Seminoles; The Cherokee Freedmen: From Emancipation to American Citizenship* (Santa Barbara: Greenwood Press, 1978); *The Chickasaw Freedmen: A People Without a Country* (Santa Barbara: Greenwood Press, 1980); Lovett, "African and Cherokee by Choice"; Sturm, "Blood Politics."

21   Carter, *Dawes Commission;* Littlefield, *Chickasaw Freedmen.*

22   Hale, "Cherokees Vote Out Freedmen," and "Freedmen Issue on Today's Ballot"; Sturm, "Blood Politics."

23   Littlefield, *Cherokee Freedmen; Africans and Seminoles.*

24   Minges, *Born in Slavery: Slave Narratives from the Federal Writer's Project, 1936–1938,* Texas Narratives, vol. XVI, Part 2. http://memory.loc.gov/ammem/snhtml.

25   Carter, *Dawes Commission*; Blu, *Lumbee Problem*; Berry, *Almost White*; Foster, *Negro-Indian Relationships in the Southeast*; Lovett, "African and Cherokee by Choice"; Patricia Anne Waak, *My Bones Are Red: A Spiritual Journey With a Triracial People in the Americas* (Macon, GA: Mercer University Press, 2005).

26   Collins, "Katimih o Sa Chata Kiyou?"

27   Wallace and Fogelson, "Identity Struggle"; Russell Thornton and Peter M. Nardi, "The Dynamics of Role Acquisition, *American Journal of Sociology* 80, no. 4 (1975): 870–85.

28   Almon Lauber, *Indian Slavery in Colonial Times Within the Limits of the United States* (Whitefish, MT: Kessinger, 1913); Perdue, *Slavery and the Evolution of Cherokee Society.*

29   Thornton and Nardi, "Dynamics of Role Acquisition."

30   Erik H. Erickson, *Identity and the Life Cycle* (New York: W. W. Norton, 1959), 17.

31   Debo, *Rise and Fall of the Choctaw Republic.*

32   Roy D'Andrade, "Schemas and Motivation," in *Human Motives and Cultural Models,* ed. Roy D'Andrade and Claudia Strauss (New York: Cambridge University Press, 1992); Holland, *History in Person*; Naomi Quinn, "The Motivational Force of Self-Understanding: Evidence from Wives' Inner Conflicts," in *Human Motives and Cultural Models.*

Peter McFarren

1   Peter McFarren, ed. *An Insider's Guide to Bolivia* (Quipus Foundation, 2003).

Ron Welburn

The writer is personally indebted to musicians Jacques Butler, Buck Clayton, Jo Jones, Lewis McMillan, and Silas Whitman; writers Stanley Dance, Gene Lees, and Maxine Gordon; Miffie Shunatona Hines and Carol Bayhylle for sharing their knowledge. Research sources and authors include Emanuel J. Dreschel, Heriberto Dixon, Will Friedwald, Patricia Galloway, Gary Giddens, Alan Lomax, Joseph Roach, William Russell and Charles W. Smith's *Jazzmen*, the Rutgers University-Newark Institute of Jazz Studies, Michael P. Smith, and the Jelly Roll Morton Library of Congress recordings.

PHOTO CREDITS

The sources of the images featured in this volume are gratefully acknowledged below; in some cases, photographers and lenders are credited in the caption text. Images from the Photo Archives of the National Museum of the American Indian (NMAI) are identified by photograph or negative number where they appear.

Cover (top), courtesy Sam DeVenney; cover (bottom), courtesy Foxx family, photo by Kevin Cartwright, NMAI; title page, NMAI, © Smithsonian Institution; 9, courtesy Museum of Contemporary Native Arts, Santa Fe, New Mexico; 10, © John Running 2009; 13, courtesy Billings Gazette; 14, photo by Graham F. Page, courtesy Experience Music Project and Science Fiction Museum and Hall of Fame; 17 (top), courtesy John W. Franklin; 17 (bottom), courtesy National Archives at Fort Worth; 20, Used with permission of Documenting the American South, The University of North Carolina at Chapel Hill Libraries; 22, © President and Fellows of Harvard College, Peabody Museum of Archaeology and Ethnology, 41-72-10/20; 28, courtesy The State Archive of Florida; 31, photo by Francis Miller/Time & Life Pictures/ © Getty Images; 34, NMAI, © Smithsonian Institution; 37, courtesy Biblioteca Estense Universitaria, Modena, Italy; 38, 40, courtesy Millie Knapp; 42, 44 (top), courtesy University of New Mexico Center for Southwest Research; 44 (bottom), courtesy Museum of the American West, Autry National Center, Los Angeles; 99.1.1; 48, courtesy Gilcrease Museum, Tulsa, Oklahoma; 51 (top), courtesy James H. Nottage; 51 (bottom), courtesy The New York Public Library; 52, courtesy Library of Congress, Prints and Photographs Division; 55, courtesy Center of Southwest Studies, Fort Lewis College; 56, courtesy the Architect of the Capitol; 59, courtesy Library of Congress, Manuscript Division; 60, courtesy Cullman Rare Books Library, Smithsonian Institution; 62, 63, NMAI, © Smithsonian Institution; 65, courtesy Breamore House, Hampshire, England; 66, NMAI, © Smithsonian Institution; 68, courtesy Blake-Scott family, photo by Kevin Cartwright, NMAI; 70, courtesy DNA Consultants, Phoenix, Arizona; 73, courtesy Fred Nahwooksy; 76, 79, 80, 83, courtesy Angela Walton-Raji; 84, NMAI, © Smithsonian Institution; 87, courtesy Hampton University's Archival and Museum Collection; 89, courtesy Angela Walton-Raji; 90, photo by Nancy Kenet Vickery, NMAI; 93, courtesy Dr. Joseph O. Palacio; 94, © 2009 Artists Rights Society (ARS), New York/VG Bild-Kunst,

Bonn; 98, courtesy Yale University Art Gallery; 102, courtesy The Montreal Museum of Fine Arts; 103, courtesy Fenimore Art Museum, Cooperstown, New York; 105, courtesy Yale University Art Gallery; 108, NMAI, © Smithsonian Institution; 111, courtesy University of Virginia Library, Special Collections; 113, courtesy Sylvia and Bill Davis; 114, NMAI, © Smithsonian Institution; 116, courtesy National Archives and Records Administration; 117, photo by R.A. Whiteside, NMAI; 121, photo by Rick McCormick, courtesy Marilyn Vann; 125, © 2007 Marty G. Two Bulls, Sr.; 127 (bottom), courtesy Glenn Nelson of ESPN HoopGurlz; 128, NMAI, © Smithsonian Institution; 131, NMAI, © Smithsonian Institution; 132, courtesy Phil Wilkes Fixico; 134, photo by Kate M.W. Oliver, UT Institute of Texan Cultures at San Antonio, 068-1107, loaned by Texas Southern University; 138, courtesy the Architect of the Capitol; 141 (top), courtesy Library of Congress, Rare Books Division; 141 (bottom), Jacques LeMoyne, *A Fortified Village*, 1564, courtesy University of South Florida, Center for Instructional Technology; 143, courtesy Research Division of the Oklahoma Historical Society; 144 (top), courtesy Long Island Collection, East Hampton Free Library; 144 (bottom), photo by Robert Cushman Murphy, courtesy The Whaling Museum, Cold Spring Harbor, New York; 146, Courtesy Greater Astoria Historical Society; 154, Courtesy Glenbow Archives, NA-177-1; 155, courtesy Picture History; 156 (top), © Getty Images; 156 (bottom), photo by Don Cravens/ Time Life Pictures/ © Getty Images; 158, 160, 161, courtesy Sam DeVenney; 162, 164, 166, courtesy Ann "Sole Sister" Johnson; 168, courtesy Darnella Davis; 169, 170, 171, courtesy Adrienne Walker Hoard; 173, courtesy Robin Chandler; 175, 176, courtesy Regina Vater; 178, courtesy Sarann Knight Preddy; 182, NMAI, © Smithsonian Institution; 183, photo by Carolyn L. Forbes; 185, courtesy Foxx family, photo by Kevin Cartwright, NMAI; 189, courtesy Library of Congress, Manuscript Division; 191, courtesy of Elizabeth Field, *Ithaca Community News*, Tutelo Homecoming Festival, September 2006; 196, 198, 199, photos by Peter McFarren; 200, 206, 207, courtesy Institute of Jazz Studies, Rutgers University; 209, photo by Clark James Mishler, courtesy Pamyua; 210, courtesy The Historic New Orleans Collection, 1974.25.23.54; 212, NMAI, © Smithsonian Institution; 216, 218, Karl Kernberger Pictorial Collection, Center for Southwest Research, University Libraries, University of New Mexico; 220, courtesy David Amram; 221, courtesy Rick Reinhard; 222, courtesy W. Thunder Williams; 224, courtesy Maceo Leatherwood.

ACKNOWLEDGMENTS

It goes without saying that any museum project requires the work of many people and organizations. Funding support for *IndiVisible* came from both the National Museum of African American History and Culture (NMAAHC) and the National Museum of the American Indian (NMAI), and we thank the Akaloa Foundation and the Smithsonian Latino Center for their generous contributions.

Penny Gamble-Williams (Chappaquiddick Wampanoag), Thunder Williams (Afro-Carib), and Louise Thundercloud have long encouraged NMAI to address African-Native American issues within the museum setting. As advocates and educators from the D.C. metro area, their promotion was critical to getting *IndiVisible* off the ground. Our project partners at NMAAHC were also our partners more than in name only and worked with us on content and funding. I offer my gratitude to NMAAHC Director Lonnie Bunch, curator for collections Michèle Gates Moresi, and education specialist Candra Flanagan for their dedication and counsel throughout the process.

The tremendous success of the *IndiVisible* traveling exhibition would not be possible without the enthusiasm and expertise of our colleagues at the Smithsonian Institution Traveling Exhibition Service (SITES). My specific thanks to SITES Director Anna Cohn, project director Katherine Krile, and the SITES staff for making it possible to share this project with more than forty museums and other venues in Indian Country and across the nation.

Of particular note, the curatorial team for *IndiVisible* has provided the scholarship on which the project has been founded. The team included Angela A. Gonzales (Hopi), Robert Keith Collins (African and Choctaw descent), Judy Kertész, Penny Gamble-Williams, and Thunder Williams. They have produced an outstanding body of work, which I believe will both stand the test of time and open doors to further examination.

Under the direction of NMAI Associate Director for Museum Programs Tim Johnson (Mohawk), *IndiVisible* was first organized and managed by Fred Nahwooksy, who served as community exhibitions program coordinator, with senior exhibitions coordinator Karen Fort seeing the project to its final outcomes. Publication development was ably led by co-editors Tanya Thrasher (Cherokee Nation) and Arwen Nuttall (Four Winds Band of Cherokee), with support from senior designer Steve Bell and intern Sara Lynch-Thomason. Rights and permissions were coordinated by a team that included Christopher Turner, Sandra Starr, and freelance researchers Claudia Monaco and Bethany Montagano. The exhibition's compelling media piece was produced by Kathy Suter, Augusta Lehman, and Kevin Cartwright, and the interactive website and NMAI's first-ever public blog site developed by Cheryl Wilson and Joe Poccia engages our audiences like never before. Eileen Maxwell, Leonda Levchuk (Navajo), and Abigail Benson successfully promoted the exhibition and its related programs, including teacher workshops developed by Genevieve Simermeyer (Osage) and Megan Byrnes and a major symposium organized by Elizabeth Kennedy Gische. Graphic design for the exhibition was provided by David Lanford.

The list of writers and researchers who have been part of this project is very large. Community and academic scholars are listed in this publication, and my sincere thanks go to all of them for their insightful analyses and observations. Their work provides a broad range of perspectives that we all need to ponder.

—Gabrielle Tayac (Piscataway)

CONTRIBUTORS

DAN AGENT (Cherokee)

Mr. Agent is a writer and photographer who retired as editor of the *Cherokee Phoenix* in 2007. He served as director of the Cherokee Nation Communications Department, and was a public affairs specialist at the Institute of American Indian Arts Museum, Santa Fe, New Mexico, and the Smithsonian's National Museum of the American Indian, where he also served as editor of the *Smithsonian Runner*. His career includes work as a film scriptwriter.

JOSÉ BARREIRO (Taino)

Dr. Barreiro hails from Cuba and is a writer, journalist, and professor. Dr. Barreiro was founding editor of *Native Americas Journal*, the flagship publication of Akwe:kon Press at Cornell University's American Indian Program. He is also assistant director of research for the Smithsonian's National Museum of the American Indian.

TIFFINI BOWERS

Ms. Bowers provides consulting services to numerous museums, cultural institutions, and entertainment organizations helping them to establish guidelines for administrative policies, collections governance, project management, staff training, educational programming, and exhibition development. She is currently a curator at the California African American Museum, Los Angeles.

LONNIE G. BUNCH, III

Dr. Bunch is founding director of the Smithsonian's National Museum of African American History and Culture. Previously, he served as president of the Chicago Historical Society, associate director for curatorial affairs at the Smithsonian's National Museum of

American History, and curator of history for the California African American Museum, Los Angeles. He specializes in interpreting African American history in American museums and the black American experience in California.

ROBERT KEITH COLLINS (African and Choctaw descent)

Dr. Collins is an assistant professor of American Indian studies at San Francisco State University. His expertise includes research in African and Native American interactions in North and South America, as well as in person-centered ethnography and the formation of public and private identities. Collins also specializes in Choctaw language and culture and has authored several book chapters on Black Choctaw lived experiences.

SAM DEVENNEY (Comanche)

Sam DeVenney, from Lawton, Oklahoma, serves as the unofficial Comanche tribal historian and is sought out by his contemporaries for information and visual documentation. He serves as a Comanche language instructor and teaches at the university level and in the local Comanche community.

PHOEBE FARRIS (Powhatan-Renape)

Dr. Farris is a professor of art and design and women's studies at Purdue University and also the arts editor for *Cultural Survival Quarterly*. As an independent curator, photographer, professor, author, and art therapist, Dr. Farris explores issues involving race, gender, indigenous sovereignty, Native American studies, peace, social justice, and the environment. Her books, *Voices of Color: Art and Society in the Americas* and *Women Artists of Color: A Bio-critical Sourcebook to 20th Century Artists in the Americas*, create a dialogue about the intersections of social activism and the arts. She is also the curator and a participating artist in the U.S. Department of State traveling exhibition, *Visual Power: 21st Century Native American Artists/Intellectuals*.

PENNY GAMBLE-WILLIAMS (Chappaquiddick Wampanoag)

Ms. Gamble-Williams is an educator, artist, and community activist and the executive director of Ohke Cultural Network, Inc., in Maryland. She conducts teacher training and works with children of all ages using storytelling, art, music, and movement to teach Native and African American histories. She produces and hosts a radio talk show called the "Talking Feather," which explores the history and culture of Native Americans, African Americans, and indigenous peoples around the world.

ANGELA A. GONZALES (Hopi)

Dr. Gonzales is an assistant professor of development sociology and American Indian studies at Cornell University. Her latest research explores the creation and manifestation of conceptual categories of race. Earlier work included community-based research of sociological processes underlying identity, development, and community health on Indian reservations. Dr. Gonzales strives to refine our understanding of the processes and outcomes of social change affecting Native peoples, tribes, and nations.

KEVIN GOVER (Pawnee)

Mr. Gover is director of the Smithsonian's National Museum of the American Indian and former professor of law at the Sandra Day O'Connor College of Law at Arizona State University (ASU). He also served as co-executive director of ASU's American Indian Policy Institute. Before joining the university faculty, Mr. Gover was assistant secretary for Indian Affairs in the U.S. Department of the Interior, where he oversaw programs in Indian education, law enforcement, social services, treaty rights, and trust asset management.

RICHARD W. HILL, SR. (Tuscarora)

Mr. Hill is an artist, writer, curator, and professor and teaches at the First Nations Technical Institute (FNTI) in Tyendinaga Mohawk Territory, Ontario. He has lectured and written extensively on placing Native American art history, history, and culture in its proper context, as well as on museum-history issues such as the impact of consultation, repatriation, stereotyping, and cross-cultural education.

MARK HIRSCH

Dr. Hirsch is a historian in the research unit at the Smithsonian's National Museum of the American Indian, where he has worked since 2001. He holds a Ph.D. in American social history from Harvard University and an M.A. from the Center for Social History at the University of Warwick, England.

JUDY KERTÉSZ

A Ph.D. candidate in the history of American civilization at Harvard University and assistant professor of history at North Carolina State University, Ms. Kertész's work focuses on colonial, revolutionary, and antebellum U.S. cultural history; American Indian histories and cultures; American nationalism; material culture; African American studies; and tribal sovereignty issues.

BRIAN KLOPOTEK

As a faculty member of the Ethnic Studies Program at the University of Oregon, Dr. Klopotek teaches courses on American Indian ethnohistory and issues of race in the United States. His research has focused on federal recognition of Indian tribes, Indian education under Jim Crow, Native Americans and gender, American Indians in the cinema, and the impact of material culture on tribal identity.

DANIEL LITTLEFIELD

Dr. Littlefield is director of the Sequoyah National Research Center at the University of Arkansas at Little Rock. He is cofounder of the Center's American Native Press Archives, which collects and archives the products of the Native press and Native writers and conducts and publishes original research on topics of importance to Indian communities.

PETER MCFARREN

Mr. McFarren is the CEO of the Inter-American Culture and Development Foundation. He is also a professional photographer/filmmaker and author whose work has appeared in numerous publications, including *Life*, *The New York Times*, *Newsweek*, and several Bolivian newspapers. For twenty years, his nonprofit Quipus Foundation has built museums and promoted the arts and information technology in his home country of Bolivia.

TIYA MILES

Dr. Miles is an associate professor at the University of Michigan in the Program in American Culture, Center for Afro American and African Studies, Department of History, and Native American Studies Program. Her research and creative interests include African American and Native American interrelated and comparative histories (especially nineteenth century); black, Native, and U.S. women's histories; and African American and Native American women's literature.

BETHANY MONTAGANO

A curator, writer, and scholar, Ms. Montagano recently co-organized a Fritz Scholder exhibition at the Snite Museum of Art at the University of Notre Dame, Indiana. After completing her graduate fellowship with the National Museum of the American Indian, conducting research on African-Native American convergence, she received her M.A. degree in museum studies. Ms. Montagano has also served as the assistant curator of exhibitions at the Eiteljorg Museum of American Indians and Western Art, Indianapolis.

KEVIN MULROY

Dr. Mulroy is the associate university librarian for academic services at the UCLA Library. Before that, he held positions at the University of Southern California and the Autry National Center. Dr. Mulroy is the author of the award-winning *Freedom on the Border: The Seminole Maroons in Florida, the Indian Territory, Coahuila, and Texas* (1993) and *The Seminole Freedmen: A History* (2007).

JOSEPH O. PALACIO, SR. (Garifuna)

A Belizean Garifuna activist and social anthropologist, Dr. Palacio teaches at the Belize campus of the University of the West Indies and was instrumental in the founding of the Caribbean Organization of Indigenous Peoples (COIP). He has extensive experience in aboriginal organizational efforts at a regional and international level. Dr. Palacio serves on the editorial board of *KACIKE: The Journal of Caribbean Amerindian History and Anthropology*.

THEDA PERDUE

Professor of history at the University of North Carolina at Chapel Hill and the Atlanta Distinguished Professor of Southern Culture, Dr. Perdue focuses her research on the Native peoples of the southeastern United States and on gender in Native societies. She speaks and writes on a wide variety of topics, including Indians in the segregated South and Indian women's history and how it can change the master narrative of U.S. history.

MWALIM (Morgan James Peters [Barbados/Mashpee Wampanoag])

Mwalim is a performing artist, writer, filmmaker, and educator and considered by critics and peers alike to be one of the true modern masters of the oral tradition. He is a tenured associate professor of English and African/African American Studies at the University of Massachusetts at Dartmouth and much of his research has focused on the oral and performance traditions of African American, Afro-Caribbean, and northeastern Native American peoples.

KIMBERLY TALLBEAR (Dakota)

Dr. TallBear is an assistant professor of science, technology, and environmental policy at the University of California at Berkeley. Her research crosses the fields of science and technology studies, feminist science studies, anthropology of science, cultural studies, and Native American studies. Her work informs policies designed to increase the regulatory, economic, educational, and human resource capacity of Native American tribes and other indigenous groups.

GABRIELLE TAYAC (Piscataway)

As a historian with the Smithsonian's National Museum of the American Indian (NMAI), Dr. Tayac conducts research focused on Native American identity issues across the Americas. Her areas of specialty include international human rights and the Native peoples and histories of the Chesapeake Bay region. She curates exhibitions at NMAI, lectures widely, and has published an award-winning children's book.

HERMAN J. VIOLA

Dr. Viola is a curator emeritus at the Smithsonian's National Museum of Natural History. A specialist on the history of the American West, he has served as director of the museum's National Anthropological Archives in addition to organizing two major exhibitions for the Smithsonian. Before joining the staff of the Smithsonian, he was an archivist at the National Archives of the United States. His research specialties include the American Indian, the Civil War, and the exploration of the American West.

ANGELA WALTON-RAJI (Choctaw)

Ms. Walton Raji recently retired as director of graduate school recruitment at the University of Maryland, Baltimore. She has conducted extensive research on African/ Native American genealogy with a special focus on the records of former Black Indian slaves and their children who were eventually given citizenship in the Five Civilized Tribes. She is co-founder of the AfriGeneas online website and she moderates the longest-running message board devoted to African and Native American genealogy. She is also now owner and host of the *African Roots* Podcast, a weekly podcast devoted to African American genealogy.

RON WELBURN (Assateague/Gingaskin/Cherokee)

As a professor of English at the University of Massachusetts Amherst, Dr. Welburn teaches American literature surveys, critical writing, Native American literature, and American Studies courses. He also directed the undergraduate Native American Indian Studies Certificate program. His research interests include ethnohistory of eastern Native America, postmodernism, cultural studies, and jazz studies. Dr. Welburn is also a widely published poet.

SELECTED BIBLIOGRAPHY

Anacostia Neighborhood Museum. *Blacks in the Westward Movement.* Washington: Smithsonian Institution Press, 1975.

Bier, Lisa. *American Indian and African American People, Communities, and Interactions: An Annotated Bibliography.* Westport, CT: Praeger, 2004.

Brooks, James F., ed. *Confounding the Color Line: The Indian-Black Experience in North America.* Lincoln: University of Nebraska Press, 2002.

Brown, Cloyde I. *Black Warrior Chiefs: A History of the Seminole Negro Indian Scouts: A True Story.* Fort Worth: C. I. Brown, 1999.

Downs, Dorothy. "Possible African Influence on the Art of the Florida Seminoles." In *African Impact on the Material Culture of the Americas: A Conference Presented by Diggs Gallery at Winston-Salem State University, Old Salem, the Museum of Early Southern Decorative Arts*, pp. 1–10. Winston-Salem, NC: Winston-Salem State University, May 30–June 2, 1996.

Forbes, Jack D. *Black Africans and Native Americans: Color, Race, and Caste in the Evolution of Red-Black Peoples.* New York: Blackwell, 1988.

———. *Africans and Native Americans: The Language of Race and the Evolution of Red-Black Peoples.* 2nd ed. Urbana-Champaign: University of Illinois Press, 1993.

Guinn, Jeff. *Our Land Before We Die: The Proud Story of the Seminole Negro.* New York: Jeremy P. Tarcher/Putnam, 2002.

Harris, Julia. "The Black-Indian Connection in Art: American Portraits, Soulscapes, and Spirit Works." *International Review of African American Art* 17, no. 1 (2000): 2–40.

Howard, Rosalyn. *Black Seminoles in the Bahamas.* Gainesville: University Press of Florida, 2002.

Hudson, Charles M., ed. *Red, White, and Black: Symposium on Indians in the Old South.* Southern Anthropological Society Proceedings, no. 5. Athens: University of Georgia Press, 1971.

Katz, William Loren. *Black Indians: A Hidden Heritage.* New York: Atheneum, 1986.

Katz, William Loren, and Paula A. Franklin. *Proudly Red and Black: Stories of African and Native Americans.* New York: Atheneum, 1993.

Lindsey, Donal F., Jr. *Indians at Hampton Institute, 1877–1923.* Urbana: University of Illinois Press, 1995.

Littlefield, Daniel F., Jr. *Africans and Seminoles: From Removal to Emancipation.* Westport, CT: Greenwood Press, 1977.

———. *Africans and Creeks: From the Colonial Period to the Civil War.* Westport, CT: Greenwood Press, 1979.

———. *The Cherokee Freedmen: From Emancipation to Citizenship.* Westport, CT: Greenwood Press, 1980.

Littlefield, Daniel F., Jr. and Mary Ann Littlefield. "The Beams Family: Free Blacks in Indian Territory." *Journal of Negro History* 41 (January 1976): 17–35.

May, Katja. *African Americans and the Native Americans in the Creek and Cherokee Nations, 1830s to 1920s: Collision and Collusion.* New York: Garland, 1996.

Miles, Tiya. *Ties that Bind: The Story of an Afro-Cherokee Family in Slavery and Freedom.* Berkeley: University of California Press, 2005.

Mulroy, Kevin. *Freedom on the Border: The Seminole Maroons in Florida, the Indian Territory, Coahuila, and Texas.* Lubbock: Texas Tech University Press, 1993.

———. *The Seminole Freedmen: A History.* Norman: University of Oklahoma Press, 2007.

Nash, Gary B. *Red, White, and Black: The Peoples of Early America.* Englewood Cliffs, NJ: Prentice-Hall, 1974.

Naylor, Celia. *African Cherokees in Indian Territory: From Chattel to Citizens.* Chapel Hill: University of North Carolina Press, 2008.

Opala, Joseph A. "Double Homecoming: American Indians with African Roots Return to the 'Rice Coast.'" *West Africa* 3778 (January 22–28, 1990): 97.

Parry, Ellwood. *The Image of the Indian and the Black Man in American Art, 1590–1900.* New York: George Braziller, 1974.

Perdue, Theda. *Slavery and the Evolution of Cherokee Society, 1540–1866.* Knoxville: University of Tennessee Press, 1979.

———. *The Black Seminoles: History of a Freedom-Seeking People.* Edited by Alcione M. Amos and Thomas P. Senter. Gainesville: University Press of Florida, 1996.

Saunt, Claudio. *Black, White, and Indian: Race and the Unmaking of an American Family.* New York: Oxford University Press, 2005.

Viola, Herman J. *After Columbus: The Smithsonian Chronicle of the North American Indians.* Washington: Smithsonian Books, 1990.

Walton-Raji, Angela Y. *Black Indian Genealogy Research: African American Ancestors Among the Five Civilized Tribes, an Expanded Edition.* Westminster, MD: Heritage Books, 2009.

Wright, J. Leitch, Jr. *Creeks and Seminoles: The Destruction and Regeneration of the Muscogulge People.* Lincoln: University of Nebraska Press, 1986.

Zellar, Gary. *African Creeks: Estelvste and the Creek Nation.* Norman: University of Oklahoma Press, 2007.

INDEX